Siciliana: Studies on the Sicilian Ethos

Legas

Sicilian Studies Series

Series Editor: Gaetano Cipolla

Volume XII

Other Volumes Published in this Series:

1. Giuseppe Quatriglio, *A Thousand Years in Sicily: from the Arabs to the Bourbons,* transl. by Justin Vitiello, 1992, 1997;
2. Henry Barbera, *Medieval Sicily: the First Absolute State,* 1994, 2000;
3. Connie Mandracchia DeCaro, *Sicily, the Trampled Paradise, Revisited,* 1998;
4. Justin Vitiello*, Labyrinths and Volcanoes: Windings Through Sicily,* 1999;
5. Ben Morreale*, Sicily: The Hallowed Land*, 2000;
6. Joseph Privitera, *The Sicilians,* 2001;
7. Franco Nicastro and Romolo Menighetti*, History of Autonomous Sicily,* Transl. by Gaetano Cipolla, 2002;
8. Maria Rosa Cutrufelli, *The Woman Outlaw,* Transl. by Angela M. Jeannet, 2004;
9. Enzo Lauretta, *The Narrow Beach,* trans by Giuliana Sanguinetti Katz and Anne Urbancic, 2004;
10. *Sweet Lemons: Writings with a Sicilian Accent*, ed. by Venera Fazio and Delia De Santis, 2004.
11. *The Story of Sicily*, by Sandra Benjamin, 2005

Gaetano Cipolla

Siciliana:
Studies on the Sicilian Ethos

Library of Congress Cataloging-in-Publication Data

Cipolla, Gaetano, 1937-
Siciliana : studies on the Sicilian ethos / Gaetano Cipolla.
p. cm. — (Sicilian studies series ; v. 12)
ISBN 1-881901-45-9 (pbk. : alk. paper)
1. Sicily (Italy)—Civilization. 2. Italian literature—Italy—Sicily—History and criticism. I. Title. II. Series: Sicilian studies ; . 12.
DG865.6.C57 2005
945'.8—dc22

2004029678

Acknowledgements

The publisher is grateful to Arba Sicula for a generous grant that in part made the publication of this book possible. Many thanks to Johanna Lynch for her help in editing and proofreading this volume.

Printed in Canada

For information and for orders, write to:

Legas

P.O. Box 149
Mineola, NewYork
11501, USA

3 Wood Aster Bay
Ottawa, Ontario
K2R 1D3 Canada

legaspublishing.com

I dedicate this book
to my wife Florence

Table of Contents

Preface

Writing an introduction to a book of essays like this forces one to look back and retrace in one's mind the journey that led to the present. In revisiting how I came to devote most of my energies to studying and disseminating Sicilian culture, one fact stands out. It happened almost by default. Before turning to Sicilian culture, I had built a university career as a scholar with a predilection for Jungian psychology (my Ph.D. dissertation was entitled *The Archetype of the Labyrinth and Its Manifestations in Petrarch*). Before the 1980s, I had not written a word about Sicily, nor had I devoted any time to study the Sicilian language and literature. Having been born in Sicily I carried Sicilian culture in my blood. I lived it in my life without acknowledging it. But starting around 1979-80, I became interested in a group of people who had started an organization known as Arba Sicula whose goals were to study, preserve and disseminate Sicilian culture. In the first few years I participated in the events of the organization, but played a marginal role. But I started to devote more and more time to studying Sicilian poetry, especially the poetry of Giovanni Meli and it wasn't long before I began translating some of his works into English. First I translated *L'origini di lu munnu* and then the *Don Chisciotti e Sanciu Panza*. The second work took me nearly four years to translate. Nevertheless the experience was so rewarding that it changed the course of my career. I remember reading the poem at night in bed and laughing out loud. I had never made such an intimate connection with a poet as I did with Meli. The reaction to his poetry reinforced my conviction that the poetry that really grabs a hold of your emotions in a visceral way can never be written in any language other than your native tongue. Meli's Sicilian spoke to me at a deeper level . When I read his famous poem that begins with "Ucchiuzzi niuri" that Goethe himself liked and translated into German I felt an emotion that could not be described, an emotion that could not be duplicated if the line were written in Italian, for example, or German. "Occhiucci neri" does not produce in me the same emotion. There were other epiphanic moments that made me realize the importance of returning to my roots. It was impossible not to heed the call.

My involvement with Arba Sicula, first as its Editor and then its President, thrust me further into Sicilian culture than might be expected of a university professor who makes a living by teaching Italian language and literature. I have had to learn things outside the scope of my training as a professor of Italian. Not being trained as a translator, I had to train myself; not being a linguist, I had to make a critical study of the Sicilian language; and not being a historian/sociologist I had to examine Sicilian history and traditions. As a result, the essays in this book are a record of my learning experiences. Through them I tried to educate myself about the various issues confronting Sicilian culture. When I first wrote the essay on the Jews of Sicily I knew nothing about their history on the island. The same can be said about the presence of the Arabs. I knew more about the Greeks because that was part of the classical education. The essay on the Sicilian language required a radical change in mindset. I had to shed some of the prejudices against the so-called dialects that are built into people of my profession. But perhaps none was more difficult to write than the essay entitled "What Makes a Sicilian?", which was published first as a 32-page booklet. It was difficult because the questions regarding the essence of being Sicilian touched me on a personal level as well. In trying to define Sicilians I was also defining myself. It was difficult also because Sicilians are a complex people whose essence defies characterization. As soon as you think you have isolated a feature, a common thread that binds, the exception to the rule pops up, leaving you with the belief that all you can do is capture the mirror reflection, a likeness, an approximation of reality. And that is basically all I have managed to accomplish with these essays: to provide the reader with a mirror reflection of the Sicilian ethos.

The second part of the book is devoted to Sicilian literature, that is, to writers with whom I feel more at home. They too represent aspects of what Sciascia called "sicelitude", a way of coming to terms with being Sicilian. Meli, Pirandello, Martoglio, Brancati and Camilleri, in their diversity, share a common thread that binds them to mother Sicily. Each in his own way, these writers give a voice to their "sicelitude" and teach us something new about the island, adding a piece of the puzzle.

The following essays are published here for the first time: "The Muslims in Sicily," "Sicily and Greece," "Vitaliano Brancati," and "Translating Camilleri". "What Makes a Sicilian?," "The Jews of Sicily," "The Trinacria, the Symbol of Sicily" and "Is Sicilian Language or a Dialect?," have appeared all in *Arba Sicula*; the essay on Giovanni Meli was published in different versions as introductions to my translation of the *Don Chisciotti and Sanciu Panza* (Legas 2003) and *Moral Fables and Other Poems* (Legas 1995). The article "On Translating Giovanni Meli's Poetry" first appeared in *Da Malebolge alla Senna: Studi letterari in onore di Giorgio Santangelo* (Palermo: Palumbo, 1985) and the piece on Martoglio is a revised and expanded version of the introduction to my edition of *The Poetry of Nino Martoglio* (Legas 1992); the article "Pirandello's Poetics of the Labyrinth" was published in a much shorter version in *Pirandello:*

Poetica e presenza, (Roma: Bulzoni Editore, 1987). "Pirandello: Don Quijote or Don Chisciotti?" was first published in *Quaderni d'Italianistica.*

It is my hope that this book will provide the reader with enough pieces of the puzzle that Sicily represents to make a coherent and understandable picture.

What Makes a Sicilian?

It is ironic that the majority of Americans recognize the name of Sicily, in spite of the fact that it is a small island, barely one fourth the size of Cuba, whereas they probably would have difficulty locating even larger countries on a globe. So perhaps the first thing we can say about Sicily is that it occupies a place of renown in modern American and European consciousness that is not commensurate with its present economic or political importance. This apparent disproportion, however, rather than being an unusual feature, is the norm for the island. Both for what it has contributed to the world and in people's perceptions of it, there seems to be an element of hyperbole and exaggeration that colors everything Sicilian. Sicily, as Ben Morreale said in a recent article, has been a talisman for the powerful: the domination of the Mediterranean has always been tied to the possession of the island. Inversely, the loss of Sicily has marked the decline of empires. When Sicily was lost to the invading Vandal hordes, Rome declined; the Byzantines lost their dominance in Italy when Sicily fell to the Arabs; the Bourbons lost the Kingdom of the Two Sicilies when they lost Sicily to Garibaldi. Sicily has been the gateway to Italy and Europe. No wonder that the Allies chose it to begin their assault on Europe in 1943. Its geographical position has guaranteed for it a place of prominence far beyond what one would expect from its size, something it shares with Italy. People have come to Sicily to fight their wars on its soil, to plunder its wealth, to leap from it into Europe. From the beginning of recorded history, it has been the point of contact between the various civilizations that have left their mark on the lands of the Mediterranean sea, the meeting point between East and West, between Africa and Europe

The beauties of the island attracted the seafaring Phoenicians who founded Palermo; the mysterious and elusive Elymians established a cult of Venus, the goddess of love, high on Mount Erice; the Carthaginians controlled much of the western half of the island; the Greeks considered the island a promised land and once they established themselves as Sicilians they outdid their brothers in the grandeur of their achievements; Rome grew into the most powerful empire in the world after its conquest

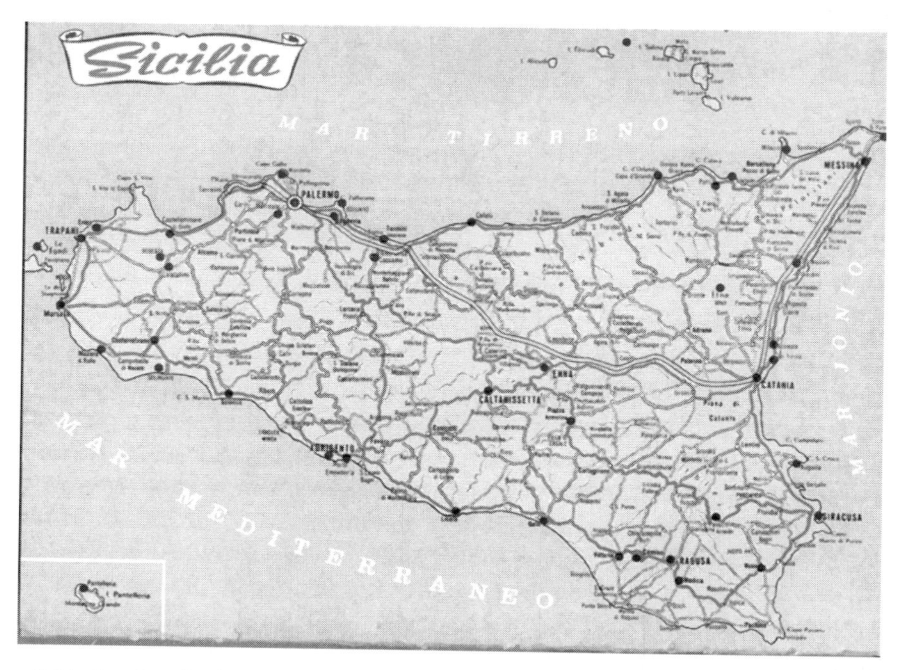

of Sicily; the Arabs transformed it into the Garden of Allah; the Norman warriors made of it the most advanced state in Europe; and Frederick II, the great emperor who was born eight centuries ago, made it the most important center of learning in Europe

But Sicily and Sicilians do not enjoy a good reputation. In the United States, or in any other part of the world for that matter, when people hear the name of Sicily, images of mayhem and violence are inevitably displayed before their mind's eye and knife-wielding villains with dark hair stand ready to do mischief against law and order. The media has portrayed Sicilians so exclusively as belonging to the Mafia that the two nouns go together linguistically like "bread and butter". The mafioso's *modus operandi* has been extended to all Sicilians and they are seen as greedy and ruthless individuals. Many actually believe that Sicilians carry the seeds of criminality and lawlessness in their blood. The gulf between real Sicilians and the image concocted by the media is very wide indeed and growing wider, judging by pictures like *True Romance* by Quentin Tarantino which characterizes Sicilians as degenerate liars and goes so far as to question even their belonging to the Caucasian race (see the chapter on the Muslims in Sicily).

In the following pages, I'm going to try to present a more balanced picture of the Sicilian contribution to western civilization. I will attempt to give you a personal appreciation of Sicilians and of Sicily, for inevitably the history of a place is the history of the people who inhabit it. Who are the Sicilians, what values do they share, what makes them tick? What makes a Sicilian?

I'd like to begin by saying that the reputation Sicily and Sicilians enjoy has little to do with first-hand experiences. The overwhelming majority of those who have been to Sicily have expressed their great admiration for its beauty and for the warmth of its people.

The many travelers who have written about the island, beginning from the account of Ibn Giubair, an Arab traveler in the 12th century to that of Roger Peyrefitte, a contemporary writer, have described it, with a few exceptions, as a kind of earthly paradise.

Nor were works of literature responsible for the negative characterization of Sicilians! Many foreign writers and poets, especially in the late 19th century, visited Sicily and left interesting diaries of their reactions. From Shelley to Byron, from Goethe to De Maupassant, from von Platen to Wagner, from Matthew Arnold to Holderlin, from Renan to Gide, Sicily has been represented as a land of rebirth. For many of these writers, Sicily was a place endowed with different qualities. It was not that things on the island were unique, but that there was more to them than elsewhere: the sun was hotter, the wine was stronger, the contrasts harsher, the beauty wilder, the passions more searing, the landscape more breathtaking! In André Gide's *Immoraliste* Sicily is a metaphor for the life force. The main character of the novel, Michel, is transformed from an "old man" into a youthful figure when he experiences the Sicilian spring. In the midst of the glorious vegetation, Michel feels reborn into a new being "Et je courais sur la route escarpèe qui joint Taormine a Mola criant, pour l'appeler en moi: Un nouvel Etre! Un nouvel etre!" (And I kept running on the steep road that joins Taormina to Mola yelling, in order to evoke him in myself: a new being! A new being!).

This sense of being reborn in Sicily was echoed by D.H. Lawrence who spoke of the island as "the dawn place". He too felt he had come into contact with his inner being the primeval island "the wonderful coast of Sicily, like the dawn of our day, the wonderful morning of our epoch".

The Romantic notion of Sicily as an earthly paradise is difficult to accept when you have felt the blasts of the bone-chilling tramontana blowing down from Mount Etna, or gasped for air in the 105-degree temperature of Catania in August. No, Sicily is not an earthly paradise socially either, when you think of the poverty of some of its people, when you know that unemployment is consistently the highest in Italy. Socially and historically, it's more like "a trampled paradise," as Connie Mandracchia De Caro declared in the title of her book.

It's obvious that generalities do not paint an accurate portrait of a people, but painting with broad strokes, and avoiding the commonplace, I would like now to identify a few Sicilian traits and the socio-historical forces that have played a part in shaping them.

Let me say that the overwhelming quality of Sicilians is not mildness, as has been underscored by many foreign observers. No doubt geographic-climactic factors have had an effect on Sicilians. For as it is true that Esquimoes are conditioned by their frigid weather and the ever-present snow, affecting their language and their *forma mentis* (mind set), it is also equally true that the wondrous contrasts present in the Sicilian landscape, the brilliant colors of its vegetation, the intoxicating fragrance of its flowers, the pitiless summer sun that parches the countryside for six months a year, the deep blue of its surrounding sea and sky, are deeply embedded in their *forma mentis.* The natural excesses of geography and weather are reflected in the character of the Sicilian people. Like their landscape, whose tonal qualities are never the "sfumato," (smoky) (see the contrast between the luxuriant vegetation on the eastern coast and the barren, lunar scapes of the interior near Enna), they are extreme in their emotions. The "chiaroscuro" predominates. They axe "ardenti amici e pessimi inimici" (the best friends and the worst enemies), as Giovanni Maria Cecchi said in the 16th century. In describing Sicilians, superlatives seemed to be the order of the day for him. They are, in Cecchi's words, "avidissimi nel mangiare…e vivono in gran gelosia delle loro donne che le tengono molto ristrette e fanno acerbissime vendette sopra a chi hanno in sospezione," (They are extremely greedy in eating…and they live with such great jalousy of their women that they will exact extremely harsh vengeance on those they suspect). Scipio De Castro, writing in the same period, considered Sicilians "sommamente timidi" (extremely timid) when it came to spending their own fortunes and "sommamente temerari!" (extremely foolhardy) when it came to spending public money.

One of the first character traits that is most evident to outsiders is the great pride that Sicilians have in themselves and in their homeland. It is significant that Sicilians, especially those who live in a foreign country, will go out of their way to tell you how proud they are of being Sicilian. I have never heard a Venetian or Bolognese say that they are especially proud of being Venetian or Bolognese. They probably are, but they feel no need to volunteer the information. Sicilians do. The special pride Sicilians profess before the world is certainly genuine, but it may be also a defense mechanism prompted by the stigma that has accompanied Sicilians through the ages. Centuries of abuse and of being told that they do not measure up to the rest of the world have taken their toll on the Sicilians' sense of themselves. Ultimately, the pride they project may be nothing more than an attempt at camouflaging a deep sense of inferiority that has been drummed into them. It is a way of protesting the world's unfair and untrue judgment of them.

Pride, defined as a sense of one's one personal worth *vis a vis* the world, seems to be a common trait among Sicilians of today as well as those of previous eras. Sicilians, in general, consider themselves superior to their neighbors, to the people from the neighboring towns, to the people from other provinces and from other regions. Needless to say, Sicilians traditionally have flaunted their own qualities and denigrated the qualities of their neighbors in poetry and songs. The people from the next town are always inferior in everything. The dummies are always from beyond the horizon. Reading a few anecdotes from *Mimi siciliani,* an interesting book written by Francesco Lanza, which has become a classic, you can see how Sicilians view their neighbors. A case in point is a tale of a foolish man from neighboring Burgio, who, worried about his wife's fear of the dark and of her spending the night alone in their large bed, did not hesitate in asking his obliging *compare*, while he was out of town, to take his place "so that nothing could happen to her."

The differences among Sicilians are probably not easily recognized by outsiders, but the difference between Sicilians as a group and other Italians are immediately evident to perceptive travellers. French writer Guy de Maupassant who visited Sicily late in 1885, made the following comparison between Neapolitans and Sicilian "No one is less like a Neapolitan than a Sicilian. In the Neapolitan of the lower classes one always finds three quarters of Punch. He gesticulates, gets agitated, is fired without cause, expresses himself with gestures as much as with words, mimes everything he says, always shows himself to be amiable in order to get what he wants, is gracious by ruse as much as by nature, and answers unpleasant compliments politely. But in the Sicilian one already finds much of the Arab. He has the Arab's gravity of gait, though he has the great liveliness of wit of the Italian. His native pride, his love for titles, the nature of his haughtiness and even the physiognomy of his face also make him more similar to the Spaniard than the Italian. But what unceasingly gives you the impression of being in the Orient, as soon as you set foot in Sicily, is the timbre of the voice, the nasal intonation of the street cries."

If Sicilians are chauvinistic among themselves and will not give way to any other Sicilian, local animosities are soon forgotten when the terms of comparison include foreigners, that is, non-Sicilians. A popular octave often heard after the island's annexation to Piedmont in 1861, claimed that a single Sicilian peasant was worth more than all the "piramuddisi" (an intentional corruption of "Piemontesi") put together. The hyperbolic expression of pride in the virtue of Sicilians may be interpreted as a lingering manifestation of what British historian Denis Mack Smith who wrote a two-volume history of Sicily, calls Sicilian megalomania. He believed that the ancient Sicilian Greeks all suffered from megalomania, characterized by their excessive, indeed, pathological need for aggrandizing their accomplishments. This trait is evident in the monuments that have remained on the Island. The Greeks who colonized Sicily, and their descendants, not unlike the people who colonized the US, manifested this need of theirs in building their temples with a obvious penchant for grandeur. Not only are the Greek temples you find in Sicily designed to surpass in size and decoration the ancient models found in Greece, but they are also strategically placed to make an everlasting impression upon the visitor. Nowhere is the Sicilians' desire to astonish more evident than in the Valley of the Temples in Agrigento. There, on a rocky ledge that forms a stage to be seen from above and from below, they built not one, for that would not have satisfied their pride, but five temples, one mile apart from one another. Guy de Maupassant was not the first nor the last visitor to marvel at the drama that Sicilian temples can evoke. Thinking of the lone and magnificent Doric temple of Segesta, he wrote: "The master decorators who taught humanity art, show, above all in Sicily, that profound and refined science that they had of effect and staging. (The temple) of Segesta seems to have been placed at the foot of this mountain by a man of genius to whom had been revealed the only place where it was to be raised up. All by itself it animates the whole landscape; it makes it living and divinely beautiful."

Sicilians inherited their sense of drama, along with their liveliness, their sense of hospitality, their gift for reasoning, their diffidence and even their physical demeanors, from the Greeks. Sicilians are much closer to Greeks in looks and attitudes than they are to Venetians or Florentines. If you were to identify those peoples with whom Sicilians have an affinity you'd have to rank the Greeks in first place, followed closely by the Arabs, the Normans and then by Spaniards. The Arabs who ruled on the island from 827 AD to about 1092 had a lasting effect on Sicilians' outlook on life. It may be said that their sense of fatalism, their persistence and their acceptance and resignation to a harsh life was inherited from the Arabs. The Sicilians' thoughtfulness and melancholy, their deep sense of nostalgia and bouts of depression are also Arabic in nature. They also have many traits in common with the Spaniards who were masters of the island for over five centuries. The Spaniards' sense of grandeur and preoccupation with how things look, their love for pomp and ceremony, for decorations and external elegance touch responsive chords in the Sicilian psyche. Yet even though they show many similarities with Greeks, Sicilians are not Greeks, nor are they Arabs or Spaniards. Sicilians like pomp and ceremony, but they don't have the same fascination with spectacles, death and ritual; they don't take themselves as seriously as the Spaniards. Bull fighting for example, never had much success in Sicily and it did not survive the test of time.

In spite of the fact that Sicily is the most southern point of Europe, Sicilians don't display the happy-go-lucky attitudes, the exuberant and quick-witted superficiality people sometimes attribute to southerners. They show in their daily behavior traits such as perseverance, determination, persistence, precision, hard work and absolute reliance on empirical reality that one associates with the northern temperament. But they are not immune to dreaming! If I were to choose someone who best epitomizes the Sicilian spirit I would single out Giovanni Meli without hesitation. The greatest Sicilian poet of all time, Meli may be considered an emblem of the Sicilian soul, always struggling between idealism and realism, between pessimism and optimism. The internal struggle that raged in Meli is embodied in the figures of Don Chisciotti and Sanciu Panza - the heroes of his long mock epic poem, written not to imitate Cervantes, but to show where the Spaniard had gone wrong. Don Chisciotti represents the poet's idealistic wish to ameliorate the lives of the poor Sicilian peasants, and Sanciu Panza represents Meli's own skeptical attitudes toward Don Chisciotti's deliriums. The battle between idealism and empiricism was eventually won by Sanciu Panza, the man who believed only what he could touch with his own hands. Poor Don Chisciotti -- whom Sanciu defined as *un omu ca non sapia cunzari na nsalata e pritinnia di cunzari lu munnu* (a man who could not fix a salad and pretended that he could fix the world) -- died a humoristic death (in the Pirandellian sense) that would have been unthinkable to the Spaniard, Cervantes. He died "a most unchivalric death," caused by a rupture. And Sanciu remarked, "Who ever heard of an Errant Knight dying of hernia?"

In Sicilians, the battle between optimism and pessimism is usually won by pessimism. Skepticism, pragmatism, realism often obtain more credence with the people, without, however, excluding their counterparts. Leonardo Sciascia once noted that Sicilians are so pessimistic about the future that in their language the future tense does not exist. Siciians will say "Dumani vaiu a Catania." (Tomorrow I'm going to Catania.) But many other languages lack the future tense. Neapolitan, for example, has no future. Yet we would not say that Neapolitans are particularly pessimistic in their outlook. The Sicilians' outlook must be seen as a continuous, losing struggle between progressive, idealistic tendencies against a more entrenched conservative and realistic philosophy. This explains the stagnation that is characteristic of Sicilian society. Had there been more visionaries, more dreamers, more Don Chisciottis, the course of Sicilian history would certainly have been different

Other peoples have played on the Sicilian stage but they too have always been considered more or less foreign to the islanders. Sicilians did not get along with the Romans, the Byzantines, the French, the Austrians and the Piedmontese and they were either hated or tolerated commensurately with the extent to which they interfered with the Sicilians' way of life. Rome was never much interested in Sicily other than as a source of cheap labor and wheat. Under the Byzantines Sicily was looted of what little remained after the Romans left. The French for their greed brought upon themselves the wrath of the Sicilian Vespers. And the Piedmontese who came following Garibaldi's invasion of the island, instead of resolving the deep-seated problems faced by Sicily, made them worse, causing the greatest mass emigration in the island's history. They were disliked for many reasons, but particularly for imposing on the traditionally antimilitaristic Sicilians an onerous eight-year long military

"La Famiglia"
by Beppe Vesco

draft. A Sicilian proverb aptly says, "megghiu porcu ca surdatu," "better to be a swine than a soldier."

The Sicilian man-made landscape speaks eloquently about the civilizations that were congenial with the Sicilian spirit and it reflects what I have been saying. The most impressive achievements of man's creativity you see there are the Punic and Greek temples scattered throughout the island, the Arab-Norman castles, the Norman cathedrals of Cefalù and Monreale and the Spanish-Sicilian Baroque.

Allow me to add a few more pieces to the puzzle of the Sicilian soul: The family occupies the most prominent place in the lives of Sicilians. The family is the single most important institution around which revolve the social behaviors of Sicilians. It's a symbol of the unity of the Sicilian people as a nation, and it is a means of defense against outsiders. For Sicilians one could really say the family is all. Each member of the family unit has precise responsibilities and duties from the father as the head, the mother as the emotional center and the children owing allegiance to their parents and their siblings. This is evident in the love that adults bestow on children. They are protective of them to obsessive measures.

The mother is at the center of the familial relationships. She holds the family together with all the powers that she possesses, she makes sure that the members behave in accepted ways. The mother is the family's emotional universe. "Casa mia, matri mia!" (My home, my mother). There is something sacred about her. While it is true that Sicilian society is eminently patriarchal, it is also eminently clear that the mother is the glue that holds a family together. The mother's role, shaped by thousands of years of history, continues to our day almost unchanged. She nurtures physically and psychologically, she performs social duties in observance of time-worn formulas, she sacrifices her whole life to her family, denying herself in the process and becoming a victim of her own dedication to others. Her devotion to her family is so complete that as a Sicilian proverb has it "La matri senti li guai di lu mutu" (The mother hears the troubles of those who are mute.) Inevitably, however, in the battle between childrens' desire for freedom and the mothers' desire to maintain the *status quo* --for this reason, Leonardo Sciascia considered Sicilian mothers a cause of the stagnation in Sicilian society -- conflicts emerge and mothers begin to consider themselves victims, adopting what may be called a martyr's syndrome. In an article published in *Arba Sicula* (Vol XIII, 1993), Angelo Costanzo suggested that Sicilian women everywhere eventually end up conforming with the image of the *matri addulurata*, that is, the sorrowful mother who grieves for the loss of her son. It is not a coincidence that in Sicily, out of all the possible scenes of the madonna's life, the most pervasive is certainly that of the grieving mother. Nor is it coincidental that women witnessing an accident immediately cry out "Bedda Matri!" Incidentally, the images of Christ that pervade the Sicilian psyche are restricted typically to those of the suffering Christ and of the Child Christ, that is suffering and innocence, an innocent victim slaughtered by powerful enemies in which one can see the suffering of the innocent Sicilian people projected unto the background of external domination and abuse. The honor of the family must be defended at all costs. Appearances become very important in this connection. "Fari na bedda fiura" (to put one's best foot forward) is a must. Everything is really subordinate to the main interest of the family. The sense of pride that attaches to the individual comes into play as well for his family. The loss of face of one member cannot fail to have some effect on the pride of the family as a unit. The Sicilian proverb "Cui perdi la bona fama, perdi tuttu!" (He who loses his good reputation, loses everything!) embodies a universally accepted sentiment on the island. A Sicilian who perceives that his honor is being attacked directly will react with astonishing fury. On the other hand, he may display unusual coolness if the attack is presented in an oblique and indirect manner. This, of course, does not mean that the offense will go unpunished or unnoticed, for Sicilians, as a general rule, have long memories, like elephants, and they will at the right time repay in kind for the insult. They are not given to forgetting or forgiving.

The great respect that Sicilians have for their dead ancestors is but an extension of the same reverence for the family. No Sicilian is ever likely to curse the dead. In fact, no curse exists in Sicilian such as the Romanesque "A li mortacci tui!" (A curse on your ancestors!). In keeping with this sense of respect for the dead, children; receive gifts on the Day of All Saints, which in Sicily is known as "u jornu dî morti" (the day of the dead). The dead ancestors are said to leave presents for children, not Santa Claus. Respect for the elderly is an expression of the same reverence.

The Sicilians' feeling for hospitality is also an aspect of the same mystique. While it is not easy to win approval and enter the close circle of friendships in Sicily, once you are admitted, Sicilians will go to extraordinary steps to make you feel at home. They are very generous with their time and money as regards guests. Hospitality is sacred.

Cicero identified three traits that accurately described the Sicilians of his day nearly two thousand years ago. He said they were "an intelligent race, but suspicious and endowed with a wonderful sense of humor." I want to expand these three traits and test them against today's reality.

That Sicilians are an intelligent people I don't think has ever been questioned, except perhaps by some pseudo-scientific reports published in the 1920's in popular American magazines. I do not know any "Sicilian" jokes as there are – without offense to the Poles - "Polish" jokes, for example. Jokes about Sicilians usually deal with other aspects of their perceived personalities. At any rate, intelligence is not a quality Sicilians lack. The proverb "Avanti cummattiri cu centu mariola, ca c'un babbu!" (It's better to struggle with one hundred con artists than with a single stupid man!) testifies to the confidence they have in their own capacity to thwart the machinations of keen minds, but they declare themselves helpless before stupidity. It is interesting to point out that Sicilians dislike stupidity so much that they do not allow their universally acknowledged fool, Giufà, to be entirely stupid. In fact, Giufà who is something of the village idiot, often doubles as a wise and just man who solves the problems of his compatriots. He is both a fool and a wise man, sharp and obtuse depending on the tale of which he is the protagonist. He is the fellow who when his mother told him "don't forget to pull the door after you" proceeded to pull it off its hinge and carry it on his back. But he is also the man who exposes the foolishness of others.

There is a rather singular visual quality to Sicilian intelligence, I think. For Sicilians, you can truly say that the eyes are the mirrors of the soul. This is hardly a scientific fact, but I can tell you from experience that Sicilians carry out entire conversation with their eyes without ever moving their lips. The Greeks had a verb for this: *ananouein.* I recall how at dinner my father had simply to look in the direction of an object on the table and my mother would immediately realize that he wanted a glass of water or the bread. The request was never made, a simple quick glance, a twitching of a finger, an imperceptible nod was all that was needed for effective communication. I have no explanation for this, except to say that Sicilians have had long experience in being spectators of history, trying to minimize their future woes from reading into people's eyes.

But the Sicilian's intelligence is not in dispute it is probably the cause of some of their difficulties. Sicilians, in their perception of their worth as individuals, tend to exaggerate, to inflate their importance. Every Sicilian believes that he is the brightest, the best at everything. In his

Gattopardo, Tomasi di Lampedusa wrote that Sicilians considered themselves demigods, perfect human beings who wanted to be left alone. This overvaluation of individual prowess which may have been inherited from the Greeks whose greatest sin was hybris, as you may recall, leads to haughtiness and arrogance, to jealousy and envy. Sicilian despise those who give themselves airs, they cannot stand for one of their peers to climb above them in terms of social or economic power, and will not accept the idea that the man who has achieved greatness has done so out of the sheer superiority of his natural gifts. It is much more comforting for them to think that luck, special circumstances, or fraud played a substantial part in catapulting that man to success. Concomitantly, Sicilians greatly admire a powerful or successful man who does not flaunt his good fortunes. In a country where titles are important and sometimes inflated a doctor-professor who introduces himself with his first name is much admired. Giovanni Maria Cecchi, whom we quoted before, was not off the mark when he said that in their haughtiness "Sicilians do not give way to anyone, unless the difference in social status is overwhelming on the side of one or the other." A Sicilian saying conveys the sense of shame that accompanies a loss of face resulting from an act of prevarication by peers: "Amaru a cui si fa supraniari! Lustru di paradisu nun ni vidi." (Woe to him who lets himself be stepped upon. He will never see the light of paradise.) The failure or inability to defend one's dignity before society results in the loss of paradise. It is no wonder that in Sicily collective enterprises do not succeed very well as a whole. The "Sicilian Vespers" of 1282, which may be deemed the first popular and national revolution in the history of the modern world, is perhaps an exception to the rule.

Let me address the second point made by Cicero: the Sicilians' "suspicious" nature. I probably would have substituted "cautious" to "suspicious". At any rate, it cannot be denied that Sicilians, as a matter of course, are not known for jumping into things. History has taught them to be wary. While Sicilians like to eat, they prize sobriety greatly (they are the most sober people in Italy according to a 1991 statistics, consuming only two liters of wine per capita per month) and they frown on frivolity. Their dislike of drinking is due to their fear of losing control of themselves or of a situation. A man who has a habit of appearing in public in an intoxicated state is looked upon with disdain ("omu di vinu, nun vali un carlinu!" (A man who loves wine too much is not worth a sou); the image of a woman who is inebriated evokes much stronger criticism. Their "caution" may be an extension of their fear of committing themselves to a course of action that could become difficult to control. Their stoicism before suffering may well be another manifestation of the same need to present a "manly" or "defensive" posture before the world. Pirandello used to say that Sicilians "have an instinctive fear of life, that's why they close them selves in, being content with little, as long as it gives them a sense of security ...It is the sea that isolates them, that cuts them off from the world and makes them alone, and everyone is and makes himself an island." The sea is responsible for giving Sicilians their proverbial insularity of spirit, it is the medium through which a thousand disasters have reached their shores. Unlike England, which used the sea to extend the vital force of the nation outwardly, Sicily has seen the sea as the medium that brought upon its shores hungry barbarians looking for the sun. Sixteen foreign dominations have left their mark on the Sicilians' soul. Cautious? Suspicious? Yes, indeed! No one has come to Sicily with gifts. They have all come to take something. They have come for its wealth, its breathtaking beauty, the fertility of its valleys, and its enviable climate. Is it any wonder that Sicilians are wary of strangers? Behind each foreign face, there lurks the fierceness of the Mameluks, the memory of the Algerian pirates who scoured the Sicilian shores to plunder and pillage, the haughtiness of the barons in Charles d 'Anjou's' retinue and the adventurers of all races who have come and gone.

In spite of the oppression that has been their lot, or perhaps because of it, Sicilians have developed a keen sense of humor, which has been recognized by the likes of Cicero and others. But their sense of humor is always tempered with a sense of fatalism. Sicilian humor is of the Pirandellian kind. Its emblem is the *Erma Bifronte,* the Janus double face that cries and laughs at the same time. And no one embodies this aspect of the Sicilian psyche better than Giovanni Meli. In a poem entitled "Lo specchio del disinganno, o sia cugghiuniata" that Pirandello himself recognized as embodying his own brand of humor his "sentimento del contrario," Meli shows that all of man's deeds are nothing but delusions, "cugghiuniati." Every octave which describes all the objects of man's desire ends with the word "cugghiuniata," which expresses his profound disillusionment with life. Love, wealth, fame, and sex -- everything man prizes highly -- are shown to be illusory prizes, a "mockery," or to use the words of a popular song "is that all there is?" One octave will suffice to show what I mean:

Oh chi bedda picciotta! Oh ch'e sciacquata!
Oh chi sangu! Oh chi vezzi! Oh chi attrattiva!

Ah! mi la vogghiu teniri abbrazzata,
ah! lu so alitu stissu mi ravviva:
mettiti bona, figghia nzuccarata,
proi ssu labbru...apri ssi cosci...oh viva!
Moviti, stringi... oh estasi biata!
Ticchi, ticchi, finiu... Cugghiuniata!

O what a pretty lass! What prodigy!
What spirit and what charm! What winning ways!
O how her very breath rekindles me!
O how I want her in my arms to stay!
O sugar-coated child do lie with me.
Give me your lips ...your thighs spread wide...hurray!
Strive now ...hold tight, o wondrous ecstasy!
In-out ...in-out...It's over! Mockery

But you don't have to quote Meli to realize that Sicilian humor is generally ironic, inward turning, self-directed. As Vitaliano Brancati pointed out, Sicilian proverbs are not malicious or sly as Tuscan proverbs are. Consider the following: "Scappari non è virgogna, quacchi vota a sarvamentu di vita!" (Running away is not shameful, sometimes it can save your lfe). Running counter to the accepted mode of behavior (in Sicily, to run away from a fight is generally deemed a shameful act. You must stand your ground!), this proverb says that Sicilians are pragmatists with a sense of humor, after all. But the proverb that speaks volumes of the Sicilians' inward-turning humor is, "ringraziamu a Diu pi chiddu chi nni duna, e a lu re pi chiddu chi nni lassa!" (We thank God for all he gives us and the King for all he leaves us!), in which the Sicilians express their profound resignation to being subjects to forces beyond their control while continuing unperturbed their journeys through life. Jane Vessels in an article on Sicily published in *National Geographic* (Aug. 1995) offers us another example of Sicilian humor. Describing the creativity of Sicilian epithets heard in Palermo's congested streets, Vessels painted this delightful vignette: "Why are you honking?" a man yelled from another car. "I love the music," she replied. "I'm going to break your husband's horns," the man shouted. She retorted, "I can put them back on!" In threatening to break her husband's horns, the man is accusing the woman of being an adulteress. Not only is the woman unrepentant about her presumed adultery, but to have the last word, she brazenly asserts her intentions to engage in another extramarital affair, thus regaling her husband with an-

A statue of Giovanni Meli in Agrigento.

other pair of horns. Hence the inward-turning quality of her retort. If the anecdote is not true, it is certainly "bien trouvè!"

Why Sicilian humor should be inward-turning is inevitably something of a contradiction, difficult to understand. Sicily is a solar and luminous island, where brilliant colors dazzle the eye, where the sun is most generous (Catania boasts the highest number of hours of sunshine in Europe), yet it's inhabited by people who cannot laugh in total abandon, people who do not know the value of a guffaw. Is it folly or wisdom? I do not know! Paolo Arena, author of La *Sicilia nella sua storia e nei suoi problemi* (Palermo: F. Agate Ed. 1949), the most passionate book on Sicily I've ever read, observes that every Sicilian artist, every philosopher, every writer is a tragic figure, an introspective madman, a singer of melancholia and desolations which constrict the heart in a vice of crying, he is a heartless investigator, a man who tears himself and others apart, harsh to such a degree that the strange brotherhood of heart, spirit and temperament between our people and Dostoyevsky's Russia becomes manifest..." Sicily has produced great writers, thinkers, and poets, "but not a single smile from the Roman era forward." Is Sicilian humor schizophrenic because it embodies the rupture between how things should be and how they really are, between the longing for justice and the evident injustice, between the desire for freedom and independence and its perennial frustration?

One last point remains. Historically Sicilians have shared the following attitudes and feelings: a general dislike for the police and for the system of justice; a cautious disregard for laws; a deep mistrust of governmental institutions and politicians; a fiercely individualistic nature; allegiance to a code of behavior known as *omertà* which today is understood as a see-nothing-hear-nothing attitude before investigating authorities, but which in the original formulation meant manliness, behaving as a man should. *Omertà's* etymology is *omu* (man) and according to Cesare Mori *(The Last Struggle with the Mafia,* London: Putnam 1933, p. 224), it meant "complete self-confidence, a high sense of honor, duty and personal dignity, a gallant heart, a balanced judgment and self control." In his view, it was a form of aristocracy of character. Sicilians universally and openly acknowledge maxims according to which it is better to cheat than to be cheated, better to outsmart an enemy than to be outsmarted, better to say less than more, better to be secretive about family matters, better to exclude rather than to include people into the inner circle of family and friends. Sicilians have always looked with contempt on the police who traditionally have enforced the laws of the rich and guaranteed the oppression of the poor, and it has always been a point of honor for them not to cooperate. Being a spy was in fact the most damning act a Sicilian could commit. But this also means that historically Sicilians found it difficult to go to the police to report that they have been victims of a crime, preferring, if they could, to right the wrong hemselves.

These modes of behavior, developed through many centuries of experiences as the least harmful method of coping with external and hostile forces, can be espoused by the majority of Sicilians. They must be considered defense mechanisms developed by all societies that have known freedom only in flashes soon to be obscured by the most abject submission to external forces. They represent strategies of survival for a people that has known oppression, neglect and abuse at the hands of many foreigners. As it happens, the traits I've briefly described are similar to the general codes of behavior under which the Mafia operated until recently. The term *mafiusu* actually meant *good-looking, manly, handsome, impressive* in Sicilian. It described a man who through the use of violence or a network of influences at his disposal was able to obtain respect and protect what he perceived to be his rights. Ultimately, I think that the mafia was spawned by an overvaluation of individual worth combined with the arrogance of power: a case of intelligence that does not hesitate to use violence at the service of greed. The mafia, like other secret societies, such as the *Beati Paoli,* which was an effective and feared Sicilian organization, may have been perceived in the past as representing a form of justice where there was no justice, a way of righting wrongs that otherwise would have gone unpunished. But Sicilians are the first victims of the mafia. Indeed, they are doubly victimized by it, in their reputation and in their pockets. But now Sicilians are saying "basta!" with increasing loudness and resolve. There has been a dramatic change, both as regards the relationship of Sicilians *vis à vis* the police and the mafia, especially after the murders of Judges Falcone and Borsellino,and as regards the codes of behavior under whichthe organization itself operates. The number of *pentiti,* mafia members who are offering to cooperate with the police, is increasing, as is the number of Sicilians, private citizens, political and religious leaders who are willing to challenge the mafia publicly.

The fact that many Sicilians share a substratum of values that has spawned such a dreadful organization, however, should not be used as an indictment of the vast majority of Sicilians who are an energetic, talented and industrious people whose positive personal values far outweigh the negative. The mafia, if you were to assign a value to it in the large picture of Sicilian contributions to Western civilization, would be no more than a perversion, a wayward path that issues out of the main lane, a deviation at a crossroads. As such it should not be of allowed to stand as a stigma, as an all-encompassing blot that defines everything else Sicilian.

Sicilians have contributed a great deal to Western civilization in every field. A great number of important tools, inventions and products were introduced into Sicily and were exported eventually into Europe. The sun dial, Arabic numbers, silk, different citrus fruits, sugar cane, cotton, rice, and ice cream, to mention a few things, found their way to Europe through Sicily.

They have excelled in poetry so much so that a popular Sicilian saying declares to the world "Cu voli puisia vegna in Sicilia, ca teni la bannera dâ vittoria" (Whoever wants poetry, let him come to Sicily which holds the banner of victory). Stesicorus of Imera (VI c. B.C.), who is regarded by the ancients as the first poet to treat mythological and epic tales in a lyrical way, was Sicilian. Critics consider him a lyrical Homer, the creator of poetic language. Virgil based his myth of Aeneas's landing in Italy, and thus his founding of it on an account by Stesicorus. Another Sicilian from Siracusa, Theocritus (III c B.C.), invented bucolic poetry. The following were Sicilian, too: Giacomo da Lentini who invented the sonnet. The Sicilian School to which he belonged was responsible for inventing a new literary language that launched Italian letters; Giovanni Aurispa from Noto, a 14th century humanist and book merchant who collected 578 Greek manuscripts, including Homer's *Iliad*, greatly contributing to the Italian Renaissance; Antonio Veneziano "the Sicilian Petrarch" who wrote in Sicilian "because he did not want to be a parrot and speak somebody else's tongue." Veneziano's poetry was deemed worthy of paradise by Cervantes, who was held by pirates in the same Algerian cell; Giovanni Meli (1740-1815), who was known as the new Anacreon and was responsible for bringing the Sicilian language to its greatest heights; Meli's contemporary and rival, the legendary Micio Tempio, whose reputations has suffered because of the unabashed eroticism of his poetry, and

"L'Annunziata" by Antonello da Messina Palermo.

in our century, Salvatore Quasimodo, who won the Nobel Prize for literature in 1959.

In philosophy, because of the special aptitude of Sicilians for arguing, Cicero believed that rhetorics was born in Sicily. Gorgias of Lentini, one of the founders of Greek philosophical thought, often traveled to Greece to lecture on the art of rhetorics; Empedocles, whom Bertrand Russell considered the father of philosophy in the West, was so gifted in everything that he was regarded as a god by the people of Agrigento. Empedocles fascinated Matthew Arnold who wrote a poetic drama on him, *Empedocles on Etna* and Frederick Horderlin, who wrote *Derbd Tod des Empedocle,* in which he imagined that the philosopher chose death by jumping into the crater of Mount Etna.

In science, Archimedes of Siracusa was probably the greatest mind of the ancient world: he calculated the power of Pi, devised a way to burn Roman ships in the harbor by directing the sun's rays on them with huge metal reflectors. He is the scientist who while taking a bath realized the principle of water displacement by a solid body and started running naked through the streets of Siracusa, shouting "Eureka! Eureka!" (I've found it!). The legend says he was so engrossed in his calculations that he did not even see the Roman soldier who slew him.

In law, Charondas from Catania was one of the greatest lawgivers of the ancients. He practically put an end to the practice of sycophants, false accusers, by requiring those who swore false testimony to wear a wreath so people would know their crime. Charondas also promoted the idea of public education for those who could not afford it. Charondas had promulgated a law according to which no one could carry arms into the council chambers, under pain of death. One day he had been called to put down a rebellion and on the way back from the battle he entered the council chambers without realizing that he was armed. When someone pointed out his crime, he drew his sword and killed himself. It's true

Sicilians have a highly developed sense of honor, but by modern standards, that's carrying the notion a bit too far!

In politics and government, the Normans created the first centralized and absolute government in Europe, and Frederick II, "stupor mundi" strove to make his beloved Sicily a model for all other parts of his empire to imitate; he wanted Sicily to be a mirror for the world.

In art, Antonello da Messina introduced oil painting into the Italian Renaissance. Sicily has produced many world class painters, sculptors and architects. Pietro Novelli, known as "the Monrealese," was the greatest Sicilian painter after Antonello, Giacomo Serpotta was a master stucco sculptor and Filippo Juvara, the architect who built the Superga Basilica in Turin. Who does not know the rapturous music of Vincenzo Bellini, the "swan from Catania," whose name is practically synonymous with "bel canto" or Alessandro Scarlatti?

Nino Martoglio, Rosso di San Secondo, and Luigi Pirandello, (Nobel Prize for 1934) occupy important places in the theater. In fact, it's hard to imagine modern theater without the revolutionary work of Pirandello. And if we wanted to go back two thousand years, we could add that comic theater was perfected by another Sicilian named Epicarmus.

Guido Piovene was correct when he said that Sicily had given Italy the largest number of poets and writers in the last 150 years. Beginning with the 19th century Verist writers Giovanni Verga, Luigi Capuana, and Federico de Roberto, who developed a new mode of representing the world in a more scientific and objective way, Sicilian writers have dominated Italian narrative with highly original works: Elio Vittorini, Giuseppe Tomasi di Lampedusa, Leonardo Sciascia, Stefano Arrigo, Gesualdo Bufalino, Vincenzo Consolo, Dacia Maraini and Andrea Camilleri are some of the more famous names who have written important pages in the history of modern Italian literature.

Sicilians have also been on the forefront of political movements. The Christian Democratic party that governed Italy for over 40 years was founded by don Luigi Sturzo, a priest from Regalbuto. Many Sicilian statesmen such as Ruggero Settimo, Francesco Crispi and Vittorio Emanuele Orlando, Mario Scelba, etc... played an importan role in Italian national politics.

Sicilians have been first at many things, as we learn from Santi Correnti, a professor at Catania University:

Archestrato from Gela wrote *The Sweet Taste*, the first cookbook in the fourth century B.C. establishing a great reputation for Sicilian cooking.

Empedocles was the first volcanologist.

The first solar clock in Europe was set up in Catania in 263 B.C.

The first modern state was established by King Roger II in Palermo in the 12th century.

The first map of the world was created for King Roger II by a Sicilian Arab geographer named Al Edrisi.

Ice cream was invented by a man named Procopio from Acireale. His nephew opened up *Le Procope* in Paris, an establishment much frequented by Voltaire and his friends.

The first census in history was taken in Sicily in the 16th century.

The first European sinologists and orientalists were Sicilian; Prospero Intorcetta from Piazza Armerina was the first to translate the works of Confucius.

Gustavo Branca Minuti, a plastic surgeon from Catania, invented the "art of reconstructing noses" in the 15th century.

The first labor union, the "Fasci siciliani lavoratori," which brought together farmers and artisans, was born in Sicily in the last decade of the 19th century.

And the first truly modern psychiatric hospital that abandoned the medieval method of treating schizophrenia was founded by Pietro Pisani in Palermo in 1816. The manual for the treatment of patients written by Baron Pietro Pisani is truly an amazing document of humanity and caring.

I've barely scratched the surface of this complex subject. But at least, if you've read this far, you know there is more to Sicily than people realize. I hope you will make it your goal to fill the remaining gaps.

It would be so much more rewarding, and so much closer to the truth, if instead of Sicily as a mafia-infested island, you thought of it as the place where the bougainvillea bloom the year round, where the smell of orange blossom is an aphrodisiac, where the scent of jasmine is strong and fills the nights. Think of it as a place that gave Europe a taste for "sanguinelli," -- the blood oranges that grow only there -- a place that made things sweet when the Arabs began to cultivate on its soil, that made it possible for Europeans to wrap their bodies in the luxurious feel of silk. Think of Sicily as the place where spring is born when Pluto releases Persephone from her infernal captivity! Think of it as the German Romantic poet Wolfgang Goethe did, who wrote in his diary: "Italy without Sicily leaves no trace upon the soul. Sicily is the key to everything."

The Trinacria: the Symbol of Sicily

It may seem strange that after more than forty-one years from the signing of its Special Autonomy Statute (1946), Sicily did not have an official symbol to differentiate itself from the other Italian regions. To tell the truth, this was something of a surprise to me. In fact, if someone had asked me, "What is the symbol of Sicily?" I would have answered without thinking twice, "the Trinacria," that is, the tryskelion, the three running legs with the head of Medusa in the middle. Everybody knows that that is the symbol of Sicily. And yet it had not been adopted officially until 1989. To remedy this

Fig 1

embarrassing situation, in 1982 the Sicilian Parliament decided to propose a law to adopt a banner. So it proposed one (Fig. 1) divided in four equal parts that contained, from left to right, the Norman flag in the first square: a blue field crossed diagonally by two stripes made up of little red and silver alternating squares; next to it a square showing the black eagle of the Swabians in the center. In the two squares below, at the left, in a field of silver, there's the image of the Tryskelion, all in gold, with blades of wheat instead of the classical serpents; and on the right in the last square there are the vertical gold and red stripes of the Aragonese.

This proposal, however, raised many objections. A heated debate exploded involving journalists, university professors, and scholars of Sicilian culture and history. The main objection to this design was that the tryskelion, the ancient symbol of Sicily and therefore connected with its native culture, would be put on the same historical level as the other three associated with various foreign dominations, that is, the conquerors who came from the North of Europe in the 11th century, the Hoenstaufens who came from Swabia, a region of modem Switzerland, and the Spanish Aragonese.

Two other banners were proposed in the course of the debate, recalling some historical aspects of Sicily. The first (Fig. 2) proposes to represent Sicily with its three historical plains: the plain of Mazara (Val di Mazara) is represented by a bunch of grapes symbolizing the vineyards of

Fig. 2

Fig. 3

the Belice river valley and Marsala; the second (Val Demone) shows, on a blue background common to all three, an anchor symbolizing the mariner traditions of the Messina province; the triangle below represents the plains of Noto (Val di Noto) famous for the production of wheat symbolized by the yellow blade. The three valleys are separated by a strip shaped like an inverted Y that shows the colors of the Normans. At the fork of the Y, that is, at the center of Sicily, which has always been associated with the city of Enna, known as "Hombelicus Siciliae", that is, "the belly button of Sicily", is represented by the octagonal castle of Frederick II, built in the city of Enna.

The third design (Fig 3) reproduces the classical tryskelion with the head of the Medusa, a somewhat less terrifying image than the Greek one surrounded by blades that refer to the large production of wheat in Sicily which was known in ancient times "the granary of Rome."

The borders of the oval are two stripes in which you can see the red and silver squares of the Normans. The dolphins with their heads above the waves symbolize the central position of Sicily in the Mediterranean sea.

These and other designs were proposed to the Parliament, but after a great deal of discussion, the design that was accepted by the committee contains, as was right and predictable, the tryskelion as the central element of the banner. Another preliminary design that seemed to enjoy the favor of the Regional Assembly was the one shown in Fig. 4, which has the image of the Trinacria at center with two equal fields in red and

Fig. 4

yello and with the Italian tricolor running diagonally from top to bottom. This design, however, did not survive in exactly the same form. The three stripes representing the Italian tricolored flag were eventualy removed.

After considerable bickering, the Sicilian Regional Assembly finally settled on a design for a banner that contained the Trinacria, the colors of Sicily (red and yellow) and the name "Regione Siciliana" on top, (Fig. 5). A more complex design was chosen for its escutcheon (Fig. 6), which features clockwise from top left, the white and red stripes of the Normans, the imperial eagle of Frederick II, the vertical gold and orange stripes of the Aragonese, and theTrinacria. A regional law was passed accepting it as the official escutcheon of Sicily in July 1989, (Law no. 373/90), but it

Fig. 5

Fig 6

was not long before the State Commissioner of Italy declared the law null and void, claiming that the Region had gone beyond the powers granted to it by the Constitution.

Naturally, the Assembly did not accept the verdict of the Commissioner which denied Sicily a right enjoyed by the other semiautonomous regions, and brought the case to the Constitutional Court. The Court declared that although the Special Statute of Sicily did not mention the right to choose a banner, it did not mean it did not have that right, especially since other regions whose statutes were more recent had it. Sicily won its day in Court and now it's official. No one can take the Trinacria away from Sicily.

The Origins of the Tryskelion

It's difficult to retrace the origins of this symbol. Exemplars of tryskelions have been found in many locations on the shores of the Mediterranean sea -- in Crete, Sicily, Greece, France, Asia Minor, on the North African coastline, and even on the Island of Man, between Great Britain and Ireland -- in different eras beginning from the VIII century B.C.. Recently two of them were found at Castiddazzu and Bitalemi, dating back to the VII-VI century B.C. The tryskelion, like the Swastika, can be considered one of the most ancient designs of the Mediterranean basin. There are three theories regarding its origins. According to some scholars it is of Phoenician derivation and had a religious significance associated with the semitic God Baal. The idea of the three legs in running position meant the racing of time, the annual cycle of nature. Baal was the god of

Fig. 7.

time and the three legs could have been associated with the trinity of Baal.

The second hypothesis claims that the tryskelion is a heraldic symbol associated with the Spartans. They were also known as Laecedemons and carried on their shield a bent leg which signified the letter Lambda, that is, the Greek "L" of their name. The soldiers of Dionysos I, the Tyrant of Siracusa, wanted to be recognized as Sicilians and put three legs on their shields symbolizing the three promontories that stand at the corners of Sicily: Pachino, Peloro and Lilibeo. (Fig. 7).

The third hypothesis is based on the two examples of tryskelions found at Castiddazzu (near Agrigento) and at Bitalemi (near Gela). These two, which are the most ancient ever found in Sicily show certain similarities with other tryskelions found in Crete in earlier times. This fact suggests that the Minoan civilization of Crete had contacts with Sicily in this period and exported the design. Whatever may have been the origins of the image, the simplest explanation may be that it is a solar symbol and the three running legs are in fact rays of the Sun. After all, Sicily is known as the Island of the Sun.

Fig. 8.

The name of the symbol varies according to the times. The Romans used to call it *triquetra,* which means triangle and refers obviously to the triangular shape of the island; the Greeks called it *tryskelion* which means three legs. And the name Trinacria derives from *trinakrios* which in Greek means triangle. The name Trinacria has been, in fact, another name for Sicily throughout history and it is regularly used to this day. In 1302 at the peace of Caltabellotta, which ended the French rule in Sicily, the name was used officially to designate the island. The Aragonese monarch was to be known as "King of Trinacria" and the Angevin ruler of Naples was to be called "King of Sicily".

The other important element is the head. It is obviously the head of Medusa, the most powerful and best known of the three sisters known as Gorgons. Medusa, according to Greek mythology had snakes as hair and her look was so dreadful that whoever looked at her would be petrified. The Greek hero Perseus, with the help of Athena, was able to cut her head off without looking at her directly, but through a reflection in his shiny shield. The head of Medusa became part of Athena's shield, symbolizing the goddess' invincibility. At the time of the Romans the head of the Medusa was replaced by the image of a sweet-looking young maiden with stalks of wheat protruding from her head instead of the horrifying snakes. The substitution was probably made to emphasize the fertility of Sicily. The Romans, in fact, used the island as the granary that fed its legions. Rome fought two wars against the Carthaginians to make of Sicily its first province. The substitution of the more benevolent nature goddess instead of the castrating and fearful monster, makes perfect sense in view of Sicily agricultural economy. As a goddess of nature she may represent Demeter who made Sicily her home together with her daughter Kore/Persephone. The myth of the abduction of Persephone by the god of the underworld Pluto took place, after all, on the shores of Lake Pergusa near Enna.

Images of the "triquetra" are quite common in Sicily, but it is surprisingly present in many other places. One such place is the Isle of Man where it may have been brought from Sicily by the Vikings (Fig. 9).

Fig.9

Sicily and Greece

In a Sicilian song written in 2001, Aurelio Caliri related the well-known Homeric tale of Polyphemus, the one-eyed Cyclops who lived on the slopes of Mount Etna and the Greek hero Ulysses, from an unusual perspective. As you may recall from the *Odyssey*, Ulysses and his companions had been imprisoned by Polyphemus in his cave on Mt. Etna and were being slaughtered and eaten by the monster. Ulysses succeeded in getting the Cyclops drunk and stuck a burning tree stump into his one eye while the giant was asleep. There is no question that from the Homeric perspective the villain was Polyphemus, characterized as a brute monster who practiced cannibalism, while Ulysses was cast in the role of

A mosaic depicting Ulysses and Poliphemus from the Villa del Casale in Piazza Armerina.

a civilizing hero. In the struggle, Ulysses' wit and intelligence won over brute force. This was also the perspective that I, as a Sicilian growing up in Sicily, shared as well, and I suppose that this is true for all Western civilization.

Ulysses was a part of the heritage that nourished all of us. As children, none of us identified with the Cyclops. He was the other in us, the shadowy part of our psyche, the monster within in whose defeat we saw our victory. The struggle between Ulysses and Poliphemus was a battle between good and evil, intelligence and brute force, civilization and barbarity. That part of the story in which Ulysses tells Poliphemus that his name is "No one" underscores the humiliating defeat of brute force when confronted by a superior intelligence. When the Cyclops tried to enlist the aid of his brothers by saying 'No one has blinded me," they assumed he was drunk and did not help him.

But in his song, Aurelio Caliri saw the event from the perspective of a native Sicilian. Ulysses was viewed as the first of a long line of invaders of the island, the first conqueror who trampled on a native son of Sicily. And Polyphemus who was as Sicilian as Mt. Etna, or the giants who lived in its bowels, Typheus, Bronte and Sterope, was cast as a victim of an external force who came to disturb his idyllic peace. Thus, for him, the story became emblematic of the history of Sicily that has seen 16 different dominations, give or take a few, that have come and gone attracted by the beauty of the Sicilian landscape, by its fertility, its climate, and its riches.

Caliri's point of view was baffling to me at first. As a Sicilian engaged in the promotion of the Sicilian language and culture, I should have rooted for the local fellow and not for the outsider. The fact that I didn't, however, seems to me significant. I did not consider Ulysses an outsider. I did not consider the Greeks as outsiders. They were an integral part of the history of Sicily almost from the beginning and I did not see the separation between the Sicilians on one side and the Greeks on the other. Sicily was Greek. Sicily was an important part, if not the most important, of *Magna Graecia*. I suppose that Caliri identified more with the local inhabitants of Sicily, the Siculi. But they were not indigenous either, nor were the Sikans who had come to the island before them, nor were the Elimians on the west coast. All of these people came to Sicily from different places. Scholars have been unable so far of determining where they came from, even though the Sikans and Siculi may have descended from Northern Italy, possibly the regions of Liguria or Latium.[1] So the question arises: to whom does one owe allegiance. Who were the true Sicilians? I suppose that since the Siculi gave Sicily its name, as well as important elements of its cultural and historical heritage, they should be considered as first on the list, even though the Sikans also gave us Sikania, another name for the island. From the point of view of the Sikans, the Siculi were the invaders. Indeed, the Siculi who settled on the eastern side of the island pushed the Sikans far to the west, until the two groups assimilated. Too little is known about either of these two groups for them to become a presence on modern

Sicilian psyche. The heritage of the Greeks, on the other hand, is everywhere present and in the end their higher civilization has given us the artifacts which inform our view of history. We know little of the Siculi and Sikans, (more can be learned through a more aggressive archeological program) but much more about the Greeks who managed to change the face of Sicily and become identified with it. The legend of Ulysses and Poliphemus may be interpreted heumeristically as the real encounter between the Greeks and the older inhabitants of the island characterized by the victors as uncivilized brutes. No doubt, in Homer's version, the colors are darkened for effect. The relationship between victor and vanquished was probably less extreme as we will learn from the following excursus into the island's Greek past.

A homage to the Greek landing in what is now Giardini-Naxos.

While Sicily may not have been the first place the Greeks colonized, (Cuma and what is now Ischia were credited as being the first colonies) it was certainly the place in which they invested most of their colonizing spirit. Long before some of the young men from the island of Euboea in the western Greece decided to embark on their adventurous journey to Sicily, the island was known to them through the reports of sailors. Those accounts, which probably spoke of a more luscious island than it is today, rich with many trees, many abundant rivers, and sparsely populated countrysides must have sparked the Greek imagination. Comparing it to the mountainous and barren land of Greece, Sicily must have appeared to the first daring men of Hellas as an earthly paradise, a kind of Promised Land. It is no wonder then that once the first colonists accepted the challenge, the Greeks from other cities quickly came to populate its shores and founded many cities. The Chalcidians from Euboea led the way founding the first city on Sicily at Naxos in 735 BC.[2] The dates of the founding of many cities on the east coast of Sicily vary according to the historian you read. But there seems to be agreement that Naxos was the first settlement. The town of Giardini, in whose territory Naxos was founded, recently renamed itself Giardini-Naxos to emphasize its antiquity. Siracusa was founded a year later by Archia from the city of Corinth in 734; the Chalcidians also founded Lentini in 728 and Catania in 727. Once the initial settlement was complete, the Greeks started to fan out westward from their primary settlements to found other cities. Gela was founded in 688 and nearly a hundred years afterwards its citizens, who hailed originally from Rhodes and Crete, went on to found Agrigento in 580 BC. The inhabitants of Zancle, whose city was founded nearly at the same time as Lentini and Catania, founded Milazzo (around 720-715 BC) shortly afterwards because their primary city, surrounded by mountains on all sides, had little land to cultivate. All the primary cities were founded on the coast, with the exception of Lentini which is about 15 kms. inland, in locations that gave the settlers easy access to fertile plains. Also Zancle/Messina may have been founded as a defensive post protecting the Straits of Messina, the passage between the Ionian and the Thyrrenian seas. The activity of extending their territories continued with the Megara inhabitants founding Selinunte, facing the land controlled by the Carthaginians in the southwest and the Messinese founding of Himera on the northern coast in 689/88.

The Greeks did not have as difficult a time gaining control of the island as the Arabs were to have in the ninth and tenth centuries AD, but there was resistance to their expansion, first by the Siculi and then by the Carthaginians. The initial settlement seems to have been accomplished without much fighting. The east coast of Sicily seems to have been sparsely populated and the local inhabitants moved away or became assimilated with the Greeks. There are cases in which a local rulers of the Siculi actually granted the Greeks land in which to live and build their city.[3] A *modus vivendi* was found, however, which allowed the Greek cities to grow in importance. Eventually they succeeded in Hellenizing the island completely, establishing a flourishing civilization in their cities. Until the V century BC the *modus vivendi* between the Siculi and the Greeks operated, but halfway through the century a Prince of the Siculi named Ducezio organized various pockets of resistance into open hostilities against the Greek cities, obtaining some military successes. Ducezio wrested control of Etna-Inessa from Siracusa and Motyon from Agrigento and for a time called himself King of Sicily, but he was defeated by Siracusa in 446 BC and exiled to Corinth.[4] The Greeks had little to fear from the Siculi from this point on and continued to extend their cultural and military presence in the island with few exceptions, one being the Carthaginians who held cities in the west. But as the Greeks put their mark on the island, Sicily, as it was to do with almost every domination, conditioned and shaped that culture in its own image. The Greeks from the diaspora, Siculi and Sikans eventually came to be known as Siceliots using a Greek suffix, "otu" still in use in Sicilian, to signify "belonging to" (as in *vicariotu, bazzariotu*). The culture of the Siceliots, though Greek in essence, had special characteristics that made it unique, just as the Sicilian Baroque was different from the Baroque when it found application in Sicily after the shattering earthquake of 1693.

Part of the reason for the Sicilianization of the Greek "colonies" had to do with their special nature. It's important to remember that the "colonization" of Sicily was really more of an "immigration".[5] The Greeks who came to Sicily from various cities, were not sent as representatives of their homeland, that is, they were not expeditionary forces that came and conquered, in the manner later followed by the Arabs. The Greeks were primarily men in search of land to cultivate. Considering that Greece had run out of space for its expanding population and considering their innate enterprising nature, people who had no future in their homeland sought out their "place in the Sun" in the "Island of the Sun" as Homer called it. Like the Arabs after them and unlike the many groups who have dominated Sicily, the Greeks came to stay. Once they established themselves on the island, displacing the local inhabitants to get what they wanted, they came to regard it as their homeland, in short, they became Sicilian Greeks and eventually Sicilians, even though the spiritual bond with the mother country was never broken. The Siceliots fiercely defended their independence from encroachments by people from their original homeland. The battle cry of the Siracusan soldiers as they engaged their Athenian foes was "Sicily for the Sicilians!" Another example of this newly found allegiance to the island they had come to regard as their homeland can be seen in an ancient vase with a painting of the shields of Spartan soldiers who had come to Sicily as part of an expeditionary force. The shields show the Greek letter "Lambda" that stood for "Laecedemoni" as Spartans were also known. The "l" resembles a

A metope depicting Perseus slaying the Medusa from Selinunte.

An artist's rendering of a Greek ship like those used to colonize Sicily.

human leg. Once the soldiers had chosen Sicily as their homeland, the shield decoration was changed and instead of sporting one leg, they painted three legs on it, to identify them as belonging to Sicily. The three legs referred, of course, to the triangular shape of Sicily that was known to the Greeks as Trinacria, the three-cornered island. The three-running legs, with the image of Medusa in the center, is the oldest symbol of the island and it has been chosen as the centerpiece of its regional flag. The face of Medusa has been changed to that of a mother goddess who has stalks of wheat coming out of her head, a reference to Sicily's fertility, instead of the snakes that girded Medusa's head. [6]

The Greek settlements grew into independent and powerful city-states and behaved like the city-states, the *poleis* of the homeland, who shared an important characteristic: they projected their power outward, always attempting to become more powerful than their neighbors, always reaching for supremacy. And so did the Sicilian cities of Agrigento and Siracusa. These two Sicilian cities together with Athens were the largest and most powerful cities in the Mediterranean, which at that time, meant the world. Siracusa rivaled Athens in power and one of its leaders, known as Gelone, was responsible for saving Sicily and the Italian peninsula from Carthaginian expansion by defeating their army in one of the greatest battles of ancient times in the plains of Himera in 480 BC. One of the conditions imposed on the defeated Carthaginians was the rejection of human sacrifices which until that time was practiced by the North Africans. The reach of power of the Tyrants of Siracusa, who were not always tyrannical as their title suggests, was long and dominant not only in Sicily but outside of it. Geron, for example, has been credited with stopping the Etruscan expansion toward the south by defeating their army at Cuma, near Naples, in 474 BC.

In the fifth century BC, Siracusa was the largest and most important city of the Mediterranean, especially after it defeated the Athenians in 413 BC. In spite of intermittent civil wars and continuous conflict with the Carthaginians, Siracusa came to establish almost complete control of the island under several rulers who abolished democracy and set themselves up as Tyrants, which at the time meant something like warlord, or military leader and did not have the negative connotations it carries today.[7] The first of these rulers was Dionysius I, who made Siracusa an impregnable fortress. Dion succeeded him for a short period and was exiled by Dionysius II. Timoleon was next and finally Agathocles, the last before the island became embroiled in the struggle between the Cartaginians and the Romans known as the Punic Wars that eventually saw Sicily become the first province of Rome. This constituted the beginning of the end of the most splendid eras in Sicilian history. The Romans brought exploitation and depredation that eventually made of Sicily a backwater country, useful only for producing wheat.

But when Siracusa was the predominant power on the island (despite the less than enlightened rule of its tyrants), it enjoyed nearly 150 years of stability that allowed it to develop a society that had nothing to envy in its counterpart in Greece. Indeed, in terms of intellectual activity, commerce, creativity in the arts, sports, entertainment, and theatre there was really no difference between Sicily and Greece. It has been said that Sicily was Greece on a grander scale.[8] I cannot help but make an analogy between the ancient Greeks and Sicilians on one hand and the English and Americans on the other. Just as the Americans received their language, laws and institutions, and their culture from the English and went on to develop a civilization of their own that conditioned the language and culture of the mother country, Sicily received the language, culture and institutions of the Greeks and later contributed much not only to the mother country but to the world under the aegis of Greece. If Western civilization owes a great debt of gratitude to Greece, as it certainly does, some of the credit belongs rightly to Siceliots who represented an important part of their world. Sicily, after all, together with southern Italy was called "Magna Graecia" which may be understood as "the Greater Greece".

If Sicily was Greek in customs, language, and culture, it can also be said that Greece was Sicilian in part, for the influence and exchange did not flow on a one-way street from Greece to Sicily only. It flowed in the other direction as well. Many of the great minds of antiquity that we normally associate with Greece were actually born on Sicilian soil and lived on the island most of their lives. A few names will suffice:

Archimedes, the greatest scientific mind of antiquity was born in Siracusa in 287 BC and lived there all of his life. His genius was inexhaustible and his inventions were of such scope that they changed the nature of mathematics and science. Like Leonardo da Vinci, he was a multifaceted genius. He worked on astronomy, constructing an artificial sphere in which one could observe the movement of the Sun, the Moon and the other planets. Once Geron, the Tyrant of Siracusa, asked him to prove that a goldsmith had cheated him by giving him a crown made of lesser metals than the solid gold he had asked for. Archimedes went on to prove that the goldsmith had made the inside of the crown in silver and the outside in gold, discovering in the process the principle that elements have a specific weight. He was an engineer who constructed many defensive and offensive military weapons. He devised a way to burn Roman ships in the harbor of Siracusa by directing the sun's rays on them with huge metal reflectors. It is said that such reflectors produced such intense heat that they could burn wood at a distance of 200 meters, melt lead at 120 meters and silver at 50 meters.[9] He invented the value of the Greek Pi; he invented a *cochlea*, known today as Archimedes' screw that was used in Egypt and in Sicily and elsewhere to raise water to a higher level. He said that he could move any weight with minimum effort. He once remarked that if he had a point of support he could move the earth. He also discovered many laws of physics, such as the principle of water displacement by a solid body. While taking a bath he found the solution to a problem he had been pondering and he started running naked through the streets of Siracusa shouting "Eureka, Eureka!" (I found it!). And he envisioned modern Calculus. Archimedes was killed in 212 BC while immersed in his calculations by a Roman soldier who did not know who he was. Needless to say, the contributions Archimedes made to Greek scientific thought were enormous. And this is an important example of how the exchange of information and scholarship actually flowed from Sicily to Greece and not the other way around.

Another example of how such scholarship flowed eastward across the Ionian sea to Greece from the island concerned Rhetorics, the art of public speaking, which had its beginning in Sicily. Cicero, who was one of the most famous Roman orators, acknowledged that Sicilians were the first to consider the subject a matter that could be taught. They were masters in the art. In fact, Gorgias of Lentini, (483 BC) one of the founders of Greek philosophical thought, traveled to Athens in 427 BC and astonished his listeners with his consummate skill as a public speaker. He often visited the city to instruct young Athenians. Tisias, one of his disciples, who often accompanied him, coauthored with Corax of Agrigento, the first manual on public speaking.

Empedocles, a naturalist philosopher, orator, poet, physician, scientist, whom Bertrand Russell considered the father of philosophy in the West, was so gifted in everything he did that the people of Agrigento regarded him as a god. He traveled throughout *Magna Graecia,* becoming a legend in his own time. He was also credited with being the first volcanologist. He fell or jumped into Mt. Etna, was swallowed by the volcano, and legend has it that the mountain expelled one of his sandals intact.

Sicilians contributed substantial innovations to Greek theatre through the work of Epicharmus, born in Megara Hiblea or Siracusa. Aristotle credited Epicharmus with the elevation of comedy to the level of high drama. He wrote in a language that was a mixture of Doric Greek with local Siracusan dialect and his comedies influenced Aristophanes who used some of Epicharmus' scenes in his plays. Sicilians were also responsible for assigning a different role to the chorus in their plays and for introducing the *Mime*, a new type of poetry. Siceliots loved the theater as much as the Greeks did and as a witness to this love they have left many open-air theatres carved out of the stone and set against dramatic backdrops in Siracusa, Segesta, Eraclea Minoa, Tindari, and Taormina.

In law, Charondas from Catania was of the greatest lawgivers of the ancients. He practically put an end to the practice of sycophants, false accusers, by requiring those who swore false testimony to wear a wreath so people would know their crime. Charondas also promoted the idea of public education for those who could not afford it. His laws were praised by the likes of Aristotle and Plato and were adopted in many cities of Magna Graecia.

Stesicorus of Himera (VI c. BC) was not born in Sicily but lived most of his life in Himera, a city famous for a great victory of the Siracusan army against the Carthaginians in 480 BC. Stesicorus was regarded as the first poet to treat mythological and epic tales in a lyrical way. He was considered a lyrical Homer.

Theocritus (III c. BC) was born in Siracusa and is considered the greatest poet of Hellenistic literature. He was the father of bucolic poetry that inspired so many poets through the ages.

Archestratus of Gela was a famous cook who is credited with the first cookbook entitled *The Sweet Taste*, making the reputation of Sicilian cooks famous all over the known world. And Mileto of Siracusa sent his own chef to give lessons to the Greeks in the renowned culinary art of Sicily.

Evemero of Messina was the first man to interpret the theogonies in a novel way that was to have much success in the middle ages. He attributed human origins to the gods and interpreted their stories as real historical events. His name has given us the adjective "heumeristic".

Sicilians excelled in the fine arts. The coins minted in Siracusa by Eveneto and Cimone were renowned as the supreme creation of the art. Sicilian sculptors were no less gifted than their Greek counterparts, as is made abundantly evident by visiting the major Sicilian museums. In architecture, Sicilians added their own features to the majestic temples that grace the countryside in Agrigento, creating a style known as Sicilian-Doric. Historiography was also well developed under Philistus of Siracusa and Timaeus of Taormina as was the art of draftsmanship.

The relationship between Sicily and Greece was not, as I said earlier, a one-way street. Many Sicilians returned to Greece to visit the oracles, to participate in the Olympic games, to teach and to learn. And many famous Greeks visited Sicily. Plato, the great philosopher, spent a good deal of time in Sicily as a political advisor to Dion and to Dionysius II whom he wanted to mold into his own figure of the philosopher king as outlined in his work *The Republic*, without much success we might add. Aeschylus, the great tragedian went there as well and wrote a play entitled "The Women of Etna" now lost, while at the court of Geron. Some of his plays were performed in Siracusa for the first time. Aeschylus died in Gela in 456. The poet Pindar spent some time in Agrigento, which he regarded as "the most beautiful city of mortal men." Even the greatest woman poet of antiquity, Sappho, was received with great honor when she visited Siracusa. Many of Greece's most notable poets and writers such as Arion, Simonides and Bacchilides, were guests of the Tyrants.

Greek visitors to Sicily include not only poets and intellectuals. Sicily stimulated the Greek imagination much before they decided to live there. In fact the image of Sicily as it emerged from sailors' accounts and poetry was probably instrumental in engendering in those first courageous colonizers the desire to see it first hand. Greek sailors had probably circumnavigated the island four or five centuries before they decided to colonize it. The fact that they localized so many of their myths on Sicily confirms that they knew a great deal about the geography of the island. Thus, it became the locale for much of the *Odyssey*, even if we do not accept the theories put forth by Samuel Butler and others which identify Ithaca with Trapani. Ulysses spent considerable time of his ten-year peregrinations after the Trojan War in and around Sicily. And it is the setting for Greek legends and myths.

The legendary Minos, King of Crete, followed Daedalus to Sicily to seek revenge. Daedalus, as you will recall, constructed a wooden cow for Minos' wife Pasiphae so she could satisfy her desire to join with the white bull of Poseidon. Out of that union the monstrous Minotaur was born and hidden in the maze created by Daedalus. When Minos imprisoned him in the labyrinth together with his son for having given Ariadne the thread that allowed Theseus to enter the labyrinth and slay the Minotaur, Daedalus escaped by fashioning a pair of wax wings for himself and Icarus. His son eventually fell into the sea and drowned but Daedalus managed to reach Sicily where King Cocalus welcomed him. He proved his engineering skills by solving a problem posed by the King. Cocalus asked Daedalus to thread a hair through the inner coils of the spiral of a shell whose end he had broken off. In response Daedalus tied the hair to an ant and put some honey at the opposite end of the shell. The ant went through the spiral carrying the hair after it. Cocalus was impressed, and when Minos asked him to give up Daedalus to him so he could punish him, the Sicilian king gave him a warm welcome and then proceeded to have him drowned in a bathtub.

The majestic Doric temple of Segesta.

One interesting tale which can be interpreted as a mythological translation of the passage of culture from Greece to Sicily is the myth of Alpheus and the nymph Arethusa. According to the story immortalized by Ovid and Virgil, the hunter saw Arethusa in the woods of Arcadia and fell madly in love with her. When he was ready to grasp her, Arethusa begged the gods to save her and she was transformed into a stream. The little river flowed into the sea and crossed under the Ionian sea to emerge on the island of Ortygia in Siracusa. Alpheus, unable to stand the pain of the loss of the beloved, asked to be changed into a stream and thus he too crossed the sea to emerge in Ortygia, to be near his beloved. The fresh water source is known to the local inhabitants as "l'occhio di Zillica" and it flows out in the middle of the great port of Siracusa, not far from the Fountain of Arethusa. Thus Greece and Sicily were connected by an underwater river symbolizing the union of their cultures.

The Trinacria with the head of the Medusa.

The demigod Hercules is known to have visited Sicily and to have killed a local hero named Eryx, a personification of Mount San Giuliano on which the city of Erice was built. Aphrodite herself had an important cult there. But of all the myths, the most important was the myth of the Great Mother Goddess Demeter and her daughter Persephone.[10] According to the myth, Pluto kidnapped Persephone near Enna's Lake Pergusa and brought her down the underworld. The myth related how Demeter, distraught over the loss of her daughter allowed all vegetation to perish. The situation became extremely serious and required the intervention of Zeus who ordered his brother Pluto to return Persephone to her mother. Pluto acquiesced, but before releasing Persephone he made her eat a pomegranate which symbolized for the ancients the wedding vows, essentially forcing her to return to the underworld. The ancient mythographers claim that Persephone by order of Zeus was supposed to spend two thirds of her time with her husband and the remaining third with her mother on earth. But owing to the fact that Sicily has only two seasons: winter and summer, Persephone spends half her time with Pluto fulfilling her marital duties and half on earth with her mother. Thus, when she is released from the underworld, nature is reborn. Sicily is the birth of spring, probably because it is the land where the almond tree blooms first in Europe. That Sicily embodied the birth of spring is probably emblematic of how the Greeks felt about the island. Demeter brought wheat to Sicily and Bacchus was said to have given mankind wine after he discovered grapes in Sicily. The goddess Athena is credited with having given the Sicilians the olive tree. These three products, of course, identify the main staples on which Sicilian agriculture thrived at the time. Hephaestos, the smith of the gods, whom the Romans called Vulcan, had his shop in the bowels of Mount Etna; as did the Cyclops Poliphemus and the giants Bronte, Tipheus and Sterope. Many other Olympians are connected with Sicily. The god of the winds, Eolus, lived in the Eolian islands within sight of the coast of Sicily and the waters of Sicily were home to the nymphs and monsters Galatea and Scilla and Charibdis in the Straits of Messina.

The gods of the Greeks became the gods of the Sicilians. Their temples were dedicated to Aphrodite in Erice, to Hercules, Jupiter, Hera, Castor and Pollux in Agrigento, and to Apollo and Artemis in Siracusa. Even the cathedral of Siracusa was built on the site of a temple to Venus, incorporating the ancient columns into the walls of the church. Conversely, though not quite so universally, the gods of the older Sicilian population came to be associated with Greek gods. Local divinities who were clearly a product of the native imagination and who were unknown in the Pantheon of Greek gods, were given in time Greek genealogy and absorbed. A few examples will suffice. On the slopes of Mt. Etna, near Paternò, the native Sicilians were extremely devoted to the goddess Hyblaia, a telluric divinity associated with the underground rumblings of the volcano. Her cult, which involved the use of priests and diviners of dreams known as Galeotai, had already become Hellenized and may have been associated with Aphrodite or Venus as the protectress of the fecundity of the earth. Another local myth that became hellenized was that of the Palici Twins, who represented telluric phenomena and were considered the protectors of the Sicilian people under Ducezio and of the Sicilian slaves who revolted against the Romans in 210 and 113 BC. Though the more ancient tradition claims they were the sons of Adrano, the God of Etna, later mythographers tell us they were the sons of Zeus and the Nymph Talia. They were born underground because their mother feared the wrath of Zeus' wife, Hera. The divine twins were honored by the people with the erection of a great temple where people came to swear oaths. The punishment for those who failed to keep their oaths was death or blinding. No one dared to lie before the altar of the Twins. Those who were found guilty of lying were exposed to the emanations of dangerous vapors from the nearby lake Naftia which caused blindness. This fear was so great that even today when Sicilians swear to the veracity of their statements, they utter the sentence: "Privu di la vista di l'occhi" (May I lose the sight of my eyes!) Another important indigenous cult that became hellenized was the cult of the God Adrano, a personification of Mt. Etna who had a temple on the slopes of the mountain in the middle of the fields of lava before the city of Adrano was built. In fact, the city was built in sight of the temple by order of Dionysius the Elder in 400 BC in pursuit of his political aims of domination of the Etnean territory. For the Greeks he represented the god of fire and his name was often given as Hephaestus and Vulcan. As he was portrayed in statues in a defensive posture holding a lance in his hand he was associated also with Ares or Mars. Thus he was seen as a protector and defender. The legend tells of the one thousand cirnechi dogs, a breed that can still be seen in the mosaics of Piazza Armerina, that assisted the god in his task. These dogs were so intelligent that they welcomed the many visitors to the temple during the day and escorted them home at night, but those who came to the temple at night with evil intentions were quickly discovered and the dogs proceeded to eat them alive. Liars and perjurers had much to worry about with these dogs. An element of this myth remains in the phrase Sicilians commonly use to denounce liars: "chi ti pozzanu manciari li cani!" (May you be devoured by the dogs!). These indigenous Sicilian myths, together with many others we cannot address, went on to enrich the Pantheon of Greek divinities for a time but have disappeared almost completely.

The connections between Sicily and Greece extend beyond the collapse of Magna Graecia before the advancing armies of Rome. Even after the Roman conquest, Sicily did not abandon its Sicilian-Greek heritage. The people of the island continued to speak Greek even though Rome imposed its language for official functions. Greek remained the written language of Sicily alongside Latin. Indeed, even after the collapse of the Roman Empire in the fifth century AD when Sicily fell into the orbit of the Eastern Roman Empire and the Eastern religious rites were introduced, Greek became once again the predominant language. Those who survived the onslaught of the Arabs in Northeastern Sicily continued to speak Greek until the Normans reintroduced Latin in the 11th century. Through the Norman period, Greek, Arabic and Latin were the three official languages at court. Greek and Arabic began to lose ground when the new vulgar languages, Sicilian at first and Tuscan afterwards, gained wider acceptance.

It's clear that the histories of Sicily and Greece are closely bound by language, customs, and affinities of character and attitude. None of the people who came to Sicily have been as compatible with the Sicilian people as the Greeks. Sicilians, especially those from the eastern part of the island who resisted the infiltration of the Arabs, inherited from the Greeks their sense of drama, along with their liveliness, their sense of hospitality, their gift for reasoning, their diffidence and even their physical appearance. The Sicilians from the provinces of Messina, Catania and Siracusa to name the major cities of the east coast are much closer to Greeks in looks and attitudes than they are to the inhabitants of Venice or Milano. If I were to identify those peoples with whom Sicilians have an affinity I'd say the Greeks are in first place, followed closely by the Arabs, then the Normans and the Spaniards. All of the others, the French, the Piedmontese, the Austrians, and also the Romans, were considered foreigners and were tolerated, but never accepted, and did not leave much of a trace on the Sicilian psyche.

The Venus Landolina. Siracusa.

The many men whose fame extended far outside the island advanced the cause of Hellenic civilization in that they wrote and spoke in Greek or a Sicilianized version of it, but having been born and raised on Sicily they represented their homeland. Their allegiance was to the city that gave them birth. Thus, if someone happened to be born in Siracusa, he was first Siracusan and then Sicilian, especially when Siracusa was at the height of her power and controlled almost all of the island. Siracusa and Sicily at that point were one reality. Naturally, they showed pride in belonging to a larger world that included the Greek city-states because they spoke a language they understood and shared common values and customs. They had a sense of belonging to the larger context *vis à vis* the non-Greek world. They were conscious of belonging to a superior civilization and regarded the non-Greek as barbarians. The Carthaginians and even the Romans were part of the outside world.

If all the men I have mentioned were able to flourish and live in Sicily, it must be clear that they found the right atmosphere and conditions there to develop their talents. The artistic and scientific developments of the island, if we do not want to claim that it had reached even higher levels of achievements than Greece itself, certainly was on par with it. The island, together with some of the cities founded by the Greeks in Calabria and Campania such as Locri, Crotone, Sibari, Paestum, Metaponto, and which constitute *Magna Graecia*, shared Greece's intellectual orientation, the same spirit and the same life, and embodied the highest form of civilization in the world. After all, the great Greek philosopher-mathematician Pythagoras who founded the great school of thought known as "The Italic School" lived in Crotone, in Calabria for 20 years and then moved to Metaponto for the rest of his life. The philosophers who subscribed to his philosophical concepts and ideas were known as the "fisosofi italici," the Italic philosophers.

It cannot be denied that Greece gave the world the bases of a new civilization, and it cannot be denied that part of the civilization was deeply rooted in Sicilian soil. The island and the cities of Magna Graecia in Southern Italy, were in fact launching pads for the civilizing impetus that radiated northward into Europe. On this occasion, Sicily played a role that seems congenial to her, destined to be repeated in the aftermath of the Arab domination when it became the filter through which the scientific knowledge of the Arabs was passed on to Europe. But whereas in the latter case, Sicilians were relatively less involved in the elaboration of the product they were transmitting, in the former they were active participants, creators as well as transmitters of the message. If as Goethe said, Sicily represents the key for understanding Italy, it is also undeniable that Sicily also provides the key for understanding Greece. It is no wonder then that many of the European intellectuals such as von Gloeden, D.H. Lawrence, Sartre, De Maupassant, Gregorovius, and others flocked to Sicily, not to Greece, to experience firsthand the essence of Greece. They came to Sicily to discover the spark of life that had been extinguished in their northern climates. Ancient Sicily and Greece are inextricably bound by their common past. You cannot think of one without the other. To realize that this is so, consider for a moment Greek civilization without Sicily.

Notes

[1] The question of the origins of the Sikans and the Siculi does not seem to be resolved, at least until additional information is uncovered. Even the ancient writers disagree on the subject. It's generally believed that the Sikans came originally from Spain and the Siculi from Central Italy. Some believe they came from Latium and spoke a language not too dissimilar from Latin.

[2] The chronology of the foundations of the Sicilian cities is naturally opened to debate. The most complete discussion on the subject is in Jean Berard, *La Magna Grecia: Storia delle colonie greche dell'Italia meridionale*, Torino, Piccola Biblioteca Einaudi, 1963. On p. 95 Berard offers a table with the foundation dates given by Thucidides, Eusebius, Girolamo, and various other authors, none of whom seem to agree. Their differences are often minor, but nonetheless enough to throw doubt on accepting any of the dates given as the absolute truth. Eusebius for example considered Zancle the first Greek colony on Sicily, founded in 757-756, twenty-three years before Naxos.

[3] I am referring to the granting of some land to the Chalcidians by the Siculian King Iblone. The Chalcidians founded Megara Iblea and lived there for 140 years until they were forced to abandon the area by Gelone of Siracusa. See Berard, op. cit., p. 118.
[4] The figure of Ducezio has become a symbol of the struggle for Sicilian independence. A noble and generous Prince, Ducezio offered his life when his army was finally defeated by the Siracusans at Nome in order to spare retribution against the Sicilians who had participated in the revolt. The Siracusans spared his life and sent him into exile to Corinth. But the Sicilian Prince quickly returned from exile and founded the colony of Calacte (present-day Caronia). He died before he could organize another rebellion against the Greeks. After his death all the cities of the Siculi fell to the Siracusans. See Santi Correnti, *Storia di Sicilia come storia del popolo siciliano*, Longanesi, Milano 1982.
[5] See Georges Vallet, *Sicilia greca*, Napoli, Edizioni del Sole, 1988, p. 13.
[6] See Gaetano Cipolla, "A Banner for Sicily" in *Arba Sicula*, Vol XV, 1 &2, 1994, pp. 98-107 and the chapter on the Trinacria in the present volume.
[7] Brian Caven has written an interesting biography of Dionysius I in which he tries to restore his reputation which has been tainted by democratic historians inimical to dictatorships. He claims that most of the negative lore about Dionysius I—his overly suspicious nature, his fear of being assassinated to the point that he taught his daughter how to shave him or the singeing of his beard to avoid contact with barbers who might harm him, his presumed whimsical condemnation to death of poets who criticized his poems etc..—were fabrications by the political opposition in Greece. See *Dionysius I: Warlord of Sicily*, Yale University Press, New Haven, 1990.
[8] British historian Denis Mack Smith who wrote a two volume history of Sicily calls Sicilians megalomaniacs. Sicilians he says have an excessive need to aggrandize their accomplishments. This is visible in the Valley of the Temples in Agrigento which contains 5 temples, out of the nine they had envisioned, designed to surpass the ancient models found in Greece. See *A History of Sicily*, Dorset Press, New York, 1968.
[9] F.G. Arezzo, *Sicilia*, Flaccovio Editore, Palermo, p. 225.
[10] Some historians believe that the myth of Demeter was native to Sicily and preceded the arrival of the Greeks. This is Holm's view. Another German historian named Freeman believes that even the myth of Persephone was of Sicilian derivation. See Holm, *Storia della Sicilia nell'antichità*, Vol I, p. 172 and Freeman, *Geschichte Siciliens*, Vol I, p. 479. The prevailing opinion is that the two myths were brought by the colonizing Greeks from Gela. See Emanuele Ciaceri, *Culti e miti nella storia dell'antica Sicilia*, Giuseppe Brancato Editore, Catania, 1910, rpt 1987.

The Muslims in Sicily

Introduction

There are many persistent misconceptions about Sicilians propagated by word of mouth and hearsay and bandied about by the media. One of them is that Sicilians are really not Italians, which I have heard many times from Sicilian-Americans. I have always taken this as an affirmation of their pride in being Sicilian rather than a refusal of their Italian identity. Another misconception (heard less frequently and usually couched as a joke), but with enough regularity as to make me think that the thought does not appear farfetched to many Americans, even Sicilian-Americans, is that Sicilians, probably owing to the island's proximity to North Africa, are somehow Africans themselves. Having made such a leap of imagination, some people may think that Sicilians are also black. Such a conclusion, as outlandish as it seems, was featured in a movie by Quentin Tarantino entitled *True Romance*, which aired on television in 1994. While any movie in which the mafia has a role to play is usually offensive, this one seems to me especially pernicious and provocative in its treatment of Sicilians and their collective persona. Though there are many reasons for disliking this movie, I found one scene in which Sicilians are characterized as liars and descendants of black-skinned Moors particularly misleading. Allow me to describe the scene.

In an attempt to recover a suitcase full of cocaine the Mafia, represented by a dapper and soft-spoken Christopher Walken who does his best to impersonate John Gotti, traces it to a man who presumably knows the location of the suitcase. The scene that directly concerns us takes place between the mafia counselor accompanied by two Sicilian-speaking toughs, and Dennis Hopper who plays the father of the fellow who stole the cocaine. In an attempt to dissuade the father from lying, the counselor declares he is Sicilian and that since Sicilians are the greatest liars in the world, it would be pointless for him to try to deceive him. He boasts that his father—the world champion of liars—had taught him that there are seventeen ways of behaving when a person lies, except for women who have a few extra tricks up their sleeves (Cicero said that Sicilians had a sense of humor!), and suggests that he should simply tell him where the cocaine is.

A game of cat and mouse ensues in which two responses are quickly judged to be lies and punished accordingly with a short violent punch in the mouth that makes the father bleed profusely. Another lie and one of the toughs slices his palm and throws a liquid —alcohol?—over it. Then the counselor and the father engage in a seemingly amiable conversation in which the latter, who has already made up his mind that he will not betray his son's whereabouts and thus be killed for it, decides to hurl what seems to him the ultimate insult on the Mafioso. He announces that he knows a lot about Sicilians. He has read a history book, which has enlightened him about the real nature of Sicilians. "Sicilians were spawned by niggers," he says with contempt, beginning a history lesson for the Mafioso who listens with a bemused look in his face, punctuating his growing anger with outbursts of ill-boding laughter. The father continues his attack by saying that "centuries and centuries ago Sicily was conquered by the Moors who were black. Sicilians have Black blood pumping through their hearts, because the Blacks did so much f...ing with Sicilian women that they changed the bloodline forever. Before the Moors, Sicilians were blond and blue-eyed, like the northern Italians. Your great great grandmother was f...ed by the niggers and gave birth to a half-Black child. Your ancestors are niggers and so you are part "eggplant"". This last remark was met by an outburst of laughter by the Mafioso. Then he retorted "and you're a cantaloupe," hardly a clever response, unless, of course, I am missing the point and "cantaloupe" is a euphemism for something else. Needless to say, the father's bravado results in violence. The Mafioso, displaying the deceptive coolness that is a must for any self-respecting counselor of his stature—a coolness that belies his murderous intentions—goes over to the father and kisses him on the cheek (a nice touch!) to thank him for his amusing lesson, walks toward one of his men, mumbles something to him and with the gun he has just been handed shoots the man in the face, point blank, and, as he surveys the destruction he has wrought, drags spit out of his mouth with deliberate slowness so we can feel his contempt and spatters the dead man with it.

Apart from the violence, which I found extremely offensive, this scene manages to be offensive on a number of other counts. First, the Mafioso's statement that Sicilians are the greatest liars, while intending to underscore a virtue (Sicilians are astute and have the ability to see through lies) becomes a genetic character flaw. In the end, most people will remember the sentence out of context and it will become another "fact" about Sicilians. They will remember not that Sicilians are very sharp, but that they are the "greatest liars in the world". Secondly and certainly potentially more misleading is the father's "historical" reconstruction of Sicilian genealogy, not because it links Sicilians with Blacks, but because it perverts history and encourages racism. By saying "Sicilians were spawned by niggers" the father is counting on the Sicilians' presumed dislike of Blacks. I recall that in the first *Godfather* saga, at one of the meetings of the Mafia council, one of the dons who had objected to having drugs distributed in white neighborhoods, did not mind it if they were distributed among black people. "Sell it to the Blacks, they're animals anyway!" he declared. That statement serves as a kind of historical background that validates the father's epithet: movie racism that feeds on itself. The man lives in this world! He no doubt has seen the *Godfather* movies and he knows from those movies that Sicilians are not supposed to like Blacks. And based on that information he seeks out the most outrageous insult he can think of and he comes up with: "You have Black genes in your blood!"

While the question of the purity of the races is really a non-question, perverting the truth in order to offend a people is evil and should be exposed. The presumed dislike of Blacks by Sicilians is also a question that needs to be explored. Historically Sicilians have been very tolerant of other races and religions. Arabs, Jews and Christians have lived side by side in Sicily in relative peace throughout history. But that's a topic that deserves to be treated at another time. In his "historical" reconstruction of Sicilian genealogy, Mr. Tarantino, who wrote the screenplay, makes a few errors (knowingly or unknowingly?) that cannot be allowed to go unchallenged, even though I am well aware that the damage has already been done and a lot more people saw the movie than will ever read my words. The character played by Hopper says that the Moors conquered Sicily and that they were Black. This statement is a gross oversimplification of the facts. First of all, the Muslims who invaded Sicily in 827 AD and who eventually gained control of the island were tribes from many different part of North Africa and the middle East. The bulk were Arabs by which historians recognize Caucasians who had come to rule North Africa from Persia to Morocco. The second most important group of Muslims were Berbers who are also Caucasians. Their darker skin is a question of pigmentation. The Saracens (in Sicily they were called Arabs or Saracens!), according to all histories I have read were olive-skinned people from the Middle East much like the present inhabitants of the area. During the long period of warfare required to eliminate local resistance, many different armies were sent from North Africa and from other places such as Spain, and among these there were smaller groups of black-skinned Muslims. But their numbers were certainly not sufficient to change the genetic pool of Sicilians. The second error deals with the assertion that before the Arabs came to Sicily, the local population was blond and blue-eyed, like northern Italians. This is certainly not true. Until the arrival of the Arabs in 827 AD, the Sicilian population consisted of many different groups including the ruling Byzantine hierarchy mixed with Greeks, Jews, native Sicilians, and others, none of whom are blond and blue-eyed peoples. He was probably thinking of the Northmen, that is, the Normans who wrested control of Sicily from the Muslims in the eleventh century and who are responsible for the blonds and redheads with blue or green eyes you may see as you walk down a street in Palermo.

Thus misconceptions are perpetuated in people's minds. Myths are created from falsehoods and misinformation. The majority of people who saw the movie in question, not knowing anything about Sicily or Sicilians, probably took the statements at face value. Even Sicilian-Americans who have not made Sicilian history a hobby will have few weapons to use against such an irresponsible handling of history. This is why it is important for Sicilians to study the history of their homeland. So let us look at the Arabs and their Sicilian connections.

The Muslims in Sicily

Unlike the Jews, whose millenary presence on Sicilian soil was completely erased from the collective memory of the Sicilian people by the middle of the 16th century, the fate of the Muslims has not been quiet as drastic. The memory of their presence on the island remains and can be readily seen practically everywhere. Unlike the Jews who never occupied a dominant position in Sicilian society and left very little in terms of artifacts and physical structures, the Muslims were for over two centuries (from 827 to 1092) the rulers of the island. Their presence, though much shorter by comparison, can be seen especially in the Western part of the island in some of the architectural details of churches and public buildings, in the names still used by the Sicilian people, in their looks, their language and some even say in their characteristic attitudes. A trained eye can discern the traces of the Muslim presence on the island, although the same cannot be said of the general Sicilian population. If, for example, you asked one hundred Sicilians to tell you whether the name of the city of Marsala has anything to do with the Moslem world, it would be surprising if five percent of them answered correctly that the name actually means "The Port of Allah". By the same token, it would be surprising if people whose last names end with an accented "à," such as Fragalà, Vadalà, Mandalà, Crucillà, Zappalà, knew that their names are derived from Arab names, unless they were interested in genealogy. Similarly, people fail to make the connection between the hundreds of localities in Sicily, small and large towns whose names are an evident link to the Muslim domination of Sicily, or realize that their well known comic character Giufà whose tales of wit and foolishness have delighted many generations of Sicilians young and old, was in fact part of the narrative oriental tradition brought to Sicily by the Arabs.

Let us begin by taking a look at what has remained of the Saracen domination. A good place to start is with names of localities that still are known by the names given them by the Saracens, some of which have been changed back to names used before the arrival of the Arabs. Agrigento was *Karkint* or *Kerkent* under the Arabs and the local population called it Girgenti until Mussolini ordered it changed to Agrigento. Enna was known as Castrogiovanni from the Arabic *Qasryanih.* Even Catania and Taormina were known by Arabic names that were abandoned: *Madinat al-Filah* (the City of the Elephant)[1] and *al-Mucizziyah* respectively. Three typical prefixes used by the Arabs to identify a place gave birth to hundreds of Sicilian toponyms, which means that their presence was deep and pervasive, especially in the countryside. Indeed these names survived a number of

The Elephant of lava stone, symbol of Catania, with the City Hall in the background. Both are works of the 18th architect Vaccarini.

successive dominations reaching us in their original formulation nearly a thousand years after the Arabs lost control of Sicily.[2] The Arabic word *qal'at*, meaning castle, fortress is probably the most productive of toponyms in Sicily. From it we derive Caltanissetta, Caltavuturu, Caltagirone, Caltabellotta, Calascibetta, Calatafimi etc...The Arabic word for a stopping place, a way station, was *rahl* which gave rise to numerous toponyms such as Racalmuto, Regalbuto, Regalpetra, etc... And the word *manzil* which also means a stopping place or way station, has given us names of towns such a Mezzojuso, Misilmeri, Mussomeli etc...

Michele Amari, who wrote the most authoritative work on the Muslim presence in Sicily, counted 328 names of certain Arab derivation spread unevenly throughout the Sicilian landscape: 209 were in the Val di Mazara, the western third of the island that includes Palermo, 100 in the Val di Noto, corresponding to the Southeast corner of Sicily, and only 19 in the Val Demone, corresponding to the northeastern third of the island.[3] The highest concentration of toponyms in the Val di Mazara means that the area had the highest concentration of Muslims. In the Val di Noto, the Muslim presence was less pervasive but still substantial. The area in the present provinces of Messina and Catania had the island's largest remaining Christian population and put up the strongest resistance to Muslim domination, which explains the fewer Arabic toponyms. Expectedly, the last cities to fall under their control were those in the northeastern tri-

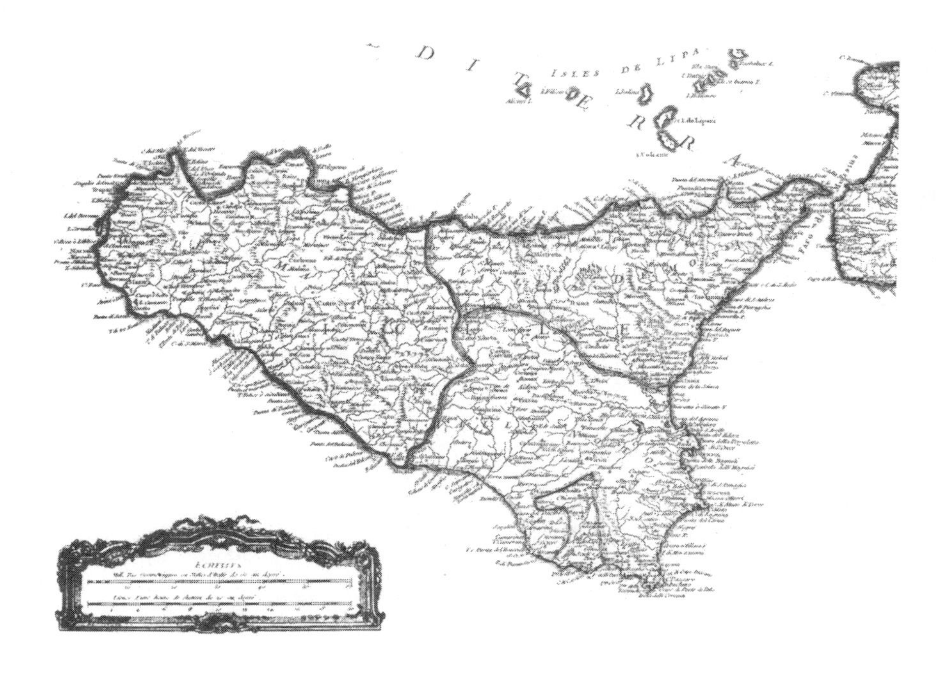

angle with Taormina, which fell in 902, and Rametta (Rometta) in 965, which was the last stronghold to fall to the Arabs.[4] From this date, the island was under the total control of the Muslims until the invasion of the Normans in 1061. Roger of Hauteville accomplished in 30 years what had taken the Arabs over a century. By 1092, all of Sicily was under Norman rule.[5]

What is the significance of this for the makeup of the Sicilian population? While many people have dominated Sicily, most of them have come and gone without leaving any trace of their presence on the people of Sicily. Nothing remains of the Goths and Ostrogoths, of the Vandals and the French, of the Austrians and the Piedmontese. Even the Normans, the Aragonese and then the Spaniards whose role in Sicilian history is a lot more important, cannot be said to have added much to Sicily's genetic pool. Their numbers were relatively few and represented the ruling hierarchies who did not mingle with the general population. The fact that the Normans were able to conquer Sicily with barely 1500 or 2000 knights against a much more numerous army of Muslim defenders is even today a source of wonder. The same can be said of the Aragonese and the Spaniards who ruled the island, but did not colonize it as farmers or artisans. Even the arrival of Lombard and Piedmontese settlers who came at the invitation of Count Roger of Hauteville to populate the towns of Aidone, San Fratello, Sperlinga, Piazza Armerina and Nicosia did not contribute much to the general make up of Sicilians. Nor was it changed by the Albanian colonies of Piana dei Greci, Mezzojuso and others who arrived in the XV century.[6] The people who have left an indelible mark on the native Sicilians, that is, those Sicilians who lived on the island before the arrival of the Greeks—the Sikans and the Siculi[7]— are the Greeks and the Arabs. It has been remarked that there appear to be two different types of people living on Sicily: one type being prevalent in the western part whose general appearance, language and mannerisms reflect the more pervasive influence of the Arabs on the area, and another in the eastern part which reflects the Greek component to a greater degree.[8]

The fact that the Arabs left such a strong imprint on the Sicilian people is probably due to the pervasiveness of their domination. At the height of their domination in the 11th century, the Muslim population may have consisted of half a million people, which represents a high percentage of a population that had been decimated by constant wars, killing, deportation, and slavery.[9] In their two hundred years as rulers of the island, they succeeded in changing practically everything: they introduced their own laws, their religion, their language, their own system of agriculture, new ways of irrigating the land, new crops that have since become closely associated with Sicily such as oranges and lemons. The Arabs, like the Greeks before them, and unlike all the others, came to Sicily to stay, and after the turbulent and bloody period of the conquest, they set to work to make the island a wonderful place in which to live. Accounts of travelers, like the one by Ibn Giubair who visited Sicily in 1184-5, speak of the island as an earthly paradise.[10] Giubair described Palermo as a great city with beautiful palaces and gardens and with 300 mosques—almost as many as the city of Cordoba in Spain—and a population of 250,000. A city of such size would be one of the largest in the world at the time. (Another Arab visitor, Ibn Hawqal, on seeing so many mosques remarked that the Sicilian Arabs were haughty and wanted a personal mosque in which to pray.)[11] The island, being part of a great empire, thrived on commerce with the eastern world, and enjoyed access to markets for a rich array of goods that it produced, from silk to cotton, from olive oil to sulfur, from sugar cane to dates. Such accomplishments are all the more amazing when you consider that with the exception of the period when Sicily was ruled almost as an independent kingdom by the Kalbite Dynasty (10th century) with only nominal allegiance to the Sultan in Cairo, their history is practically one continuous struggle, first to wrest control of the island from the Byzantines and then for supremacy among themselves. There were always tensions among the various groups of Muslims, especially between the Arabs and the Berbers.[12] In fact, one of the reasons for the astounding success of the Normans who conquered the island with a very small but determined number of knights, lies in the fact that by the middle of the 11th century the Muslims were worn out by their constant internecine wars, assassinations, usurpations of power, and internal revolts.

In spite of this, the impact of the Muslim presence on Sicily was enormous. For one thing, it severed Sicily from the orbit of the West, separating it from the other Italian provinces on the main land. Under the Byzantine domination, it had been part of the Eastern empire's Italian domain such as Calabria, Puglia and other regions in the north. Under the Arabs, Sicily came to be a part of the great Muslim empire that ran from India to Morocco. Michele Amari viewed the arrival of the Arabs as a positive development in that it freed Sicily from the stagnant and sleepy Byzantine civilization that for nearly three centuries had reduced the island, through excessive taxation and greed, to a poor and unproductive place.[13] Under the Muslims, however, the island began to reap the benefits of the Islamic civilization that at the time was the most advanced

Robert Guiscard and Roger Gran Conte receiving homage from the Muslims. Oil painting by Giuseppe Patania in the Royal Palace.

in the world. Sicily became the meeting point between East and West, Europe and Africa. Although the Arabs had established a thriving civilization in Spain which was the launching point for their intellectual heritage, part of the credit for introducing to Europe some of their scientific advances in medicine, in agriculture, in geography, mathematics and astronomy, to name a few areas in which the Arabs excelled, rightly belongs to Sicilian-based Muslims. Ironically, the channel for the transmission of the intellectual heritage of the Arabs was opened by the Normans who wrested control of Sicily from the Arabs and by the Swabians who succeeded them.

The Normans adopted a tolerant attitude towards the vanquished Arabs. They organized their new possessions along the same lines as existed under the Arabs. The new fiefs, which were distributed to Norman knights, were basically the same as the military districts the Arabs called *iqlim*. They maintained a number of key departments for the administration of the island such as the financial department known as the *Diwan*, the treasury department know as the *Diwan al-ma'mur* and others. A considerable part of the Norman military forces after the conquest consisted of Muslim soldiers, and the Muslim influence was predominant in the Norman court in terms of its titles, functions, customs, and even ceremonials. Even the *Tarì,* a coin minted by the Normans was practically the same as the *ruba'i* of the Arabs and had the same value. Instead of ousting the Muslims, the Normans actually embraced their culture. Often the Norman kings assumed Arabic names and lived in opulent palaces like the Oriental Emirs they replaced. Roger II, the most renowned King of Sicily, called himself *al-Mu'tazz-bi-lah*, William I was known as *al-Hadi bi-amri-llah* and William II was *al-musta'izz-bi-llah.* They often spoke Arabic as well as Greek and Latin. The great Emperor Frederick II, son of the last Norman queen, Constance of Hauteville, who was a great admirer of Islamic intellectual and material culture was buried in a wrapping of Arabian draperies encrusted with silver and gold, discovered when his tomb was opened in the 18th century. To the Arabs he was known as *al-anbaratur*, the Emperor.[14] His son Manfred, who shared his father's admiration for the Arabs, was denounced by the Pope as "The Sultan of Lucera" and the Lord of the Saracens. Primarily soldiers of fortune with little use for the Oriental refinements and luxuries of their predecessors, the Normans quickly adapted to the ways of the Arabs, repeating what had happened to the Romans when they came into contact with the Greek civilization. The conquerors were conquered themselves, forming the conduit through which the intellectual heritage of the Arabs was introduced to Europe.

Out of this conduit, an architectural style known as Arab-Norman emerged whose monuments are scattered throughout the island, but particularly in Palermo. In Sicily, unlike in Spain, very little remains in architecture that can be called truly called Arabic—the baths of Cefalà Diana is one of the rare examples of it, the Royal Fortress of Maredolce another. But there is a profusion of the style that was born from the collaboration between Arab artists and artisans who actually built and decorated the structures and the Norman masters who commissioned them. Out of this collaboration came such jewels as the Cathedrals of Palermo and of Monreale, the Palace of the Normans, the Cappella Palatina, the Churches of the Martorana, San Cataldo, San Giovanni degli Eremiti, which combine oriental elements, including Arabic inscriptions and motifs, with Christian religious themes and palaces like the Zisa, the Cubba and others.

But the conduit did not just bring forth a new architectural style that is, as far as I know unique, it also brought an incredible number of innovations to the west, as well as a greater understanding of science and philosophy, geography and mathematics, medicine and agriculture. Let us review some of the most important contributions:

In the twelfth century, as Aziz Ahmad wrote, "the language of science was Arabic. Translations of Greek works from Arabic into Latin antedate those made directly from Greek. Arabic commentaries on the works of Greek masters profoundly influenced European thought."[15] The medical school of Salerno was greatly helped by the translations of Arabic medical texts. The translator of the medical works of Haly Abbas, Stefano of Pisa, wrote that the medicine scholars at the time (1127) were found primarily in Sicily and Salerno and were either Greeks or persons familiar with Arabic.

In astronomy, the Arabs utilized astrolabes, star maps and celestial globes. Ptolemy's *Almagest* was translated from Arabic into Latin as early as 1138; also the works of al-Farghani, whose work was to play a role in Columbus' discovery of America, were translated at the court of Frederick II.

In geography they pioneered the use of latitude and longitude. The great Arab geographer Edrisi made the first map of the known world for King Roger II.

The Arabs invented algebra and the use of zero. The Arabic numerical system we use was introduced into Europe by Leonardo Fibonacci from Pisa who had studied in Spain and the Orient.

In philosophy, the Arabs found Greek science and metaphysics compatible. They had great admiration for Aristotle, for example, and they were instrumental in translating some of his works into Arabic. Averroes' commentaries on Aristotle were extremely important to Western medieval philosophy. The works of Avicenna and Averroes were translated into Latin. The credit for introducing the works of Averroes to the west goes to Michael Scot, one of the luminaries at the court of Frederick II. Palermo, at this time, was a center for Aristotelian scholarship. Frederick's son, Manfred, commissioned Bartolomeo da Messina to translate Aristotle's *Ethics* into Latin; he was responsible for commissioning the translation of several works by Plato. Considering the very important role played by these two philosophers in the Renaissance, one has to wonder whether the intellectual history of the period would have followed the same course without these translations.[16]

In agriculture, the Arabs introduced a new system of irrigation adopting Persian hydraulic techniques, using large reservoirs known as "gebiah," a word still used in Sicilian (*gebbia*) to describe large cement basins designed to collect rain or water from natural springs. Many rivers in Sicily were made navigable and unlike today when water needs to be rationed in many places of the island, it flowed abundantly from springs and rivers, making it possible for the islanders to engage in horticulture and gardening. In Sicily springs or water sources carry Arabic names even to this day. The many cultures introduced by the Arabs –oranges, lemons, other citrus fruits, sugar cane, mulberries, silk worms, papyrus, the sumac tree for tanning and dyeing, dates, pistachio nuts, cotton and hemp—changed the agrarian and industrial economy of Sicily. The silk industry, which became an important monopoly for Sicily had markets outside the island. Silk for export was primarily in the hands of the Arabs who had markets throughout the Mediterranean.

They also introduced the cultivation of rice, giving Sicilians one of their favorite fast food items, the *arancina*, a deep-fried golden hued – hence the name "little orange"—rice ball sprinkled with saffron and filled with meat and peas. Gaetano Basile claims that the *arancina* brought to Milan by Aragonese princesses who married heirs of the Sforza family became the famous *risotto alla milanese*.[17] But please don't let Umberto Bossi, the leader of the Lega Lombarda, hear this!

Another very important food item that has become a staple no Italian can live without resulted from the Arabs' introduction of durum wheat. Of course, we know that wheat was always the most important product of Sicily, so much so the Romans conquered it to feed their armies, but the hard wheat was imported by the Arabs and it is from this strain that pasta is made. You may read this with some skepticism—many regions of Italy claim to have made the first pasta!—But there is evidence that in the town of Trabia, near Palermo, a kind of pasta called "itria," which is Arabic for "spaghetti" was manufactured in the 10th century.[18] So much for the story that Marco Polo brought spaghetti from China in the 13th century! As masters of the milling process, they made *semolina* from durum wheat and developed another Arab specialty: *couscous* which is still prepared in the western part of Sicily. It's not part of the eastern repertory at all and that is understandable since the Arab presence was not as pervasive there.[19]

While we are talking about pasta, there's probably no other dish that's recognized as more typical of Sicilian cooking than "Pasta cu li sardi". Basile writes that this delicious dish, which can be made in many different ways in Sicily, was created during the Arab conquest by the chef of the Byzantine general Euphemius who was responsible for the Arab invasion.[20] Having to feed an army, the cook needed a dish that could be nutritious without being expensive. So he combined sardines, which are plentiful in Sicilian waters, with fennel—Basile slyly adds that the fennel was put in to counteract the smell of the sardines – and pignoli nuts—to guard against food poisoning![21]

The Sicilian sweet tooth was inherited from the Arabs. Once sugar was introduced into Sicily, people created an array of delicacies that make a trip to Sicily worth while just to taste them. The Arabs invented sherbet, which eventually gave Sicilians their famous ice cream, their fruit *granite*, their *sciauni*[22] and even their famous *cassate*. In fact, the Arabs used to mix sugar and ricotta cheese in copper pots known as *quas'at*, which probably was the origin of the *cassata,* even though its ingredients have been expanded considerably.

In fishing, the Arabs introduced a more efficient system of catching tuna. Before them tuna, which in Sicily comes near to shore to spawn during May, was traditionally caught individually with a hook. The Arabs instituted the system whereby the schools of tuna were allowed to enter a series of underwater chambers that led to "the chamber of death" where the nets were raised by men in boats tied together to form a large square pool. When the nets bring the tuna to the surface, men simply harpoon them and drag them onto the boats in a frenzy of killing. This system of fishing which has lasted more than a thousand years has given way to more "efficient" methods by the Japanese fleets which scoop up the ocean's fish indiscriminately in mile-long nets. This practice, known as the "Mattanza," is coordinated by a *Rais*, an Arabic word meaning "Chief", and has developed a tradition rich in songs and rituals that are still practiced today on the island of Favignana. Now, however, it is largely an event enacted for the entertainment of the tourists. The tuna fishing industry which in the past provided jobs to thousands of local fishermen in the Egadi Islands and on the western coast of Sicily, has all but disappeared. Some of the old tuna canning factories have been turned into hotels.

Under the Arabs, the island's metal mining industry was also expanded and silver, mercury, lead and other minerals were extracted. Sea salt production, an industry that continues to this day in the saltpans of Trapani and Marsala, became an important addition to the economy of the island as well. The production of Sicilian wine, which today represents a growing and important source of income for Sicilians, was neglected for religious reasons and then reinstated for religious reasons: the Arabs because they are not allowed to drink wine and the Christians because wine is an important element in the celebration of the mass. The production of olive oil, which had been important at the time of the Greeks, also fell, but both regained their ancient importance once the Arabs were out of power.

An important outgrowth of the application of the Muslim practice of paying their soldiers with land resulted in the breakup of very large estates known as latifundia owned by few individuals who often did not live on the land that characterized the landscape under the Romans and the Byzantines.[23] The Arabs provided incentives to small farm owners to cultivate every bit of land at their disposal with a system that reduced taxes to encourage productivity. For example, they did not tax ownership of animals used for work in the fields. The Arab system of taxation was also less repressive than the one imposed by the Byzantines. They instituted an efficient system of government, dividing the island into three sectors: the Val di Mazara, Val di Noto and Val Demone, each ruled by a *kadì*, (in Sicilian *gaitu*) who was responsible to the emirs who had made Palermo their capital instead of Siracusa that had been the capital under the Byzantines. In their administration, the Arabs followed a policy of toleration towards the Jews and the Christians. As expected, these groups were subjected to many restrictions on their personal freedoms: they had to pay a personal tax known as *giziah* and a land tax called *harag* both of which varied depending on individual circumstances. The *giziah* could be avoided by converting to Islam. Needless to say, there were other advantages in converting to Islam and many Christians did exactly that. The Christians and Jews who did not convert had to wear distinctive clothing: the Jews a white patch on their back with the image of a monkey on it. The same for the Christians except that their animal was a pig. The same patches had to be affixed on the doors of their dwellings. Although the Christians were free to practice their religion without interference from the authorities, they were not allowed to show the cross in public, ring church bells, hold processions, or proselytize, and they could not recite prayers aloud within earshot of Arabs. Even the slaves seem to have been treated better. They could become free men by converting to Islam, or go from areas that had to pay a tribute to Muslim areas where no tribute was required. In general, it can be said that once their power was consolidated and all rebellions crushed following the long and bloody period of the conquest, the Arabs did not oppress the population unduly through religious intolerance and persecutions, though as we noted earlier there may have been some pressures to convert to Islam as the following two lines from a popular Sicilian poem confirm:

C'è lu gaitu e gran pena ni duna:	The Kadì is here and gives us great woes:
voli arrinunziu a la fidi cristiana.	he wants us to renounce our Christian faith.[24]

San Giovanni degli Eremiti with its charming cloister in Palermo.

One aspect we have barely touched upon is the influence that the Arabs had on the language of Sicily, not a simple task. First of all, we do not know with any degree of certainty what languages were spoken by the Sicilian population during the Arab domination. We know that documents were written in one of three languages Arabic, Greek or Latin. At the entrance to the Cappella Palatina in the Norman Palace of Palermo there is an inscription written in these three languages testifying to their widespread use in religious rites, written documents, correspondence etc... And we know that any document written in any of these languages was considered legal for a long time.[25] Needless to say the first generation of Arabs spoke Arabic. A smaller percentage of the Christian population probably spoke or at least understood Latin. A larger percentage of them, however, probably understood and probably spoke Greek. They celebrated their religious rites in Greek. Whether they actually spoke Greek in their everyday life is difficult to say. My own feeling is that alongside Greek, Arabic and Latin a fourth language that can be identified as an early form of Sicilianwas probably spoken by many people in everyday situations. Varvaro calls this form of Sicilian "mozarabico" in analogy with the language that developed in Spain during the Moorish domination. This was not an early form of the modern Sicilian language that came into being in the 13th century, but rather an evolution of the Latin spoken before the Arabs' arrival. He claims that the Sicilian language, as we have come to know it, developed after the arrival of the Normans.[26] The Sicilian language as we know it today preserved numerous idiomatic expressions, grammatical features and lexical items that come directly from Arabic.

We have already mentioned the numerous Arabic toponyms that have been Sicilianized. A few examples will suffice. Mount Etna is known to Sicilians as *Muncibbeddu*, which is an interesting case of a mixture of Latin and Arabic both of which mean mountain: the Latin *mons* and the Arabic *gebel.* The word literally means "mountain mountain". Some Sicilians like to pay homage to their volcano by translating *Muncibbeddu* as "the mountain of mountains". The river where I learned how to swim is the *Alcantara* which is Arabic for "the bridge"; in Palermo one of the major arteries of the city is still "Cassaru" in Sicilian, which is derived from "qasr" meaning "castle". The street leads to the Norman Palace, built by the Arabs. An interesting verb was derived from this: *cassariarisi* which can be translated loosely with "ambling leisurely up and down the main street". Such words as *calia*, (roasted chickpeas), *zibbibbu* (elongated green grapes which were imported into Sicily from Cape Zebib), *zotta* (whip), *giarra* (large clay container for oil, wine) *naca* (cradle), *bazzariotu* (hawker) and many others are all of Arabic derivation. F. G. Arezzo in his very informative text *Sicilia: studi storici, giuridici ed economici sulla Sicilia* has compiled a 77-page vocabulary of Sicilian words derived from Arabic that testifies to the pervasiveness and depth of its influence.

From a structural point of view, Sicilian also has many affinities with Arabic. Arezzo listed a number of them. Not knowing Arabic, I will rely on his authority for the veracity of what follows, although I can vouch for the Sicilian part. Arezzo claims that in both Sicilian and Arabic,

1. The future tense basically does not exist. In both languages the present tense is used to convey a future idea.

2. The preterit is used instead of the present perfect, which does not exist;

3. The repetition of a noun, adjective or verb to signify a number of things, for example in Sicilian "furriau casa casa" means "he searched around from one room to the next"; the repetition of "schirzannu schirzannu" means "as I was joking around" and "parrannu parrannu" means "as I was talking".

4. The initial h changes frequently but not always in c, which exists only in Sicilian and Arabic, and not in the other European languages, as for example in *hama, Homisu* which become *cama, Comisu*;

5. Subject pronouns are attached to the end of the verbs as in *manciastivu, bivistivu.* (you ate, you drank).

6. The use of the pejorative suffix in *azzu-azza*, in both Sicilian and Arabic denotes connotation of grandness, largeness without the negativ-

ity. Thus in Sicilian, "un carusazzu" does not mean only a "bad boy" but also a "tall and impressive boy"; "na fimminazza" does not mean only "a bad woman" but also "substantial, large woman." This feature is not shared by Italian, for example, where the pejorative "accio-accia" means just that.

7. The diminutive used in a derogatory sense as in *razzina*, which does not mean little race, but bad race.[27]

Arezzo also listed a few gestures that are common to Arabs and Sicilians:

1. Pointing the thumb backward over the shoulder indicating that there are others following;
2. Placing your finger on your cheek and turning it to indicate something is chic or tasty;
3. Winking as a conventional sign; and
4. Turning your hand in the air to say that you don't care.[28]

Clearly the Arabs who made a home in Sicily were not like the other adventurers. They found the island congenial to their spirit and their nomadic tendencies were won over by the beauties of the land. Their feelings of security, especially after the conquest was complete, allowed them to devote themselves to pursuits other than war. Thus, the Sicilian Arabs grew to participate at the highest level in the intellectual pursuits that characterized the Arab civilization, contributing to scholarship in science, philosophy, law, religion, poetry and even as military commanders. It was, in fact, a Sicilian-born Arab general who succeeded in conquering nearly all of North Africa for the Fatimid dynasty. His name was Jawahr as-Siqilli. He conquered Egypt and even founded the Azhar University there. Arabic scholars of Sicilian origin, such as the philologist Ibn Makki, the jurist and theologian al-Mazari, the linguist Ibn-Rashiq, the translator of Dioscorides' treatise on Botany Abd-Allah, wrote important books on many subjects and were regarded in the Islamic world as revered authorities.[29] Many of the Arab leaders, whether born on Sicily or outside it, enjoyed wide recognition as scholars and poets in their own right. Indeed, the 70 year old general who commanded the Arab landing at Mazara in 827, Asad b. al-Furat, was a scholar and one of the foremost jurists of Islam's first three centuries.[30] The emirs themselves were often learned men and poets who fostered intellectual pursuits. Under them, and especially under the Kalbite dynasty which enjoyed almost complete independence from the Caliphs based in Cairo, Sicily became an important center of learning and scholarship that rivaled the renowned centers of Spain. But the Sicilian Arabs developed a different relationship with the land they ruled than their counterparts in Spain. In Sicily, they represented a substantial percentage of the population, by all accounts more numerous than their subjects. In Spain, the Arabs were surrounded by a sea of Christianity, which certainly was not conducive to developing that sense of exclusive possession Sicilian Arabs had for the island. The Arabs living on the island came to consider themselves Sicilian and Sicily their homeland. To the outside world, the Arabs living in Sicily were Sicilians. The chroniclers of the time, Goffredo Malaterra and Amatus of Montecassino, who wrote histories of the Normans' conquest, identified the Muslims living in Sicily as *Sicilienses* or *Siculi* as opposed to *Normandi*. Even the Muslim writers from North Africa used the term *Siqilli* to identify their Sicilian brethren as opposed to *Rum*, a word that identified the Christians.[31] As for themselves, the Arabs living on Sicily openly demonstrated their attachment to their island. No one expressed this sense of attachment better than the Arabic speaking Sicilian poets who flourished especially around the beginning of the second millennium. Poetry was for the Arabs a crucial instrument of knowledge, a privileged way of expressing one's relationship with the world. The poets used it to extol their leaders' heroic deeds, to transmit history, to sing of the pleasures of wine and food, the passions of love from the courting of the beloved to the final joining, expressed with rare sensuality. The lexicographer Ibn 'al-Qatta compiled an anthology of the work of 170 Sicilian Arab poets entitled *The Precious Pearl on the Poets of the Island*, containing twenty thousand lines of poetry.[32] Unfortunately this and other anthologies compiled afterwards did not survive. The poets whose work has survived, however, have left us touching accounts of their affection for the island. Of these, no one was more gifted or sang with more feeling about Sicily than Ibn Hamdis, a poet born in Siracusa in 1056. He fought against the Normans and took refuge in Spain at the court of Al-Mutamial, the poet Prince of Seville. He wandered through many Arab lands and although his poetry encompasses a wide range of feelings, the most genuine note of his song is the bitterness of his exile and the heart-rending longing to return to his lost paradise, his homeland in Sicily, as the following poem demonstrates.[33] I am pleased to provide my own Sicilian and English translations of one of his poems:

The worries of white hair chase youthful cheer away.
Ah, how the soul grows gloomy in the light cast by white hair!
As youth was flowering, my fate decreed I live
far from my home when it declined and waned.

Can man find consolation for lost youth?
But men who suffer seek some remedy.
Am I to dye my hair with black *bidab?*
Am I to cover dawn with dark of night?
But how can I find dyes that will endure,
if I cannot find ways to make youth last?
A little breeze, a breath of fresh, cool air
blows gently by, as a soft whispering.
It moved at night driven by lightning flashes
and made the sky weep for the dead on earth.
You heard the thunderclap urging the clouds
as when a camel shrieks in anger at its edgy females.
The flashes of lightning burning in her flanks
were shining blades emerging from their sheaths.
I spent the night clothed by the dark.
O first brightness of dawn, bring me the light!
O wind, when you bring rain to sate the thirsty fields,
push the dry clouds my way that I may fill them with my tears.
If I could weep upon the land of my youth,
oh, life of woes, it would be always moist with tears.
Wind, run after the clouds, don't go away!
Don't let that hill where my home is suffer from thirst.
Do you know it? If not, know that the burning Sun
perfumes the growing branches.
What marvel? In that place, minds in love
impregnate the air with perfume.
There beats a heart so full that I stole all
the blood that's flowing in my veins from it.
My thoughts secretly return to those shores
like the wolf returning to its forest.
Here I was a companion to lions running in the woods;
here I found gazelles hiding in their lairs.
Across you, Sea, my paradise is found
where I lived, not in woe, but happily.
I saw the dawn of life there and now that evening falls,
you have forbidden me from living there.
Oh why did they tear me from what I longed to have
when the ocean separated me from those shores?
I would have galloped on the crescent Moon
to reach it and to hold the sun tight to my chest.

Li prioccupazioni dî capiddi janchi, scasanu l'allegria dâ gioventù.
Ah comu scurisci l'animu a lu lustru dî capiddi janchi!
O ciuriri dâ gioventù mi tuccau di viviri
luntanu da me casa quannu idda declinau e svaniu.
Si po' truvari abbentu pâ gioventù pirduta?
Picchi cu senti duluri cerca midicina.
M'haiu a tinciri i capiddi cû niuru dû *bidab?*
Ci haiu a mettiri a l'arba la notti pi cuperchiu?
Ma comu spirari na tinta ca dura,
si non haiu truvatu u modu pi fari durari a gioventù?
Un vinticeddu debbuli, ciatu di boria frisca,
ciuscia duci e murmura.
Di notti, idda si mossi guidata dî lampi
ca ficiru chianciri u celu pî morti ntâ terra.
Si sinteva a vuci dû tronu c'ammuttava i nevuli,
comu un camiddu quannu vucìa raggiatu i so fimmini nirvusi.
I lampi ardianu ntê cianchi d'idda:
era u luccicari dî spati ca niscevanu dî foderi.
Mi passaiu a notti ô scuru:
O primu alburi, portami a luci!
O ventu, quannu porti l'acqua pi ricriari ddi campi assitati,
ammutta i nevuli asciutti versu di mia,
accussì li inchissi dî me lacrimi.
Bagnassi u me chiantu dda terra unni passaiu a gioventù:
Ah, vita di svintura, fussi sempri bagnata di lacrimi.
O ventu, curricci appressu a li nevuli, non ti nni iri,
non lassari ca dda certa collina dû me paisi sintissi la siti.
Tu a canusci? Si no, ha sapiri ca l'arduri dû suli
ci fa odurari li rami.
Chi meravigghia? Nta ddi posti, l'intelletti d'amuri
mprenanu l'aria chi so profumi.
Ddà batti un cori accussì chinu,
ca io ci pigghiau tuttu u sangu ca scurri ntê me vini.
A ddi prai ritornanu i me pinseri ammucciateddi
comu u lupu ca ritorna ntô so boscu.
Ccà io fui cumpagnu di liuni ca currevanu ntê foresti;
ccà ìu a truvari gazzelli ntê so tani.
Darreri a ttia, o mari, c'è u me paradisu,
chiddu unni campaiu, non ntra li guai, ma filici.

Vitti spuntari l'arba dâ me vita e ora ca è sira,
mi vietastuvu di staricci.
O picchí mi strapparunu chidda ca bramava p'aviri,
quannu u pelagu mi separau di ddi prai?
Avissi cavarcatu a luna criscenti p'arrivari ddà
a strincirimi u suli ntô pettu.

Although many Arabs remained in positions of importance in the Norman court and their knowledge continued to be exploited for more than two centuries following their loss of Sicily, the bulk of the Saracens were enslaved, replacing the Christians at the lowest rung of the social ladder, and were eventually driven out of Sicily completely by a man who ironically admired Islamic culture, Frederick II, the Emperor who was buried in Arabian draperies in 1250.[34] Following a rebellion by the few Arabs still remaining, crushed in 1243, Frederick ordered all the Saracens out of Sicily, sending them to live in the town of Lucera in Calabria, where twenty years before, he had exiled an even greater number of rebellious Arabs. Thus, the Islamic presence on the island came to an end. But while their physical presence ended completely in 1243, their spiritual presence lingers to this day in the names, faces, foods and sounds of the Sicilian people.[35] So much so that many foreigners coming to the island for the first time cannot help associating with the Arabs the sounds and colors of Sicily, the flavors of its ice cream and marzipan fruits, the bittersweet taste of its sauces, the nasal tonalities of its songs, the unique sounds made by street vendors hawking their wares, and the bazaar atmosphere of their open air markets.

As a product of many different influences, Sicilians are unique. The great French writer Guy de Maupassant speaks for a host of travelers who have visited Sicily when he writes:

"No one is less like a Neapolitan than a Sicilian. In the Neapolitan of the lower classes one always finds three quarters of Punch....

But in the Sicilian one already finds much of the Arab. He has the Arab's gravity of gait, though he has the great liveliness of wit of the Italian. His native pride, his love for titles, the nature of his haughtiness and even the physiognomy of his face also make him more similar to the Spaniard than the Italian. But what unceasingly gives you the impression of being in the Orient as soon as you set foot in Sicily, is the timbre of the voice, the nasal intonation of street criers. One finds it everywhere, the sharp note of the Arab, this note that seems to come down from the front of the throat, while in the north it rises from the stomach to the mouth.

And the dragging, monotonous and soft song heard as you pass the open door of a house, is quite the same in rhythm and accent, as the one sung by the horseman dressed in white who guides travelers across the great bare spaces of the desert."[36]

Notes

[1] The symbol of Catania is an elephant made of lava stone with an obelisk on its back. The monument sits in the center of Piazza Duomo in front of the Cathedral dedicated to Saint Agatha.

[2] For a discussion in depth of the question of names see Alberto Varvaro, *Lingua e storia in Sicilia*, Sellerio editore, Palermo 1981.

[3] Michele Amari, *Storia dei mussulmani in Sicilia*, Ed. by C.A. Nallino, Catania 1933-9

[4] The island was essentially under Arab control by the time time they took Taormina in 902.

[5] The conquest of Sicily was accomplished essentially by Roger with occasional help from his brother Robert Guiscard. There is a vast literature on the Norman conquest of Sicily: the following are essential readings on the subject: Michele Amari, *Storia dei Mussulmani in Sicilia*, op.cit.; J.J. Norwich, *The Normans in the South*, London, 1966 and *the Kingdom in the Sun*, London, 1970; D.C. Douglas, *The Norman Achievement*, London, 1960; S. Tramontana, *La monarchia normanna e sveva*, Turin 1986; D. Mack Smith, *A History of Sicily, Medieval Sicily, 800-1313*, New York 1968; Donald Matthew, *The Norman Kingdom of Sicily*, Cambridge, 1992; Edmund Curtis, *Roger of Sicily and The Normans in Lower Italy*, New York, 1912.

[6] The Lombards and the Albanians were brought into Sicily primarily to counterbalance the presence of the more numerous Muslim population. They constitute islands within an island. They have managed to keep their distinctive language and traditions that are very different from Sicilian. Today, however, those who speak the Gallo-Italic dialect lament the fact that Sicilian has made some inroads and has basically altered it. In Piana degli Albanesi they continue to speak Albanian.

[7] The Elimians who founded Erice, of whom little is known, represented too small a percentage of the population to make any difference.

[8] F. G. Arezzo, *Sicilia*, Palermo, Flaccovio Editore, 1950, p. 7.

[9] Aziz Ahmad, *A History of Islamic Sicily*, Edinburgh, Edinburgh Univ. Press, p. 23

[10] See Giuseppe Quatriglio, *I viaggiatori in Sicilia*, Palermo, 2001

[11] A reference to the geographer Ibn Hawqal who regarded the Sicilian Sufism with disdain because of its excesses and preoccupations with earthly concerns. See Ahmad, op. cit., p. 40.

[12] There were profound differences between these two groups. The Arabs who may be identified as nomadic people of North Africa tended to live off the work of the slaves they had gained in the conquest. The Berbers tended to farm the

land they conquered.

[13] Michele Amari, op.cit..

[14] Constance of Hauteville was the heir to the Normans. She married Henry VI of the Hoenstaufen dynasty, Frederick Barbarossa's son. She gave birth to Frederick II in Iesi in a tent in front of many people so as not to quell any doubts that the heir was really her son. Many people questioned her ability to produce a child because she was over forty at the time, twice the age of her husband.

[15] Ahmad, op c.it., p. 88.

[16] In the Renaissance the two philophers were studied in depth and were considered the pillars of philosophy. A famous fresco by Raphael in the Vatican known as "The School of Athens" shows Plato and Aristotle at the center of an active world of intellectual speculation that represents the ideals of his age.

[17] Gaetano Basile, *Sicilian Cuisine through History and Legend*, Legas, New York, 1998.

[18] Basile, p. 24.

[19] The couscous made in Trapani, Marsala and Mazara is made with fish, not meat, as it is normally prepared by Arabs far from the sea. This is probably due to the fact that the Arabs who came to Sicily were from coastal areas of North Africa.

[20] Euphemius was a general who rebelled against the Eastern Emperor because he had been chastised for his amorous pecadillos—the legend says he married a nun against her will—Instead of submitting to punishment he declared himself Lord of Sicily until he was defeated by one of his subordinates. He fled to North Africa where he enlisted the aid of the Arabs with the understabding that he would remain in charge of Sicily and pay a tribute to the Arabs once the conquest was accomplished. He was killed in battle during the siege of Siracusa. The Arab became masters of Sicily through an intermediary and they lost Sicily when one of their leaders enlisted the aid of the Normans. Machiavelli a few centuries later was to coin one of his fundamental principles according to which a weak leader should never enlist the help of stronger allies!

[21] Basile, p. 25.

[22] The *sciauni* is a deep fried, thin pastry shell filled with ricotta cheese and sprinkled with sugar that probably has different names throughout the island. But the ingredients and the technique of preparation are very likely of Arab origins.

[23] Michele Amari, op. cit., p.

[24] The lines were taken from a poem quoted by Santi Correnti, *Storia di Sicilia, come storia del popolo siciliano*, Milano, Longanesi, p. 83.

[25] See Varvaro, op.cit., p. 162.

[26] Varvaro, op. cit., p. 116-24.

[27] Arezzo actually listed some thirty points of affinities between Arabic and Sicilian, op c.it., pp. 21-4.

[28] Ibid.,

[29] The list of Sicilian-born scholars would be too long to include. See Ahmad, op. cit. pp. 88-104.

[30] Ahmad, op. cit., p. 42.
[31] For a discussion on the languages in use in Islamic Sicily, see Alberto Varvaro, op.cit.
[32] *Poeti arabi di Sicilia*, op. cit., p. 6.
[33] The surviving poetic texts of the Sicilian Arab poets have been collected and translated by Michele Amari in his companion work to the *Storia dei Mussulmani in Sicilia*. We are referring to the *Biblioteca Arabo-Sicula*, III Vols. Torino-Roma 1881. Small pocket editions of some Sicilian Arabic poetry are available such as *Poeti arabi di Sicilia*, ed. by Carlo Ruta, Palermo, Edi.bi.si. 2001.
[34] Interesting parallels can be drawn between the fate of the Jews and the Arabs as regards Sicily. The year 1492 marked a bitter day for both, when Ferdinand and Isabella of Spain defeated the last Arab stronghold in Granada and signed the edict expelling the Jews from their realms, which included Sicily. The Arabs and the Jews who got along very well in Sicily (in fact under the Arabs, the Jews were somewhat better off than the Christians) shared a common fate. But whereas the Jews never returned to Sicily, Arabs from across the Channel of Sicily are returning in boatloads as illegal aliens to Mazara del Vallo, the city they first conquered. See Francesco Renda, *La fine del giudaismo in Sicilia*, Palermo, Sellerio, 1986, for an excellent treatment of the subject.
[35] It is tempting to see the *Opera dei pupi*, the Sicilian puppet theater, as another remnant of the Arab presence on the island, but, in spite of the ubiquitous references of the struggle for the possession of Europe between the Knights of Charlemagne and the Saracens, these chivalric legends were imported into Italy by the Normans and became a topos of Italian literature later in the Renaissance with Boiardo and Ariosto. This form of entertainment grew in popularity in the 18th century. Still the decorations on the panels of Sicilian *carretti* often display menacing Saracens in battle with Christians. And their faces probably remind Sicilians of the time when the Arabs lived on their island.
[36] Guy de Maupassant, *Sicily*, Palermo, Sellerio, 1990, p. 30.

The Jews of Sicily

As I search my memory for anything associated with Jews during my years of growing up in Sicily, all I can come up with is a ditty in Sicilian which was repeated by children as they performed acts of cruelty on lizards and frogs (how painful to recall the mindlessness of it!). The ditty was "non fu io e mancu Deu, fu la spata dû giudeu!" (It was not I, nor was it God, it was the sword of the Jew!) which in retrospect took a lot of gall on our part. There we were about to sever a lizard's tail or worse and we were accusing the Jews! The anti-Semitism contained in the ditty, however, was not of a personal nature; it had to do with the biblical guilt of the Jews as the people who had failed to recognize the divinity of Jesus and had killed him, which is what Catholics were taught through catechism (that is, before the Church adopted a more enlightened approach). I and my comrades had no personal knowledge of Jews as persons of flesh and blood. They were an ancient people who had lived "in illo tempore." As far as I knew, (and I regard my experiences there as typical and representative) there were no Jews in Sicily, nor had they ever lived on the island. It is not that I was particularly uninformed or oblivious to my surroundings. There seemed to be no physical signs in Sicily from which you could infer that Jews once inhabited the island in large numbers. I had never seen a synagogue, or a ghetto, or a building that could be identified as Jewish. I knew no word in Sicilian that betrayed the presence of Jews on the island. I knew no food that could be recognized as Jewish.

On the other hand, I could easily spot influences of other groups that have inhabited Sicily throughout its tormented history. Physical signs of the presence of Phoenicians, Greeks, Romans, are commonplace, as are those of the Arabs, Normans, Swabians, French, Aragonese/Spaniards, and even Americans, who were the last to enter Sicily as conquerors. If you look at a map of Sicily and see cities such as Caltanissetta, Caltagirone, or Caltavuturo, you have an example of the Arabic presence on the island, —"Kalt" means "castle" in Arabic—; if you hear Sicilians speaking their ancient language, you will recognize traces of the various languages its people have spoken at different times in their three thousand year history: Phoenician, Elymian, Siculian, Greek, Latin, and

Sicilian; words like "bruccetta" (fork) or "custureri" (tailor) are echoes of the French domination ("brochette, couturier"). If you read a Sicilian love poem chances are that some of the imagery and words are derived from the Provençal tradition that Sicilian exploited as they created the first vulgar language worthy of poetry in the XIII century; the Normans come to mind while admiring the cathedrals of Monreale and Cefalù; the Romans' presence is ubiquitous as is the presence of the Greeks, the Arabs and the Phoenicians. But nothing of the Jews was visible to my uninitiated eye. Of course, they never conquered Sicily like the others and they never left monuments to themselves for posterity. But they lived there for fourteen long centuries, sharing bad times and good times, side by side with pagans, Christians, Greek Orthodox Byzantines and Muslims, in relative harmony, as teachers, merchants, doctors, farmers, textile workers, dyers, and shoemakers, contributing not little to the economic and cultural life of Sicily. Yet today, those fourteen hundred years of history seem to have been erased from the consciousness of Sicilians.

Who were these Sicilian Jews, where did they live, what did they contribute to Sicilian history and what made them disappear from our collective consciousness? In trying to answer these questions, even as incompletely as I can on this occasion, I was attempting to fill a void in my understanding of Sicilian history, a part of which has been wiped off the slate. I was attempting to come to terms with a puzzle whose pieces finally began to fit although the history of the Jews in Sicily has not been fully explored and much more remains to be learned.

Fortunately things are changing and that history is beginning to be written. In November 1992, in Salemi (province of Trapani), a convention was organized by the Institute of Jewish Culture "SLM," headed by Titta Lo Jacono, to discuss the historical importance of Jewish communities in Sicily. The weeklong convention, attended by important Catholic and lay personalities, represented a solid beginning and an invitation to start studying those things not destroyed by time: the documents that gather dust in town archives and libraries.

The date of the conference was chosen, of course, to coincide with the five hundredth anniversary of a momentous event in history. No, not the 1492 discovery of America by Christopher Columbus! I am referring to another event that echoed even more loudly in the hearts of European Jews: the edict by Ferdinand and Isabella of Spain, the Catholic Monarchs, expelling the Jews from all their realms. This was a tremendous blow to Judaism comparable to the Exodus from Egypt with one

A memorial stone in the city of Salemi.

qualitative exception: in the first exodus, the Jewish masses could look forward to finding the promised land at the end of their journey, but in the expulsion from Sicily, the Jews had few places in the world that wanted them, no promised land awaited them, only the beginning of a hopeless dispersal to the four corners of the known world.

So let us begin from the end of the sojourn of the Jews on the island they had called home for fourteen hundred years from which they were evicted, not by popular animosities of their neighbors and townsmen, but by the actions of a distant king from a distant land. Sicilian Jews were caught in the vortex of a turbulent drama that began elsewhere, precisely in the Spain of Ferdinand and Isabella, the Catholic Monarchs, to whom Sicily belonged at the time.

Having driven the Moors out of Granada, their last stronghold on the Iberian peninsula, Ferdinand and Isabella, who considered themselves the champions of Christianity, wanted to eradicate from Catholic Spain any other religious groups and set about the task by ordering a massive campaign to convert or drive out the Jews. Under pressure from the Grand Inquisitor Torquemada, Ferdinand and Isabella signed an edict in which they accused the Jews of proselytizing and eating away at the well-being of Christians with their usury, and ordered them to leave all Spanish realms within three months on pain of death and the confiscation of all their wealth. Their expulsion from Spain was deemed essential to "extirpate... the apostasy and iniquitous perversion of the Jews who by their practice and conversations have induced many Christians into heresy and in some errors". The only way to circumvent the expulsion was to convert to Christianity. If the Jews abandoned their faith and embraced Christ, they would be considered Christian subjects having the same legal liberties and rights. In Sicily, which was governed at that time by Viceroy Don Ferdinand de Acugna, (remembered as one of the better Viceroys) the anti-Semitism rampant on the Iberian Peninsula was not shared by the majority of Sicilians, and they did not want to see their numerous and long-standing Jewish communities leave the island. The Viceroy, sensing the enormous impact that the edict was going to have on the island, did not make it public until June 18, 1492, two and a half months after its proclamation in Spain (March 31, 1492), perhaps hoping that its implementation would not take place. No doubt he knew that an action of that magnitude was bound to create animosities, especially among the powerful members of the Sicilian Camera Regia (Sicilian Parliament) which could have objected not only on legal grounds — that body had not been consulted on a matter that was of the utmost importance to them — but also for moral and economic reasons. Losing the entrepreneurial skill of the Jews would be catastrophic to the island and the elite knew it. The Viceroy also knew that public opinion was firmly against the mandate because the Jews, having lived in Sicily for so long, were well integrated into the social fabric of the country.

A painting of life at the court of Frederick II. From a French miniature.

No doubt all of the reasons listed above were true, but it should not be surprising to find that the opposition of the Sicilian officials had additional motives for objecting to Ferdinand's edict. Francesco Renda made it abundantly clear in his *La fine del giudaismo siciliano* (The End of Sicilian Judaism) that the Sicilian authorities were attempting to safeguard some of the privileges and constitutional guarantees that the Sicilian *Regnum* had enjoyed for a long time against Ferdinand and

Isabella of Spain's centralization moves. The version of the edict that was sent to Sicily was different from the one published for the Spanish provinces. In the Sicilian edict Ferdinand cites a more determinant role for the General Inquisitor Torquemada in his reaching the conclusion that the Jews had to be expelled for the good of the nation. Renda suggests that the difference was due to Ferdinand's attempt to wrest control of the Holy Inquisition which in Sicily was administered by the Roman Church through its Sicilian bishops, even though the General Inquisitor Torquemada had jurisdiction on the island. But Torquemada's power was ineffective in Sicily. In actuality, his representative was without power over the island because the ecclesiastical hierarchy there strenuously defended, with the covert help of the Roman Curia, its jurisdiction over matter of faith. Thus, the matter of the expulsion of the Jews was tied to other sticky political questions that involved the Papacy in its long-standing relationship with Sicily, the Sicilian Parliament, and Ferdinand's desire to gain greater control over his realms and possessions.

Whatever the power politics at play, once the edict was made public, Sicilians in positions of authority, which included the count of Adernò, Tommaso Moncada, Grand Justice of the "Regnum," as well as the Judges of the Magna Curia, the Masters of the Royal Patrimony, the Treasurer of the *Regnum*, wrote a petition to Ferdinand and Isabella to stop the edict from taking effect. Other bodies protested to the Viceroy with letters and personal appearances. In essence, these petitions briefly contradicted the religious rationale given by the King for the expulsion order and focused on a number of points of legal, economic and social importance. Specifically, they pointed out that

1. In Sicily the Jews did not try to convince Christians to abandon their faith nor did they cause heresies;

2. The Jews spent nearly one million florins a year to feed and clothe themselves and if they were evicted the island would lose this enormous sum (Titta Lo Jacono, in his *Judaica Salem*, estimates this sum to be equivalent to three quarters of a billion dollars);

3. The commerce between Jews and Christians would come to an end and cause much hardship on Christians;

4. The island would come to lose the iron works industry, which was totally in the hands of Jews. And this would have disastrous consequences on shipbuilding;

5. The island would come to lose low-wage workers employed in the construction of city defenses against incursions by pirates;

6. The state coffers would come to lose the income from taxes levied on the Jews;

7. Some of the islands belonging to Sicily, like Malta, Gozzo and Pantelleria, which were inhabited in large numbers by Jews would become deserted;

8. With the exception of a few individuals and families, Jews were generally so poor that if the three months limit was not extended, many would starve to death.

The tone of the petition, written in Sicilian, is one of dismay, sadness and disbelief. In a second letter written to the Viceroy by the municipal government of the City of Palermo, and similar in tone, the Jews were cleared of the accusation of proselytizing and of usury: the letter stated categorically that there are no reasons for proceeding against the Jews since the accusations are not founded on fact: "And for this reason the action must not be continued against this "regnum" since there are no reasons for it, nor can the cause be that the mentioned Jews are usurers for in this kingdom it has never been known that the Jews practiced usury publicly."

Sicilian Jews were in fact not engaged in money lending, even though Jews had been given permission to charge 10% on loans by the Emperor Frederick II in his Melfi Charter of 1231. Thus, even if some of the Sicilian Jews practiced usury, they were not committing a crime, unless they charged more than the permitted rate of ten percent interest. The expulsion of the Jews was considered an act of violence against their natural rights and against the position of the Popes reiterated on a number of occasions that the Jews were allowed to live among the Christians in the hope that they might convert and see the Christian light of truth. Nevertheless, the edict stood and was carried out on the legal justification that pertained to their special status as "servants of the King".

Let us clarify this concept. The status of "servants of the King," was instituted by Frederick II in the 13th century. It was a way to legalize the presence of non believers in the Christian societies of Europe and it remained as an institution in the Catholic monarchies of France, Spain, England and Germany even in free city-states and principalities. The status of "servants" was considered a form of punishment for the Jews' involvement in the crucifixion of Christ and their unwillingness to recognize the divinity of Jesus by the Christian monarchs and by the Catholic Church. They were condemned to a condition of eternal serfdom. That does not mean that they were slaves. The Jews could not be bought or sold like the Muslims, for example. They were able to organize themselves as a political community in accordance with special statutes and were allowed to live among Christians, always in a position of inferiority. Ironically, during the domination of the Arabs, (827-1062) the Jews occupied a middle rung in the social ladder with the Christians on the lowest step. When the Normans ruled, (1062-1266) the Christians replaced the Arabs at the top and the Arabs slid to the bottom and became slaves, while the Jews remained pretty much in the middle as before. At any rate, in Sicily the Jews lived there as servants, subjects and vassals of the King. They did not depend on the Church or the feudal nobility or even on the magistrates of the cities where they lived. Their safety, protection and guarantees were provided by the King through his representatives. The Jews did not have to serve the King in any way, that is, they had no duties to perform for him. But as the King's servants, their right to own and keep property, to practice their faith and to engage in commercial activities were protected by the King and his officials. They were allowed to live in Sicily at the King's pleasure. Indeed, their bodies literally belonged to the King as property. And this special status was in fact given as a legal justification for the expulsion edict proclaimed for the Sicilian Jews. No mention of it was made in the edict that was published for the Spanish Jews. Obviously, foreseeing the negative reaction of the Sicilian authorities and their protestation against the baseless charges of usury and proselitzing made against the Sicilian Jews, Ferdinand and his ministers added a legal claim that could not be denied. In effect, Ferdinand's edict could be considered morally and ethically unsound, but the special status of the Jews as his "servants" gave him the cover he needed. Basically, the King said that the Jews were his property and as such he could dispose of them as he wished. Here is an excerpt of the Sicilian edict that is tellingly absent from the one that was proclaimed in Spain:

"And since the Jews owing to their own guilt are subjected to perpetual serfdom and they are Our servants and dependents; and if they are tolerated and allowed to live through our compassion and grace and if they forget this condition of theirs and show their ingratitude by not living quietly in accordance with the above mentioned condition, it is just that they should lose our grace; and that without it they should be treated as heretics and purveyors of such heresy and apostasy {...]. And considering that all the bodies of the Jews who live and reside in our realms are our property and we can dispose of them at our will through our royal power and supreme authority, using such power to remedy such an urgent cause, we command that all the said Jews, male and female, young and old, who live in our realms and dominions in the west and in the east be expelled and we expel them...."

The Sicilian officials, having broken a lance in behalf of the rights and privileges of the Sicilian Parliament, had to acquiesce and thus began a painful and traumatic experience for the Jews of Sicily who were Sicilians, spoke Sicilian, indeed contributed no small part to the development of the Sicilian language, that culminated in their abandonment of their native land where they had lived in relative safety for over a thousand years.

The presence of the Jews in Sicily and in Southern Italy goes back in time to the first century before the modern era. While conquering Roman armies operating in the Mediterranean basin brought a good number of Jews into Italy as slaves, the largest number of them were brought back by Pompey after he sacked Jerusalem in 63 BC and by the Roman Proconsul Crassus who is said to have sold thirty thousand of them as slaves. To these groups a good number of merchants trading with Rome and operating out of the Eastern Mediterranean, and particularly Alexandria, may be added to make up the first nucleus of Jews to reside in Sicily. In time, the small communities of Sicilian Jews grew in size and importance through immigration from other parts of the Mediterranean. By the time they were expelled, there were fifty-two

The Greek theater of Siracusa carved from the rock.

Jewish communities throughout the island, the largest being in Palermo with 5000 people. Trapani, Messina, Catania, Marsala, Sciacca, Agrigento, and Mazara had large communities ranging from 2000 to 3600 people; medium sized communities ranging from 350-1500 individuals existed in Bivona, Caltagirone, Caltabellotta, Mineo, Modica, Noto, and Polizzi; smaller communities existed in Salemi, with 320 Jews, in Taormina, Castroreale, Randazzo, Augusta, Erice, Paternò, etc... It is difficult to quantify the actual number of Jews living in Sicily. According to some scholars the total Jewish population of Sicily was 100,000 people, which is estimated to represent 10% of the total Sicilian population. Others adopt a more conservative estimate of 50,000. But even if the lower estimate is accepted, it still constitutes a large nucleus whose weight in the life of the community, owing to the restless activism of the Jews who traveled back and forth between their communities, was certainly felt. It also identifies Sicily as the land with the highest percentage of Jews in Europe. Consider that at the time of the expulsion from Spain the number of Jews was estimated to be 200,000 which represents barely 2 percent of the total Spanish population. In Sicily even if we accept the lowest estimate of the number of Jews, they represented 5 percent of the population. This number may not seem like much, but the percentage varied from town to town and in a few cities Jews represented nearly half the total population, as in Marsala for example which had 46.9 %. The highest percentages of Jews relative to the rest of the population were in Sciacca (31.9%), Trapani, and many other places with percentages higher than 10 such as Agrigento (12.4), Randazzo (11.3), Castroreale (15.2), Savoca (11.2), Palermo (14.9), and Polizzi (11.6). Such high percentages confirm that the Jews must have had an important role to play in the life of their communities. Even though they lived in "giudecche" their presence in such numbers could not be ignored and had to have an impact on the daily lives of their fellow townspeople. Such a long and uninterrupted presence in Sicily is also proof of the relative integration of the Jews into the larger society. The Sicilian people as a whole shared a long tradition of tolerance for different religious beliefs, and Jews, Muslims, and Christians had lived in relative tranquility side by side for many centuries. Indeed, in the height of the Middle Ages, while Europe was experiencing savage repression and massacres of an ethnic and religious nature, Latins, Greeks, Muslims and Jews lived in harmony in Sicily, practicing their individual religions and beliefs without interference from the government. It was so under the Arabs and it continued under the Normans and the Swabians, and to a lesser degree under the Aragonese.

By far, no other dominant group had as much influence on the Sicilian Jews as the Arabs did. The Jews enjoyed certain privileges, together with the general population, including the right to own real estate and to have synagogues, but they were forbidden to carry arms, to enter the army, and to build more synagogues. They had to pay, like other groups, a tax known as "ghezia" for practicing their religion freely and they had to wear a distinctive sign — a yellow belt and a special turban — that was instituted for the first time ever in Sicily in 887. These measures notwithstanding, the similarity of customs, culture and languages between Arabs and Jews worked in favor of the Jews who became the natural liaison between Arabs and Christians. The Jewish community in Palermo flourished and became the largest in Italy. Other communities existed in Agrigento, Siracusa and Catania. Sicilian Jews had even constituted a small community in Egypt.

The golden age of Judaism in Sicily came during the twelfth and fourteenth centuries, under the Norman-Swabian dynasties. Under the Normans who came to power in 1066 and remained in Sicily until the last of their dynasty, Constance of Hauteville married Henry VI, the son of Frederick Barbarossa, the Jews enjoyed parity of civil rights with other citizens. They could hold public office, own property, except for Christian slaves. They were free to engage in any commercial activities, to travel and work. Benjamin of Tudela, a medieval traveler, who was not unlike Marco Polo in spirit of observation and interests, has left us a detailed description of the various Sicilian Jewish communities he visited between 1170 and 1173, giving information as to their numbers and occupations. He describes Sicily as a kind of earthly paradise and the Jews who live in it as a large and flourishing community. The Jews were engaged in many activities too diverse to list here, but two occupations in which they held a monopoly were the silk and dyeing industries. The Arabs brought the silk worm into Sicily, and built a thriving industry, but it was the Jews who eventually made it grow into a monopoly. King Roger II returning from an expedition against Byzantium in 1147 stopped off in Thebes, Greece, where the silk industry was in the hands of Jews. He captured the town and took the Jewish silk workers with him to Palermo giving a great boost to the native industry and guaranteeing for Italy four centuries of domination of the market. The dyeing industry, which required special skills, was another favorite occupation of the

Jews. They were also adept as fishermen, artisans and skilled workers of every kind.

But the happiest and most productive time for the Jews came when Frederick II ("Stupor mundi", the wonder of the world) came to occupy the throne of Sicily, Southern Italy and Germany. While he was forced by political necessity to adopt policies that at times seemed inimical to Jews — he accepted the dictates of the Fourth Lateran Council that required Jews to wear a distinctive sign, an orange-colored TAU of his own design, he confirmed that they should continue to pay taxes to the bishops — he expressed his true feelings for them in his Melfi Charter, published in 1231, in which he declared that Jews were under his personal protection and that they had the same rights to justice as all other citizens. In addition, for the first time in history and against the power of the Church, which had just lifted its excommunication from his head, he declared that money lending, as noted earlier, was not illegal for the Jews as long as they did not charge more than 10% interest. While Jews did not immediately embrace money lending, it was to become an important activity for them. The Church, of course, had maintained throughout that charging interest on money lent was sinful. The Jews figure prominently in Frederick's plan for economic reforms. He gave them absolute control of the silk monopoly. The Emperor at one point closed all dyeing shops in the realm except those in Capua and Naples, placing these under the direction of two Jews, as a way of monopolizing that industry as well. These two Jewish directors in turn could authorize the opening of other shops. In addition, as a way of stimulating commerce, Frederick organized fairs in various cities with Jews participating prominently in them. Under Frederick's rule, Jews prospered, being able to conduct their activities with the support of the sovereign and under his protection. Their highly specialized skills with silver, gold, (the Jews were linked to these arts so much that "orefice," a word that signifies "goldsmith" used as a family name indicates that family's Jewish ancestry), coral and iron made their contribution to the economy of their island nearly irreplaceable. One activity illustrates the sense of safety and continuity they felt in Sicily: many Jews were farmers and grew vineyards while living in small towns. Always weary of the sudden change in political climate, Jews have tended to be an urban people, as a natural defense against the unpredictability of historical events that might force them to liquidate their assets quickly and run. Such an eventuality must have appeared remote to the Sicilian Jewish farmers who invested everything they had in the land. Frederick II was only one of the last in a long line of rulers who by their action instilled such abiding faith. But he was the one who was the most appreciative of the business acumen of Jews, and also of their spiritual and cultural patrimony. Things changed for the worse, however, after the death of Frederick and his successors and the arrival of the French, in the person of Charles d'Anjou, in Southern Italy and in Sicily.

The destinies of the Jews and the French in Southern Italy parted when Sicily rebelled against the greed and abuses of the French in 1282 and threw them out, slaughtering every Frenchman in sight. Sicily became a separate kingdom under Charles of Aragon, while Southern Italy remained under the Anjou dynasty. While there is no question that Sicilian Jews fared a lot better than their counterparts under French domination, it is true that in the Kingdom of Sicily which lasted from 1302 to 1402, when it was demoted to a Vice regency, the Jews suffered a setback — although they did not suffer in the same measure as the general population —due to deteriorating economic conditions. A crisis caused by dynastic strife and infighting among local barons engulfed the island. In addition, as the economy changed from industrial/agricultural to strictly agricultural, the Jews who had occupied key positions in the silk manufacture and dyeing industries were forced to shift their attention to trading in agricultural products. Slowly their wealth diminished. The political climate also changed. Under the Aragonese, harsher laws against Jews were enacted. Jews could not practice medicine on or give medicine to Christians, they could not hold public office or associate openly with Christians. But as happened in the Vatican, these laws were not adhered to in daily practice. In fact, Jewish doctors were allowed to frequent the Court and were received honorably there as "familiars."

No doubt, many of the problems that rose between Christians and Jews can be ascribed less to the Aragonese government than to the action of the Church, which through preachers, inflamed the population against the "murderers of Christ" and was in part responsible for episodes of brutality against the Jews. Typically, the time of the year Jews dreaded most was Holy Week which culminated in the reenactment of the passion of Jesus, a reenactment that still takes place in costumes and with elaborate productions worthy of Hollywood in many Sicilian towns. Jews in fact, stayed indoors as a matter of course during the last three days of Holy Week. It was customary to stone Jewish homes during the days of the Passion of Christ. It was known as the "sassaiuola santa" ("Holy stoning"). On occasion the stoning deteriorated to setting the

Jewish homes on fire, or worse, killing the terrified Jews locked up inside. The fury of Franciscan and Dominican preachers who denounced Jews from the pulpits caused many to abandon what is truly a Sicilian way of life: "vivi e lassa viviri" (live and let live). Still, such outbreaks were sporadic, temporary and causally linked to outside agencies whose actions were condemned by the Viceroys who had to intervene in defense of the Jews. They were momentary departures from the normal behavior of Sicilians. Although some terrible atrocities were committed against Jews, fanaticism is normally alien to the Sicilian "modus vivendi". Sicilians are very pragmatic people. They are extremely rationalistic and will not perform acts of brutality unless family honor is at stake. Sicilians, as Tomasi di Lampedusa observed, have a way of changing everything that comes to them from the outside and the hot wind of anti-Semitism in crossing the Mediterranean sea became much cooler when it reached Sicily, and even then it was not easily tolerable. Racism, as Titta Lo Jacono wrote, is an imported plant, but unlike the prickly pears or orange, it has never taken root in Sicily.

By and large, in the 15th century Jews continued to enjoy autonomy as a collectivity, have their own synagogues, cemeteries, ritual baths, slaughter houses; they were free to choose their work, own property, and they could own slaves, except Christian ones. These privileges were not cheap, however, since the authorities frequently made demands on the Jews for special purposes, to renew a license, for example, or to extend a right or confirm a privilege already obtained. One of the most ironic "donations" the Jews ever had to make was when they paid Ferdinand 2,500 Ounces in 1481 and another 1000 Ounces again in 1489, ostensibly to obtain assurances from him that their previously established rights were not going to be altered. In actuality the money helped finance the war against Granada, the outcome of which destroyed the last stronghold of Arab power in Spain and sealed the destiny of the Jews. Unwittingly, they contributed to their own expulsion!

But that was not the only irony. Once the edict was announced and the machinery set in place to extract as much wealth from the departing Jews as possible, the Spanish authorities registered and sequestered Jewish properties to make sure that any outstanding debts or obligations were paid. The most outrageous of ironies was a demand by the government to be reimbursed for all the future taxes that it was not going to collect from the Jews! They were forced to pay one hundred thousand Florins to have their properties released to them, as well as five thousand Florins to the Viceroy as a special donation. The two sums were not far from the actual value of the properties seized by the government. In other words, the government expropriated these properties and left the Jews the task of transforming them into cash in the hope that something would be left over, after satisfying Christian creditors. In the end, little was left, in fact, to the Jews who out of the meager pooled resources the community had to pay for the indigent being expatriated, which for the city of Palermo alone was 1/8 the Jewish population. Those who were too poor to pay for their transportation out of the country were to be provided by the community with "una coperta di lectu...cum unu paru di linczola usati et uno mataraczo usato di pocu precio et la somma di tre tarì per testa." (a blanket for the bed with a pair of used sheets and an inexpensive used mattress and the sum of three tarì per person.)

Needless to say, the departure from Sicily was traumatic for both those who remained and those forced to leave. The expulsion order, however, had different effects in Sicily than it had had in Spain. Out of 200,000 Jews in Spain, 150,000 accepted banishment rather than convert to Christianity. In Sicily, there seems to be agreement among historians that a great number of Jews, and particularly those that belonged to the upper classes, preferred to convert rather than lose their capital and their homeland that had been very hospitable to them. The town of Salemi, where out of thirty Jewish families only four decided to accept exile, represents a special case and is certainly not typical of how Sicilian Jews reacted to the expulsion order. Nor can what happened in San Marco and Castronovo, where the scale tipped in the other direction, be considered representative. In San Marco 723 out of 728 Jews preferred to leave; in Castronovo, 120 out of 130. The percentage of those who left is difficult to calculate but it is generally accepted that most of the poor Jews preferred to leave, no doubt hoping to find better economic conditions elsewhere. There were also many who accepted conversion but continued to be Jews within the sanctuary of their homes. It is safe to assume that at least a quarter of the Jewish population and perhaps more than that accepted baptism in order to remain on the island. That was the percentage of Jews who opted for conversion in Spain where the conditions were a lot harsher on account of the relentless pursuit of the Spanish Inquisition of those whose conversion was not deemed sincere. But in Sicily in 1493 and until 1500, the Inquisition was still in the hands of the local bishops and was relatively mild in comparison. Thus the marranos, that is, the converted Jews could be Christians to the outside world but practice Judaism—a difficult thing to do considering they had no access to books, temples, and all the other necessary objects of their faith— within the confines of their home. The Spanish style Inquisition took over in 1500 but it did not begin working as it had in Spain until the arrival of Viceroy Ugo Moncada and the new Grand Inquisitor Alonso Bernal in 1511, personally appointed by King Ferdinand. Thus began an intense campaign to seek out the marranos who were suspected of practicing Judaism. The Spanish inquisitor who bypassed local laws and institutions was responsible directly to the King and had ample powers to act. From 1511 through 1515, 120 converted Jews were burned at the stake, 79 of them in person and 41 in effigy because they were either dead or absent. In the period between 1511 and 1560, 441 marranos were condemned to be burned alive. The relentless campaign to eradicate every trace of the Jewish presence in Sicily was indeed successful. All the synagogues were either destroyed or converted to Christian churches. They were sold at auction and bought by wealthy Sicilians. The synagogue of Messina became the Madonna della Candelaia, those of Salemi and Calascibetta were renamed after Santa Maria della Catena. All the Samuels, Abrahams and Davids became Giovanni, Francesco and Salvatore, the three most common Christian names chosen by the marranos. For an idea of how complete was the obliteration of the Jews was let me make a few parenthetical remarks. When this article first came out, an old friend pointed out that I should have known at least one typically Jewish artifact, the so-called "marranzano" which sometimes Sicilians also call "scacciapinseri" and which in English is known as a "Jews' harp". The observation threw me for a loop for a little while. Why did I not think of it as Jewish? Primarily because I , as a youth growing up in Sicily, did not know that a "marrano" was a converted Jew. Thus, I saw no connection between "marrano" and "marranzano". After some research I discovered that the Sicilian definition of the word "marranu" differs from the Italian definition. In Italian the word is "an offensive title given to the Moors or the Jews recently converted to Christianity," which is similar to the English definition of the word. In Sicilian, however, "marrano," according to Piccitto's dictionary, means "villano, individuo zotico" (peasant, uncouth individual). The meaning given for the adjective is "maledetto, scomunicato" (damned, excommunicated). In the provinces of Catania, Enna etc... it actually means "storpio, sbilenco" (crippled, crooked), and in Messina it means "cornuto" (cuckold). The meaning of converted Jew is not part of the Sicilian dictionary. The Jews, as you can see, were eradicated even from the language.

The Jews who had lived in Sicily since the first century BC left the island they called home on January 12, 1493, never to return again. Many of them went to Rome, where the Popes surprisingly adopted a generally protective attitude towards them. Even the Borgia Pope, Alexander VI, who was a Spaniard did not share the Spanish monarch's preoccupation with Jews and offered them his protection, even against the petition by local Jews who feared that the influx of many others would cause problems in their community. The city that received the largest number of Sicilian Jews was Reggio Calabria where the Jewish communities of Messina and Siracusa moved en masse. They were welcomed by King Ferrante of Naples who offered them his protection and ordered that the new arrivals be treated as though they had been longtime subjects of the crown. But it was not long until Ferdinand took control of Naples, marking the end of their sojourn there. In 1515 most of them were forced to leave again. A small number of rich families remained in Naples for another 30 years. But in 1541, when these families were forced out, the history of the Jews in Southern Italy came to an end. Many went north, and especially to Rome and Ferrara, others preferred farther destinations in Albania, Greece, Syria and Palestine. The authorities made two attempts, in 1740 and in 1747, to recall the Jews in the hope of stimulating economic activity in the realm, but no Jewish communities ever returned to Sicily or Southern Italy. Yet the memory of their residence in these places lived with them for a long time, for when midway through the 16th century, they established themselves in Salonicco, Constantinople, or even the island of Corfù—, many "Aljiamas" bore the names of the places they had been forced to leave. In Salonicco a dozen synagogue-communities were called "Sicilia" "Puglia" Calabria" "Otranto" and "Messina."

What's left of the fourteen centuries of Jewish permanence in Sicily? As I said at the beginning, not much remains to the untrained eye. But serious efforts are being made to try to recover a part of the past because respect for history is a barometer of civilization. Much work remains to be done. Each of the fifty-two towns in Sicily had its own "giudecca," its own cemeteries and synagogues. While a great number of the physical remnants of the Jewish presence have been destroyed or transformed, a great deal remains; town archives contain masses of documents that need to be studied and catalogued. The most visible evidence of the Jewish presence is probably in the use of names that are very common in Sicily. Names of cities such as Messina, Catania, Palermo, Piazza. Trapani usually denote a Jewish background because they were adopted by them with great frequency; as were names of professions like Orefice, (goldsmith) Ferraro, Ferro (iron monger was a profession almost exclusively reserved to Jews). Barbera (with its many variants — Barbieri, Barberini, Barberis — identifies people who worked as barbers but who also performed small operations, pulled teeth etc.), Zavatteri, Zapateri identified shoemakers. Jews frequently used last names such as Angelo or D'Angelo. It was translated directly from the Hebrew (Angelo is Malechai in Hebrew). Palumbo was a translation of the name Jonah; other common Sicilian Jewish names are: Sala, Lo Presti, (probably a variant of Pristo-Preste, priest which is a translation of the Jewish "Cohen"), Forte, Leone and Moncada (this last name, belonging to one of the most renown aristocratic families of Sicily was common among the *conversos*). The name Jaffe became Bello, Lo Bello. Those who converted were given permission to use the names of noble Sicilian families such as Torres, De Castro, Martines who sponsored them, and when they had no other name to fall on they chose the days of the week. Some maintained their Jewish names, but that was deemed suspicious by the Inquisition who interpreted the choice as an unwillingness to embrace their new Christian identities.

The integration of the Jews with the rest of the population left marks on Sicilian customs and traditions, even if we are not aware of them. The Jews continued culinary traditions imported by the Arabs and brought them north after the expulsion.[12] Until the 1600s, Sicilians normally used animal fats for cooking. Gradually they began to favor olive oil, which was part of the Jewish culinary tradition. A typical Sicilian dish of Jewish origin is meat fried in olive oil with garlic and sage. Another is "Artichokes a la giudea." Who knows what other Jewish customs have entered the mainstream of Sicilian life? Who knows how many people of Jewish origin walk among Sicilians without knowing anything about their ancestors?

Notes

1. Isidoro La Lumia (1823-1879), who wrote an excellent history of the Jews in Sicily, *Gli ebrei in Sicilia*, Palermo: Sellerio, 1984, tells the story that while an emissary of the Spanish Jewish community was asking the King and Queen to reconsider the edict, by offering them thirty thousand ducats, Torquemada entered the room and taking a crucifix from under his cape and placing it on the table, said: "Judas Iscariot sold his master for thirty pieces of silver, would you sell him for thirty thousand?"

Having said this he turned around and brusquely walked out, leaving the Queen astonished and stunned. As for the king, La Lumia added slyly : "Ferdinand was also stunned or so at least made believe he was." La Lumia believes that Ferdinand, whose greed and ambitions are well known, was more interested in expoliating the Jews than in safeguarding Christians from the evil influences of heresies.

2. This is part of the text in Sicilian made public by Viceroy D'Acugna, which presumably translated the original Spanish documents. See Attilio Milano, *La storia degli Ebrei in Italia*, Torino: Einaudi, 1963, p. 218.

3. This is I. La Lumia's judgment, op. cit., who viewed the Viceroy's delaying tactics in implementing the royal mandate of expulsion, which was made public on June 18, 1492, two and a half months after its proclamation in Spain, as an expression of his sympathetic attitude toward the Jews.

4. Lo Jacono, *Judaica Salem*, Palermo: Sellerio, 1990, p. 47.

5. The text of these two letters is in La Lumia's volume, pp. 59-65.

6. Ibid.

7. According to Attilio Milano (p. 178), in the 250 years since the publication of the Melfi Charter, very few availed themselves of the privilege. Jews in Sicily were accustomed to more direct means of producing wealth. In fact, in some agreements stipulated in 1363 and in 1398 between various chapters of the Jewish community of Siracusa, the article that Jews were forbidden to practice usury amongst themselves and with Christians was introduced at the request of the community itself. Christians, of course, were not allowed by Christian doctrine to lend money at interest.

8. Benjamin's writings are summarized by Milano, op. cit., and by others. They are a valuable source of information for twelfth century Italy.

9. Lo Jacono, op. cit., p. 49.

10. See Carmelo Trasselli, "Gli Ebrei in Sicilia" in *Nuovi Quaderni del Meridione* VII, p. 44. His views are shared by Titta Lo Jacono, *Judaica Salem*, op. cit. and by Aliyahu Ashtor, *The Jews and the Mediterranean Economy 10th-15th Centuries,* London, Variorum Reprints 1983, p. 241.

11. Titta Lo Jacono claims that the persecutions suffered in Spain by the Jews had given them a stronger sense of belonging to a special group and a stronger attachment to their traditions. The fanaticism of the Christians begat the fanaticism of the Jews who refused to give up Judaism. But in Sicily where only sporadic explosions of hatred against the Jews had been seen and mostly as a result of religious propaganda, Jews felt more at home.

12. Mary Taylor Simeti's *Pomp and Sustenance*, New York: A. Knopf, 1990. Simeti speculates that Jews were responsible for helping develop the "cucina baronale."

Is Sicilian a Language or a Dialect?

In the performance of my academic duties I am often called to advise students who want to study Italian. When I inquire whether they have some knowledge of Italian some of them admit somewhat sheepishly that they know what they characterize as "bad Italian". Owing to the fact that Sicilian immigrants represent between 40 or 50% of the Italian-American population, that "bad Italian" often turns out to be Sicilian. But Sicilian is not the only "dialect" that is classified by my students as being "bad Italian". Neapolitan, Barese, Calabrian, Molisan, to name a few southern Italian "dialects" all are characterized as corruptions of that lofty language that is Italian, inferior linguistic expressions without beauty or grace that lack nobility and elegance, so much so that they can only exist in the confines of one's home, away from the ears of outsiders who might form a negative impression on the dialectal speaker's worth. The embarrassment displayed by these students as they admit to understanding or even speaking such lowly idioms is a constant source of amazement to me as well as anger that I try to put aside quickly as I attempt to encourage them to consider the linguistic skills they have acquired as an asset rather than a liability, a help not a stumbling block to learning Italian. Inevitably, however, I reflect on the long and tortured road that the so-called Italian dialects have traveled through the centuries, "losing a chord every day" to use Ignazio Buttitta's famous poem "Lingua e dialettu," chased out of the classroom by intransigent teachers ("don't say *racina*, that's Sicilian dialect, the correct Italian word is *uva!"*), forbidden to appear in public by a dictatorial regime, vilified as a poor and unwelcome relative, wrongly accused of being a poor tool in the hands of an unskilled artisan, and unwelcome in government offices and among polite society.

For this reason, in an attempt to bolster students' confidence, I tell them that Sicilian is not really a dialect, but another language. I usually qualify the term "dialect" which most people understand as a subcategory of language in relation to another more dominant linguistic medium, by saying that Sicilian is certainly not a corruption of or an inferior form of Italian. Often, depending on the situation, I expand upon the answer, giving some facts about the privileged position of Sicilian among the first languages that developed from Latin and about the Sicilian School of poetry that flourished under the Emperor Frederick II in the early part of the 13th century. I point out as well that standard Italian, the language spoken on Italian radio and TV, that everyone in Italy understands more or less, was derived from the Florentine language of the middle ages, which like Sicilian was derived from Latin. I point out as well that the Sicilian language reached a more mature stage of development earlier than Florentine and that in fact Sicilian was the first of the so-called "vulgar" languages (vulgar from "vulgus" meaning popular) to be considered worthy of use in poetry. Indeed, as Dante himself acknowledged in his *De Vulgari Eloquentia*, a treatise that evaluated the 14 known "dialects" spoken in Italy in search for one that was sufficiently "lofty" to be used as a common literary medium, Sicilian was not only the first but also the dominant language for poetry in Italy in the 13th century.[1] The fact that Florentine evolved into what we call standard Italian is an accident of history, a confluence of historical and cultural factors that might have issued different results if one or more components had been absent. In fact, I like to think that if Frederick II had not died in 1250 and the Ghibelline cause had been successful, the linguistic history of Italy would have been very different. Had the Imperial armies not been defeated at Benevento in 1266, a battle that ended the Ghibellines' influence in the political scene of the peninsula, today we might have spoken Italian with a Sicilian accent. [2]

Such informal discussions work wonders, turning students who were afraid to open their mouths in class for fear speaking in the dreaded "dialect" into eager participants whose understanding of Italian by far surpasses those students who have had no prior experience with the language. But the stigma attached to Sicilian and to the other dialects does not only affect students. It touches the lives of the many millions of courageous Italian-Americans who came to the United States seeking economic and social freedom, knowing only the language spoken in their little village. Knowing that the bulk of the Italian immigrants came from the six southern regions of Italy and that they came at a time when even in Italy the population was still essentially speaking "dialects" it is safe to conclude that the majority of Italian-Americans are dialect speakers, as are their offspring although to a lesser degree. Thus, the stigma attached to speaking a dialect touches millions of Italian-Americans any time they come into contact with Italian bureaucracies, Italian schools and even Italians of a more recent immigration.

If you speak Sicilian or Neapolitan with people who do not know you, your interlocutors will consider you illiterate. A person's inability to speak Italian correctly can be a source of embarrassment and ridicule. Playwright and poet Nino Martoglio in his *Centona* and in many of his plays, got a lot of mileage out of making fun of his fellow Catanese who are constantly tripped up by their poorly learned Italian. Dialect speakers who constantly mangle the Italian language are a staple of Italian dialectal theatre, reflecting long-standing Italian attitudes.[3] Clearly then the refusal to speak Sicilian in public is directly connected with the desire to avoid the stigma attached to it. And it is not surprising that the first thing Italian –Americans abandoned when they came to the US was their language.

The first generation of immigrants begins to lose their communicative skills by speaking a kind of pidgin Sicilian that they alone understand. Thus Sicilian-Americans have no difficulty understanding "u storu", "a bega", "u sobway" "a giobba" " a ccichina" "u sanguicciu" "u bussu" "u bossu" etc... By the second generation the transformation is nearly complete. The offspring of Italian-Americans rarely go beyond a passive knowledge of the dialect. They understand a lot but they will rarely communicate in the dialect. By the third generation the dialect has all but disappeared. Perhaps a curse word or epithet in dialect may remain but that is the extent of it.[4] The stigma accompanying the dialect speakers is primarily responsible for their ready acceptance of English. The sad thing is that they, too, like those who look at the dialect with disdain, are convinced that they are speakers of an inferior, corrupted idiom.

In the following pages, I am going to discuss the historical relationship between Sicilian and Italian, and I will attempt to answer the question in the title: "Is Sicilian a language or a dialect?" Since this is a touchy subject that involves regional pride, identity and politics, I will try to answer the question without falling victim to that dreaded social disease known as "campanilismo," a faint echo of which still characterizes Italian society.[5]

The relationship between Italian and Sicilian is indeed very complex and must be understood within the larger context generally known as "la questione della lingua," that has plagued Italy since the Renaissance and which arises out of a uniquely Italian dilemma centering on which language Italians ought to use in written communication and in literature. Other European nations did not have to face the same problem because early in the formation of their countries, one language became the dominant medium of communication that everyone accepted and used to the exclusion of other localized idioms. The French language developed around the French spoken in the capital Paris; the Spaniards adopted Castilian and the English the language of London. But in Italy, which did not become a nation until 1861, and which consists of twenty regional cultures that have existed in one form or another since the time of the Romans, the regional differences in history, tradition and most importantly, in language, have remained. Italy is in effect many different countries in one. The Italian landscape is so diverse that if you travel from North to South you'd think you are crossing an entire continent. This is so in the physical shape of the cities, in the attitudes of the people who live there, in their faces and in their languages. Turin, to give an example, has more in common with Marseille or Geneva than it does with Palermo. The differences are so extensive and remarkable that, once Italy became one nation under the Savoy King Victor Emanuel II, Massimo D'Azeglio quipped: "Now that we have made Italy, we have to make the Italians." Indeed, the notion that all the people who inhabited the Italian peninsula were Italians struck Romans, Venetians, Neapolitans, Piedmontese and Sicilians as a curious idea not easily digested. Considering that after the collapse of the Roman Empire each region and each city within it, carried on through the centuries a course of their own, isolated or with little contact with the other regions, it would be surprising if they had developed a sense of belonging to the same country. Thus the inhabitants of each region, nay each city, looked at the inhabitants of other cities and regions, even those that were geographically near, if not with suspicion, certainly with a sense that they belonged to a different world.

In the eighteenth century, as Carlo Goldoni, the Venetian playwright wrote in his memoirs, the inhabitants of Turin, the capital of Piedmont whose royal family led the struggle to unify Italy, considered even the people of Milan, Genoa and Venice as foreigners.[6] The Romans regarded the inhabitants of Lombardy as "buzzurri" and certainly would be hard put to embrace them as Italians (to put it mildly,) as the following lines from a sonnet by Giggi Zanazzo make clear:

E so' Tajani, di', 'sti ciafrujoni?
Si loro so' Tajani, car'Andrea,
me fo taja' de netto li cojoni.[7]

And these barbarians you call Italians,
If they're Italians, my dear Andrea,
I'll have my balls chopped off completely.

Even after unification, Sicilians who had many reasons to resent the new "Italian" government, referred to the Piedmontese with the term "piramuddisi," claiming that a single Sicilian peasant was worth ten Piedmontese.[8] The reasons for the reciprocal distrust and antipathy among the regions were many, but certainly one of the most important was the fact that they did not speak the same language. Sicilians spoke Sicilian, Neapolitans spoke Neapolitan and each region spoke a native language that was different from the Tuscan that had become accepted, more or less, as the literary language of the peninsula. The term "dialect" appears for the first time in the Italian context in the second half of the 16th century.[9] Florentine, which was a Romance language, like Sicilian or Venetian--that is, a language that evolved from the mother tongue, Latin--had grown to be the most prestigious language because of a number of historical factors: its high literary prestige (owing to the fact that the three greatest poets of the middle ages and humanism, Dante, Petrarch and Boccaccio, wrote in Florentine), and its economic and political importance beginning in the 13-14th centuries and culminating in the Renaissance. With the establishment of Florentine as the literary language of choice, all the other regional languages, including Sicilian, came to be regarded as dialects, creating a unique situation that Italians have struggled with to this day. It must be made clear at this point that the term "dialect" was understood as a language that was operating in the context of a more prestigious language. The term does not carry connotations of superiority or inferiority in terms of its ability to convey meanings. It was a question of perception. Those who opted for Florentine perceived it as the more refined, the more elegant tool, which had the possibility of reaching a greater number of people in a written work.

It also must be made clear that we are talking about the written language, not the spoken language. The two must be viewed separately because their histories follow different paths and can be summarized as follows: Tuscan became the *de facto* language of choice for government bureaucracies to communicate with the people, the courts, and poets and writers who wanted to reach a larger audience. The rest of the people carried on their daily affairs in their native languages.

This was the linguistic situation in Italy at the time of the unification. Few of the thirty million people who lived in Italy in 1861 understood or spoke Tuscan. The estimates of the actual percentages of the population who knew Tuscan varies from a low of 2.5%, probably more believable, to a high and improbable 10%. Victor Emanuel II, the first King of Italy, spoke French, not Italian, and Ferdinand II, the King of the

Two Sicilies, spoke Neapolitan. Understanding and speaking Tuscan implies the ability to read, unless you happen to be born in Tuscany. To get an idea of how many people understood Tuscan in Sicily in 1871, consider that when Rome became the capital of Italy, 85.26 % of the Sicilian population were illiterate and that it took the Italian government forty years to bring it down to 58.81% in 1911.[10] This means that from the time Sicilian was born as a language until well into the 20th century the great majority of Sicilians—the situation was not different in other regions of the South like Calabria, Basilicata and Apulia— had only one language at their disposal: Sicilian. And since 85% were illiterate, Sicilian remained for them essentially an oral medium of communication.

With the advent of the modern age that brought compulsory education to all and made radio, cinema and television accessible to the masses, the situation changed dramatically. There has been a reversal of sorts. Most Italians now will understand and speak, more or less correctly, a variety of Italian that has been coined by the media. The number of people who rely exclusively on the regional languages to communicate is getting progressively smaller and linguists have been sounding, somewhat prematurely in my opinion, the funeral bells mourning the death of dialects for the last 50 years. There has been a substantial erosion in the use of regional languages, but in a few regions such as the Veneto, Sardinia and Sicily, the dialect still constitutes a viable means of communication although it has become ever more restricted to specific situations. Generally, Sicilians will not use the Sicilian language when they go to the bank to cash a check, unless they know the teller, they will not use it to apply for a document in a public office, or when they speak to someone they do not know. But the language is not dead nor is it in the throes of death. The critic Lucio Zinna once made a statement about Sicilian that I like to believe is true. He said that the Sicilian people are becoming more jealous of their language than they are of their women. Knowing how Sicilians view such things, I think Sicilian is safe for the time being.

Let us step back and look at the early history of Sicilian. While there is no question that Sicilian is derived from Latin, linguists are not of one mind as regards the timing of the transformation. Ignazio Sucato in his *La lingua siciliana*, actually believes that Sicilian is the oldest of the Romance languages.[11] He argues that the Siculi who replaced the Sikans as the original inhabitants of Sicily were a people from the region of Latium who spoke a language that was very similar to the Latin of the Romans. Thus the language of the Siculi developed along the same line as Latin and eventually became a Romance language. Another interesting theory put forward by Dr. Joseph Privitera in a forthcoming book, also claims that Sicilian was the first of the Romance languages. But his views of its development are different. He states that Spanish, French, Portuguese etc... began to develop as new languages after the collapse of the Roman Empire in the fifth century AD. But Sicilian had already existed since after the Punic Wars when Sicily became the first Roman province. Owing to the large presence of Roman soldiers and colonizers who were there to cultivate the wheat that made Sicily the granary of Rome, as well as to the fact that the island was a forgotten place, a new language began to emerge much sooner than in the other provinces where the Roman presence was more felt.[12]

A Castle built by Manfredi Chiaramonte in Mussomeli (Caltanissetta).

These two views represent more radical interpretations of what we know. But the history of Sicilian is as complex as the history of the island. Without going back to Sicilian prehistory, we know that the people who have inhabited the island have spoken Sikan (the first ethnic group to live there), Siculian (the second and more aggressive ethnic group that subdued the peaceful Sikans), Elimian (a smaller group living in the area of Erice, Trapani), and Phoenician (the people of Carthage who controlled most of the western part of the island). These languages have left little trace on Sicilian, but several languages have played a near hegemonic role in its three-thousand year history: Greek, Latin and Arabic. Greek was spoken everywhere on Sicily from the time of the colonization (7 century BC) well into the III century AD. Even after Sicily became a province of Rome, Greek continued to be a language of great prestige. After the Punic Wars (ended in 243 BC) Latin grew in importance, but it did not replace Greek completely.

Indeed, under the rule of the Byzantine, Greek (from the 6th to the 9th century) reestablished its hegemony. When the Arabs ruled Sicily (827-1061), Latin and Greek were both languages of great prestige, while Arabic was spoken by the populace.[13] When the Normans took over the island they reestablished the importance of Latin. By that time, Sicilian which must have been developing for a long period at the same time that Greek and Latin were the languages of prestige, began to emerge. We know that languages do not develop overnight and it is safe to assume, although no written documents exist, that Sicilian was spoken long before it appeared as a full fledged written language in the 13th century. It's generally accepted that Sicilian developed earlier than other regional languages such as Florentine and Venetian or Apulian. As the language at the Court of Frederick II, Sicilian was used by the bureaucrat-poets in his entourage. It was the preeminent language of poetry, used not only by Sicilians but also by poets who were not Sicilian. This means that for about a century it was what Florentine would later become. Some apologists for the supremacy of Sicilian, pointing out that Sicilian and Florentine in the 13th and 14th centuries were structurally almost identical, advanced the idea that Florentine was nothing other than an evolution of the Sicilian language. We know, of course, that very little of the Sicilian literary production has reached us in its original form and that what we can read of the Sicilian School has been Tuscanized by Florentine *amanuensis* who copied the texts. In reality, the Tuscan poets were the successors of the Sicilian School and certainly borrowed poetic forms and vocabulary.

Writing in reaction to Pietro Bembo's *Prose della Volgar Lingua*, that advised poets to imitate the language of Petrarch and Boccaccio, in 1543 Claudio Mario Arezzo, from Siracusa, published a treatise entitled *Osservantii di la lingua siciliana et canzoni in lo proprio idioma*, in which he put forth a thesis that was destined to be popular with Sicilian intellectuals: he claimed that Tuscans had appropriated the Sicilian language, saying that "the vulgar language that the major Sicilian poets used in the 13th and 14th centuries is nothing other than what Tuscans are using today and the same as that in which Dante and all the others wrote their poems."[14]. This thesis was restated again a century later by Giovanni Ventimiglia (1624-65) from Messina. While he does not accuse the Florentines of having "appropriated" the Sicilian language, he says that if the language used by Petrarch existed in Florence, it wasn't different from Sicilian. So his advice to Sicilians was that they should use Sicilian in their compositions not because Sicilian was the first but paradoxically because Sicilian was basically Tuscan.[15] So much for the dominant misconception among Italians today that Sicilian is nothing more than a corruption of Italian.

The points of view of the Sicilian writers expressed above clearly show that the struggle for supremacy for the written word between Sicilian and Tuscan had already been decided in favor of Tuscan. An examination of the written documents from the fourteenth and fifteenth centuries shows that by then Sicilian had replaced Latin and was used almost exclusively for legal documents, Parliamentary records, inheritances etc... The ruling Jewish counsels in the 52 Giudecche spread out in the major cities of Sicily all used Sicilian in their official documents, contributing substantially to the development of the written form of the language.[16] Franco Lo Piparo has compared the written records for the opening sessions of the Sicilian Parliaments. Since the statements followed basically the same formula and used the same wording for successive years, Lo Piparo was able to see the slow process of Tuscanization of the texts. Spanning a period of over 60 years, such records provide clear evidence of the changeover to the Tuscan language. It began first by substituting Tuscan endings to Sicilian words. For example, words like the Sicilian "humili" was written as "humile" in later records, past participles of verbs that normally ended in "u" were changed to the Tuscan ending of "o," as in "deliberatu, votatu e conclusu," which barely three years later became "deliberato, votato e concluso." The process of Tuscanization of the written documents, which began in the first decade of the 16th century, was essentially completed by 1543. Lo Piparo says that after that date Parliamentary documents written in Sicilian are rare.[17]

Of course, this does not mean that Sicilians stopped writing in Sicilian. It simply means that a certain segment of the writing public, bureaucrats and scientists, essentially adopted Tuscan. Sicilian, however, continued to be used for other purposes such as poetry.

The slow but progressive inroads made by Tuscan were acquiesced with resignation by most, but some reacted with vigor and asserted their prerogative to continue writing in Sicilian. For many it is a question of choice, a statement of national pride. The case in point is best expressed by the great poet Antonio Veneziano whose collection of poems entitled *Celia* was admired by Miguel Cervantes as worthy of paradise. (The two were captured by Algerian pirates and spent some time in jail together). Veneziano defended his choice to write in Sicilian by saying that every great writer has written in his native language. So why should he, being a Sicilian, write in a language other than Sicilian? "Am I, who am Sicilian, to become a parrot of others? Oh the Tuscan language is more common, it's understood more. That is true in Italy, not in Sicily, nor by Sicilian women whom the majority of poets aims to please and serve."[18]

But Veneziano made an excellent point at the end of his explanation that certainly resonates today that dialect poetry in Italy, precisely because it is the language one has breathed since childhood, is a more responsive tool at the service of the poets' inspiration. He said: "Let everyone accept that a great emotion is best expressed in the maternal language and thus we can see when someone is extremely angry or very cheerful that he reverts to his own native tongue, even though he may have the command of other languages too."[19]

In spite of the fact that over 90% of the Sicilian people did not read or understand Tuscan, official documents and even those occasional official announcements directed to the general public continued to be written in that language. Considering the high rate of illiteracy, I suppose, it made little difference to the general public whether an announcement was written in Tuscan or Sicilian. They needed intermediaries to interpret the announcement in any case. This simply meant that the interpreter would also have to act as a translator.

The two languages continued to coexist developing a niche of their own. Owing to the overwhelming presence of the written Italian, and to the necessarily small percentage of people who used Sicilian for literary endeavors, Sicilian came to be associated more and more with a spoken language. Since those Sicilians who knew how to write did so in what little Italian they had mastered, Sicilian grew to be primarily a tool of oral communication.

The role played by the Catholic Church in the consolidation of Sicilian as a spoken idiom was absolutely determinant. The Roman Church, which had always maintained strong relations with the people of Sicily, prescribed that catechism and preaching be done in Sicilian so as to better communicate with the faithful. From the middle of the seventeenth century through the latter part of the eighteenth century the Sicilian people learned Christian Doctrine in Sicilian from books written especially for them such as *Gli elementi della dottrina cristiana esposti in lingua siciliana* (1764) by the Archbishop of Monreale, Francesco Testa. As you see, the title is in Italian, which points to the peculiarity shared by all these texts. The parts of the book that were addressed to the priests were written in Italian, while the parts of the Christian Doctrine destined for memorization by the masses were in Sicilian. Owing to the high rate of illiteracy, the Church taught catechism to Sicilians by rote, by memorization. The faithful were asked to repeat the prayers orally until they had learned them by heart. Naturally, the Sicilian masses never saw the written word. They only heard the prayers spoken by the priests. This was a missed opportunity not only to eliminate or at least reduce the plight of illiteracy, but also to give back to the Sicilian language an element that is essential in the development of a language, its written form. Had Sicilians learned how to read and write Sicilian, it might have made a difference in the course of the history of the language. Did the

A clay Trinacria from Castelmola.

Protestants not teach their members how to read and write so they could better study the holy books? Do the Jews not teach Hebrew so the members of their communities can recite their prayers? Unfortunately for Sicilians, they learned their Avemarias and Paternosters by heart. They never saw those prayers written anywhere. Such absolute reliance on memorization of the Doctrines of the Church reinforced the notion that Sicilian is only an oral idiom. Of course, we have seen that the notion is false. Sicilian had a long tradition as a written language as well. The people who see the journal of *Arba Sicula* for the first time never fail to marvel at seeing Sicilian written. They are not accustomed to the sight. The most ironic consequence of this is to see a person who is a perfectly fluent speaker of Sicilian fumble and stumble over the written Sicilian word.

My mother, who speaks Sicilian perfectly, struggles with the written word and must first split it into syllables to recognize it and then pronounce it correctly.

Unfortunately, history records many other missed opportunities that could have given back to the Sicilian idiom its natural and logical function as the language of the Sicilian people: We all know today that a people's identity is inextricably bound to the language it speaks. Language is a repository of the genius of a people. We do not have to quote the now famous poem by Ignazio Buttitta "Lingua e dialettu" in which he equates the loss of the Sicilian language with the loss of the Sicilian identity.[20] The intellectuals of the Age of Enlightenment already subscribed to such a notion. We have known for a long time that language is one of those important elements, together with customs, history and climate, that distinguish and separate the people of the world. It is not farfetched to say that the language one speaks influences even the way a person looks. Consider for example that when Americans speak they adopt a more relaxed position for the organs of speech, as evidenced by the sounds they make as they pause in search of words. They make phatic sounds with their mouths slightly open and with a relaxed jaw, as they say "huh". Italians in the same situation adopt a more rigid stance, the mouth is nearly closed and the muscles of speech are more tense as they say their "bè, eeh". Surely such different stances produce a visible effect on the faces of the speakers. At any rate, the notion of one people one language was the model in the eighteenth and nineteenth centuries. Today it's possible to envision nations that have a multilingual society, such as Canada, but the subject arouses strong emotions and controversies. A case in point is the United States where the move to declare English the official language of the nation has evoked strong protests by some of the other ethnic people who are an important part of the society.

The linguistic problems of Sicily really cannot be separated from politics. If Sicily had become an independent monarchy, as seemed possible when the British gave it its own Constitution in 1812, then its language could have become the national language. The massive political action required to implement such a radical reversal has never been possible. The supporters of Sicilian as the national language of Sicily have always been ineffective. There have been some attempts worth noting, however, in defense of the Sicilian language. In 1796 the Accademia Nazionali was founded with the expressed objective of cultivating and defending the Sicilian language. Its Constitution, written by the greatest poet who ever wrote in Sicilian, Giovanni Meli, was a curious document

The greatest Sicilian novelist Giovanni Verga.

that prescribed that its poets had to write only in Sicilian about Sicily, making sure not to treat politics, theological matters, or any subjects that might be considered offensive to any individual, no matter how ignoble or low a citizen he may be. The poets were required to submit their compositions to the censors. The constitution as written paradoxically would have caused the expulsion of Giovanni Meli himself from the ranks of the Accademia. Meli was a "contestatore" as Giorgio Santangelo said,[21] and may have penned the constitution by resorting to his well known and well documented penchant for irony (see my own introduction and notes in the *Don Chisciotti and Sanciu Panza*, (New York: Legas 2003).[22] I am inclined to believe that Meli wrote the Constitution in code, that is, using such completely opposite notions as he had always subscribed to that those who read them knew exactly that he meant the opposite of what he said. But in terms of the renewal of the Sicilian language Meli created an illustrious Sicilian, which borrowed much from Tuscan and from the bucolic/Arcadian vocabulary then in vogue. It was not the language of the people, though he interspersed his text with local color. It was an illustrious written language, however, that could be understood by all Sicilians who had an education. Meli created an opus that was to give him a stature that went far beyond the confines of Sicily and Italy and certainly deserves greater recognition as one of the major figures in the European literature of the 18th and early 19th centuries. And he is credited with engendering a kind of Renaissance of Sicilian poetry both in terms of poets who followed his school (poets such as, Francesco Carì, Francesco Nascè, Giovanni Alcozer and Ignazio Scimonelli),[23] and those who adopted a more realistic and popular approach to the use of the Sicilian language (Micio Tempio, and Giovanni Maraffino from Catania and Giuseppe Marco Calvino from Trapani).[24] But neither the Accademia Nazionali's efforts, which were devoted to safeguarding a Sicilian literary language far different from the spoken idiom nor those of poets such as Tempio whose language was much closer to the popular idiom heard in the streets of Catania were directed toward the establishment of Sicilian as the national language of Sicily.

That would be the task of another Accademia founded in Acireale at the end of the eighteenth century, known as the Accademia degli Zelanti. The intellectuals belonging to this academy, especially when they glimpsed the possibility that Sicily might become an autonomous nation, began to challenge Tuscan in a more systematic and coherent way than it had ever been done before. The Zelanti wanted Sicilian to be taught in school, claiming that one of the reasons there was such rampant illiteracy in Sicily was that teaching was essentially done in a foreign language. Tuscan, rightly so, was a foreign language to Sicilians and mastery of it not only required a great deal of study, but always remained elusive for most people, whereas if teaching were done in the Sicilian that everyone understood, the time spent in the study of Tuscan could be devoted to mastering other subjects. The language of the people, the idiom learned from the mothers, would be, in the opinion advanced by the Accademia, much more effective in educating the masses. In order to free the Sicilian nation from its cultural bondage, the Zelanti felt that the Sicilian language had to be the medium of communication in school and in the writing of public and scientific treatises.[25]

Unfortunately for the Sicilianist cause, the views expressed by the Zelanti of Acireale were never embraced by the political movements that promoted Sicilian autonomy in the various revolutions of 1820 and 1848. Naturally once Sicily became part of Italy in 1861, the new Nation, as mentioned before, became engaged in making Italians out of many different people, and the political climate favored a monolingual nation. It is not surprising that under Fascism the so-called dialects were subjected to a relentless campaign intent on obliterating them from the cultural landscape.[26] Such campaigns were so successful that the Sicilian language was never mentioned in the Autonomy Statutes of 1946 when Sicily was granted the widest latitude of control over its destiny. The Statutes were granted primarily in recognition of its different historical background, traditions, and language, as well as to put to rest the separatist movement that threatened to cut Sicily's ties with Italy and perhaps make of Sicily the 50th State of the US.[27] That was another failed opportunity to redeem the Sicilian language. The Sicilian politicians who succeeded in obtaining a marvelous document for self-determination, on paper at least, somehow never considered making Sicilian the language of the newly created political body: the Sicilian Region. And it must be said that during the

A citati di Palermu è u capulogu dâ Reggioni.

Titulu I

Organi da Reggioni

Art. 2 – Organi dâ Reggioni sunnu: l'Assemblea, a Giunta e u Presidenti dâ Reggioni. U Presidenti regionali e a Giunta costituisciunu u guvernu dâ Reggioni.

Sezioni I

Assemblea Regionali

Art. 3 – L'Assemblea reggionali è costituita di novanta diputati eletti ntâ reggioni a suffraggiu universali direttu e secretu, secunnu a liggi pubblicata di l'Assemblea regionali in basi a principii stabiliti dâ Costituenti in materia di elezioni politichi.

L'Assemblea regionali veni eletta ogni cincu anni.

Li elezioni dâ nova Assemblea regionali sunnu stabiliti dû Presidenti dâ Reggioni non menu di trenta e non cchiù di quarantacincu jorna prima dâ scadenza dî cincu anni e p'un iornu prima dû sissantesimu iornu successivu â scadenza dû periodu di cincu anni.

A nova Assemblea s'havi a riuniri entru i vinti iorna dâ proclamazioni di vincitori dopu a cunvucazioni dû Presidenti dâ Reggioni in carica.

I diputati regionali rapprisentanu l'intera Reggioni.

Art. 4 – L'Assemblea regionali eleggi tra i so membri u Presidenti, dui ViciPrisidenti, i Secretarii di l'assemblea e i Cummissioni permanenti secunnu i normi dû so regulamentu internu, ca cunteni in chiù i regolamenti supra l'eserciziu di funzioni relativi a l'Assemblea regionali.

Art. 5 – I diputati, prima di essiri ammisi a l'eserciziu dî so funzioni, hannu a pristari giuramentu di esercitarili sulu pû scopu du beni inseparabili di l'Italia e dâ Reggioni.

Art. 6 – I diputati non sunnu processabbili pî voti dunati nta l'Assemblea reggionali e pi li opinioni espressi duranti l'eserciziu da so funzioni.

Art. 7 - I diputati hannu dirittu a fari interpellanzi, interrogazioni e mozioni dintra di l'Assemblea.

Art. 8 - U Cumissariu dû Statu (vidi l'art. 27) pò proponiri a sciugghimentu di l'Assemblea reggionali pi continuati violazioni du prisenti Statutu. U dicretu di sciugghimentu havi a essiri pricidutu dâ dilibbirazioni di li Assemblei legislalitivi dû Statu.

L'amministrazioni ordinaria dâ Regginoni nta stu casu veni cunsignata a na Commissioni straordinaria di tri membri, numinata dû guvernu nazionali siguennu a designazioni dî stissi Assemblei legislativi.

Tali Cummissioni chiama pi novi elezioni pi l'Assemblea regionali dopu a fini di tri misi.

Sezioni II

Prisidenti Reggionali e Giunta Giunta Regionali

Art. 9 – U Prisidenti e li Assissuri sunnu eletti di l'Assemblea reggionali ntâ so prima siduta, e tra i so membri, â maggioranza assoluta dî voti secreti dî diputati.

In casu di dimissioni, incapacità o morti dû Presidenti, Presidenti di l'Assemblea havi a cunvucari entru chinnic iorna l'Assemblea pi l'elezioni dû novu Prisidenti reggiona li.

Titulu II

Funzioni di l'Organi Reggionali

Sezioni I

Funzioni di l'Assemblea reggionali

art. 11 – L'Assemblea reggionali è cunvucata dû s Prisidenti in sessioni ordinaria ntâ prima simana di ogr bimestri, e in modu straordinariu, a richiesta dû Guvernu reg gionali o di almenu vinti diputati.

art. 12 – L'iniziativa di li liggi reggionali spetta ô Guvern ed ê so diputati reggionali.

I Pruggetti di liggi sunnu elabburati di Cummissioni c l'Assemblea reggionali câ participazioni di rapprisintanzi c li interessi prufissiunali e di organi tecnici reggionali.

I regulamenti pi l'esecuzioni di liggi furmati di l'Assemble reggionali sunnu pubblicati dû Guvernu reggionali.

art. 13 – I liggi appruvati di l'Assemblea reggionali e i regu lamenti pubblicati dû Guvernu reggionali non si ponnu cun siddirari perfetti si ci manca a firma dû Prisidenti reggional e di l'assissuri cumpitenti in materia.

I liggi sunnu promulgati dû Prisidenti reggionali, passati i ter mini di cui a l'art. 29, secunnu comma, e sunnu pubblicati nt Gazzetta Ufficiali da Regioni.

Ntrasinu in viguri ntâ Reggioni chinnici iorna dopu a pubbli cazioni, salvu diversa dispusizioni cumpresa ntâ liggi o regulamentu individuali.

art. 14 – L'Assemblea, dintra l'ambitu dâ Reggioni e dintr di limiti costituzionali dû Statu, senza pregiudizziu di riform agrari e industriali dilibbirati da Costituenti dû populu talia nu, havi putiri legislativu esclusivu supra i materii siguenti:

agricoltura e furesti;

bonifica;

usi civici;

industria e cummerciu, eccettu i reguli pî rapporti privati;

aumentu dâ produzioni agricula e industriali; valorizzazioni distribuzioni, difisa dî prudutti agriculi e industriali e di l attività commerciali;

urbanistica;

travagghi pubblici, eccettuati i granni opiri pubblichi di inte ressi prevaletimenti naziunali;

mineri, cavi, turbieri, salini;

acqui pubblichi, in quantu non sunnu oggettu di opiri pubbli chi di interessi naziunali;

pisca e caccia;

pubblica beneficenza e opiri pii;

turismu, vigilanza albirghera e tutela dû paisaggiu; cunserva zioni di l'antichità e di l'opiri artistichi;

reggimi di l'enti lucali e di l'enti pruvinciali;

ordinamentu di l'uffici e di li enti reggionali;

The text of the Sicilian Autonomous Statute translated into Sicilian by the present author. The text was printed in a calendar by the FNS.

last 50 years in the Sicilian Parliament, which is the oldest in Europe, the Sicilianist cause has received very little encouragement. It's true that in 1981 the Parliament passed a law intended to promote the study of Sicilian. The Region proposed to assist those schools that undertook initiatives aiming at the introduction of Sicilian in their curricula, but it did not go far enough, in my opinion. It seems to me that the Region ought to have made the study of Sicilian mandatory for every Sicilian. Recently we have seen some positive movement in the introduction of Sicilian in the public school curricula. Indeed, two years ago Arba Sicula donated twenty copies of the *Introduction to Sicilian Grammar*, by J. K Bonner[28] and edited by the present writer to two public schools in Palermo in which Sicilian was being taught thanks to the enthusiasm of a teacher who is a member of Arba Sicula. There are many Sicilianists organized for political action that encourage the use of Sicilian. One of them is the well-known FNS, led by our friend Giuseppe Scianò, that recently translated its name into Sicilian to become "Frunti Nazionali Sicilianu-Sicilia Ndipinnenti". Unfortunately, although they are very devoted to the Sicilian cause, they represent a small minority of Sicilians. For all intents and purposes, the majority has accepted the slow fading out of their language "senza fari cìu," that is, without raising a fuss.

I realize that I have yet to answer the question with which I began: "Is Sicilian a dialect or a language?"

If we address the question from the point of view of linguistics, the answer is that Sicilian possesses all the requisites normally required of a language. Sicilian, like Italian or Spanish, operates as a complex linguistic system having a phonology of its own, a morphology, a syntax and a lexicon that are unique to it even though it may share some elements with other languages.[29] Its sounds can be transcribed accurately except for a few special sounds that are unique to Sicilian and that have consistently defied linguists to find an acceptable solution. I am referring to the special sound Sicilians make in the word "bedda" and to the initial sound of the word "ciumi". Neither the double "d" of "bedda" reproduces the sound required which is made by hitting the point of the tongue against the front palate nor the "ciu" of "ciumi," which is similar to a less explosive pronunciation of the English word "shoe".

Sicilian has a vast written literature, in spite of the fact that most people are not accustomed to reading or writing in Sicilian. That is a shortcoming for the schools. You may be surprised to learn for example, that Ph.D.s who specialize in Italian literature are not normally required to study the regional literatures of Italy.

Some people who know various forms of Sicilian sometimes will object to recognizing a different way of saying or pronouncing certain words from another province or town, claiming that Sicilian is indeed many different dialects, not one. And indeed the differences between different idioms within Sicily can be striking. For example the people of Noto and surrounding towns will invariably pronounce the "k" as "ch". To them the words "chiavi," "chiodu" are pronounced "ciavi, ciodu" which elsewhere in Sicily are pronounced "kiavi, kiodu".[30] In some parts of Sicily the name is Turiddu in other parts Turiddru. There are also many differences in lexical items from one province to another, indeed from one town to the next, even a few miles away. Yet the differences are not of such a scope as to hinder communication among Sicilians. All languages have "dialects" within them, that is local variations in pronunciation and even lexical items. A Texan who speaks with a Southern accent is still speaking English. So a man from Noto who says "ciodu" instead of "kiodu" is simply speaking a local variety of Sicilian.

A widespread belief among Italians and Italian-Americans, even among Sicilians, is that Sicilian is generally an inferior form of communication. A language performs the task of communication for the people who use it, and as long as they are able to communicate, the language is deemed sufficient. Therefore, linguists dismiss the notion of superiority or inferiority in languages as inappropriate. If a superiority of one language over another can be acquiesced it has to be a relative superiority. That is, a language may be better or more adept in one or more areas than another language. For example, English may be more adept in computer technology than the language of the Eskimos, but by the same token the language of the Eskimos will have ten terms for snow where English has only one. A language may be richer in certain sectors than another. No one would argue that Italian is richer in vocabulary dealing with abstract or technical vocabulary, but it is also true that Sicilian is far richer than Italian in the world of nature, in agricultural terms and in the utensils of work. Where Italian has only one or two terms to describe a certain type of tree, Sicilian will have six or seven for the same tree. Thus the idea of Italian being richer than Sicilian has to be put aside as untenable. Indeed most Italian writers complain that literary Italian because of its very nature as a learned language, is far too generic and lacking in precise terminology for objects and situations that occur in daily life. In his *Coscienza di Zeno*, the great novelist Italo Svevo explained to Doctor S., his psychoanalyst, why he did not describe "il grandioso deposito di legnami, vicinissimo alla casa dove noi pratichiamo la psico-analisi" (The enormous lumber depot very close to the house where we hold our psychoanalysis). Svevo writes,

> "If I had talked about it, a new problem would have arisen in my already difficult presentation. This elimination is nothing more than the proof that any confession I made in Italian could neither be complete nor sincere. In a lumber depot there are

> many different varieties of lumber that in Trieste we call with barbaric names borrowed from dialect, Croatian, German and some time even from French (*zapin,* for example, which is not equivalent to *sapin*). Who would have given me the true vocabulary? Old as I am, was I supposed to hire a Tuscan lumber merchant?" (my translation).

Svevo's statement confirms that in reality the "dialects" are far richer than standard Italian in lexical items dealing with everyday objects. The Italian literary language that has become, with some modification, the standard language of Italy suffers primarily from having paid too much homage to Petrarch rather than to Dante. The first, in fact, to use Gianfranco Contini's insight, tried to eliminate from his language the mutability of time, reducing his lexicon to a minimum number of words that could stand the test.[32] Dante's approach to language was altogether different. Instead of reducing the language at his disposal he did not hesitate to create new words on the spot if he did not have a word that expressed an inner need. *The Divine Comedy* is full of his verbal inventions.

Italian writing has suffered from this peculiar situation because writers have had to write their works in a language learned in school or from written sources. Inevitably such a language, because it has been learned from books, is not a living instrument and does not have the immediacy of the spoken tongue, the liveliness of a dialogue you might hear in the street. Alessandro Manzoni, the greatest Italian novelist, who addressed the "questione della lingua" by going to Florence to rewrite his *Promessi sposi* in a language closer to the current speech of the Florentines — his now famous "sciacquare i panni nell'Arno." He was well aware that the literary Italian lacked the specificity and immediacy of the spoken language writers require, as the following anecdote makes clear:

> "Suppose we are five or six Milanese in a house talking of this and of that in Milanese. There comes along a Piedmontese or Venetian or Bolognese or Neapolitan, and as good manners dictate, we stop speaking Milanese and begin speaking in Italian. Tell me if the conversation continues as before; tell me if we find that abundance and sureness in the choice of words we displayed a moment before. Tell me if we don't have to opt for a generic or less precise term where before we had at our disposal the special term that fit exactly our aim; tell me if we don't have to help ourselves through the use of paraphrases and

> descriptions where before all we had to do was name the thing; now we have to guess where before we were sure of the term that we wanted to use; indeed we did not have to think, because the term came by itself, now we have to resort to use the Milanese term and add the phrase, 'as we say here in Milan.'" [33]

Every Italian writer has had to struggle with the question of the language in one way or another and has had to fashion a language of his own in which his native idiom plays an important part. The case of Giovanni Verga comes to mind but many other examples could be adduced here. His Italian takes from the Sicilian its colorful and earthy nature and could not have been created without it. It is a fact that Italian writers adopt a language that is different from the one they use in their everyday living. They basically share the situation of Italo Svevo who admitted openly that

> "With every Tuscan word we use we lie! If he only knew how we enjoy relating those things for which we have the phrase ready and how we avoid those for which we would have to turn to the vocabulary. This is really the way we choose the episodes of our life worth noting. It's clear that our life would have a totally different look if it were related in our dialect."[34]

It is clear that the relationship of dialects, and Sicilian in particular, with the more dominant language, standard Italian, is very complex and that there are advantages and disadvantages in the monolingual approach. The regional languages constitute a cultural wealth that we cannot afford to lose. The monolingual approach adopted for the political aim of making Italians speak with one voice has for all intents and purposes succeeded. Most now understand and speak the variety of Italian they hear on radio and TV. It is neither a colorful nor a precise tool of communication, leaving much to be desired in its expressivity unlike the regional languages. But the campaign has been needlessly costly for it has brought most of the regional languages to the edge of the abyss while creating in those who communicate through the "dialect" unnecessary feelings of inferiority.

The colorless character of modern Italian is probably responsible for the resurgence of interest in the regional idioms. Increasingly more and more poets are turning to their native languages as a way of finding a more genuine voice for their poetic concerns. Everywhere in Italy the so-called dialects are being used by today's generation of poets in sharp contrast to their decline in daily living, almost as if everyone were trying to save them from extinction. This resurgence has been felt even in the United States. Professor Luigi Bonaffini has recently published two impressive anthologies containing the best production of dialect poetry written in the last fifty years. His *Dialect Poetry of Southern Italy* and *Dialect Poetry of Central and Northern Italy,* 1250 pages in trilingual format published by Legas, go a long way toward opening up a world of poetry whose depth of form and sensibilities rival the production in the Italian language. Projects such as Bonaffini's are born out of the awareness of a new reality that places the so-called dialects on a par with standard Italian. As evidence of this flourishing, a massive three volume anthology of dialect poetry (*La poesia in dialetto*) totalling over 4,000 pages was recently published by Franco Brevini, the foremost authority on the subject in Italy, for Mondadori.

I do not think that this resurgence of interest in the regional languages will reverse the course of history. We are not likely to see the Sicilian Region, for example, adopt Sicilian as its official language, even the Sardinians who have been more adamant about their language are not likely to go that far. But I am hopeful that in the right political climate Italy, which contains in its constitution an article (article 6) that aims to protect and preserve linguistic minorities, (although it has not lifted a finger for the regional languages—apparently the regional languages do not seem to be covered by the article) will awaken and see the light. The many languages that gave to Italian literature its distinctive "dialectality," to use a Pirandellian term, are worth preserving as are the cultures they express for in the final analysis languages are living cultures, and knowing two of them makes one doubly rich.

Notes

[1] Dante was very critical of the existing dialects and had some unflattering things to say about Genoese, Roman and the others. In his *De vulgari eloquentia* he always spoke with respect, however, about the Sicilians and their accomplishment. Petrarch also spoke of the Sicilians as the first poets: in his "Trionfo d'amore" he lists love poets of a prior time: "Ecco i duo Guidi che già fur in prezzo,/Onesto Bolognese, e i Ciciliani/ che fur già primi e quivi eran da sezzo." (Behold the two Guidos who were renowned/ Onesto Bolognese and the Sicilians/ who were once first and here they trail behind."

[2] The efforts of Frederick II to establish a new cultural canon that spoke Sicilian was directed primarily at replacing the cultural domination of the Church. It was part of a grand design that included the creation of a new type of civil servant unrelated to the Church. That is the main reason for his founding the University of Naples in 1224.

[3] As a literary ploy this is as old as the Roman *Atellanae*. Boccaccio's *Decameron* is full of bumbling peasants who mangle Latin phrases and legal jargon.

[4] Professor Herman Haller has written an interesting book entitled *A Language lost and regained?* that addresses the problems of the immigrants' language.

[5] "Campanilismo" refers to the excessive pride in the accomplishments of one's own homeland to the discredit of other towns or countries. The term comes from "campanile" (bell-tower). Needless to say Sicilians are as guilty of this as others. *Mimi siciliani*, a book by Francesco Lanza, which details the extreme "campanilismo" of Sicilians, has become a classic of Sicilian humour.

[6] *Tutte le opere di Carlo Goldoni*, ed. by G. Ortolani, Mondadori, Milano, 1935-56, Vol I, p. 295.

[7] G. Zanazzo, *Poesie romanesche*, ed. by G. Orioli, Newton Compton, Rome, 1976, p. 51.

[8] The octave in question states that one Sicilian peasant is worth ten "Piramuddisi".

[9] Franco Brevini, *La Poesia in dialetto*, Mondadori, Milano, 1999, vol I, p.XLVIII. According to Brevini, the word first appears in Varchi's *Ercolano*.

[10] Franco Lo Piparo, "La Sicilia Linguistica," in *Storia d'Italia: Le Regioni, Dall'unità a oggi*, *La Sicilia*, Giulio Einaudi Editore, Torino, 1987. Lo Piparo, who has written a comprehensive history of the Sicilian Language, provides some interesting statistics on this subject. pp 787-93.

[11] Ignazio Sucato, *La lingua siciliana*, Edizioni la Via, Palermo, 1975.

[12] Joseph Privitera, *The Sicilian Language*, an unpublished manuscript.

[13] For a discussion of the various languages spoken in Sicily at different times of its history see Alberto Varvaro's *Lingua e storia in Sicilia*, Sellerio editore, Palermo, 1981.

[14] As quoted by Franco Lo Piparo, op.cit., p. 747

[15] LoPiparo, op.cit. p. 749.

[16] Francesco Renda, *La fine del giudaismo in Sicilia*, Sellerio, Palermo, 1989.

[17] Lo Piparo, p. 741

[18] *Opere di Antonio Veneziano*, ed. by S. Arceri, F. Giliberti, Palermo, 1861. The quotes are from the "Epistola dedicatoria" to his *Celia*.

[19] Ibid.

[20] The poem appeared in English for the first time in the first issue of *Arba Sicula* and has become identified with the objective of the organization.

[21] Giorgio Santangelo, *La "siepe" Sicilia*, S.F. Flaccovio Editore, Palermo, 1985.

[22] G. Meli, *Don Chisciotti and Sanciu Panza*, introduction, notes and translation by G. Cipolla Legas, New York 2003.
[23] See G. Santangelo, op.cit., the chapter of "La poesia dell'Arcadia: Meli" pp. 55-197.
[24] Domenico Tempio, known as Micio Tempio and G. M. Calvino appear in English in an anthology of erotic poetry entitled *Sicilian Erotica*, ed. by Onat Claypole, Legas, New York, 2001.
[25] For a discussion of the work of this organization see Lo Piparo. Op. cit.
[26] The Fascist Regime forbade the publication of dialect poetry in newspapers as contrary to the ideals espoused by Fascism.
[27] Such a possibility was indeed a matter of discussion in certain American quarters. But the plan was scuttled when the Russian Foreign Minister Andrei Vishinsky paid a quick visit to Sicily to voice his government's opposition. The political and military implications of such a move would have shattered the balance of power in the Mediterranean.
[28] J.K. Bonner, *Introduction to Sicilian Grammar*, edited by Gaetano Cipolla Legas, New York, 2002
[29] There is an excellent and comprehensive discussion of the question in Salvatore Riolo's article "Considerazioni sulle traduzioni dialettali," in *Dialetto e letteratura*, ed. by G. Gulino and E. Scuderi, *Atti del 2 Convegno di studi sul dialetto siciliano*, Pachino, aprile 1987.
[30] Corrado Avolio in his introductory study to the *Canti popolari di Noto*, Forni Editore, Bologna, rpt 1970, concluded that this particular sound showed that the Siculi were a people who came from the area of Liguria, contrary to what Ignazio Sucato said, because the Ligurians even today have the same peculiar ´sound in response to a Latin k sound.
[31] Italo Svevo, *La Coscienza di Zeno, La Rigenerazione, Racconti e altri testi*, ed. by M. Lavagetto, Einaudi, Torino, p. 409.
[32] Gianfranco Contini, Introduction to Petrarch's *Canzoniere*, Einaudi, Torino, 1970
[33] As quoted by Franco Brevini, op. cit., p. LXXI.
[34] Italo Svevo, op.cit., p. 409.

The Sounds of Sicilian

A Pronunciation Guide

Introduction

The pronunciation of Sicilian should not present insurmount able difficulties for anyone. It will be especially easy for those who are familiar with romance languages like Italian, Spanish, French, Portuguese and Rumanian. Sicilian was the first of the regional languages of Italy to gain acceptance as a medium for poetic expression. It flourished under the reign of Frederick II in the first half of the thirteenth century. The poets who belonged to the Sicilian School, some of whom were not native of Sicily, wrote in the language spoken at the imperial court. Sicilian was the language used to record the actions of the Sicilian Parliament until the middle of the sixteenth century when Florentine replaced it in official documents. Until the first half of the twentieth century, Sicilian continued to be the only language of most inhabitants of the island. Italian was learned in school and even though official business was conducted in Italian, the majority of Sicilians used their language in their daily lives and they still do so today. Although linguists announced its imminent disappearance 50 years ago, Sicilian has proven to be resilient. Though its range has been restricted to use within the family, among friends and relatives, Sicilian is still spoken and understood by most people on the island. Although Sicilian political institutions have not done enough to preserve it, interest in it as the language of poetry and the performing arts has been growing. Many people in Sicily and in the United States are interested in seeing the language preserved. In the United States, Arba Sicula has devoted all its energies to the study, preservation and dissemination of Sicilian for the past 25 years. The present undertaking, long in coming, answers a need often expressed by our members and by those who want to make a connection with the language of their ancestors. Used in combination with our bilingual journal and with our other publications on Sicilian grammar, this guide to the pronunciation of Sicilian will be a very useful and welcome tool of study.

The sounds of Sicilian are basically similar to those of the other romance languages and, needless to say, they are closest to Italian, even though Sicilian has a few sounds that are not present in Italian, such as the retroflex sound that linguists transcribe with "dd" and sometimes with dots under the "dd" as in *beddu* (beautiful), and the sound of "ciu" in "ciuri" that linguists have represented in various ways for centuries without ever reaching agreement. Though not unique to Sicilian, these two sounds represent one of the distinguishing features of the language. If you are not a native Sicilian, people say, you will have difficulty producing them, especially the "dd" sound. We are confident, however, that with practice you will be able to master them. We will see how these sounds can be produced later.

The Sicilian Alphabet

There are 23 letters in the Sicilian alphabet. The letters "k," "y", "x" and "w" are not used except in words of foreign origin. There have been some attempts to revive some of these letters to return to the spelling Sicilians used centuries ago, but today those who write in Sicilian often do not abide by generally accepted rules of spelling. This has resulted in a less than uniform system of writing. The 23 letters of the Sicilian alphabet are:

Letter	Name of Letter	English Pronunciation
A	a	ah
B	bi	bee
C	ci	tchee
D	di	dee
Dd	ddi	ddhee
E	e	eh
F	effi	ehffee
G	gi	jee
H	acca	ahkha
I	i	ee
J	i longa	eeh longah
L	elli	ehllie
M	emmi	ehmmie
N	enni	ehnnie
O	o	oh
P	pi	ppee
Q	cu	ckoo
R	erri	ehrrie
S	essi	ehssie
T	ti	ttee

U	u	ooh
V	vi or vu	vvee, vvooh
Z	zeta	dzetah

The Sicilian Vowel System

Let us begin with the vowel sounds. Unlike Italian, Sicilian has only five vowel sounds and they are:

a e i o u

Italian recognizes 7 vowel sounds because the "e" and the "o" can be pronounced as an open or closed sound. Sicilian pronounces the "e" and the "o" as open sounds as in such English words "bet" "let" and "not" "more". Sicilian vowels, unlike English vowels, are always pronounced in one way, no matter where they occur.

Thus the "a" of "casa," and "pani," is like the "a" in "father";
the "e" of "genti," "meti" is like the "e" of "let";
the "o" of "mori," "robba" is like the "o" of "over";
the "i" of "Pippinu," "minnali," is like the "i" of "machine";
the "u" of "subbitu," "omu" is like the "oo" of "stoop"

Sometimes, however, Sicilian vowels, because they are in unstressed positions, tend to be pronounced as a blend of two vowels. This occurs usually in the third person plural of the present or imperfect tenses and in some words. For example, the present and imperfect tenses of verbs like *purtari* (to bring) can be heard as *portanu,* or *portunu; purtavanu* or *purtavunu*; words like *subbitu* (right away) can be heard as *subbutu.* These vowels are called uncertain because the speaker does not stress the vowel in question and its pronunciation can be heard as either "a" or "u".

The Sounds of Sicilian Consonants

Sicilian consonants for the most part are pronounced almost exactly as the Italian counterparts. There are, however, a few exceptions, as we will see. English speakers will not find it very difficult to pronounce Sicilian sounds.

B

B has the same sound as the "b" in "bed". This letter presents a peculiarity that is true of other Sicilian letters such as the **"d,"** **"r"**, and the **"z"**. In initial and also in medial position, the "b" is pronounced double. Words normally written with one "b" are pronounced double as in the following: *bonu, beddu, bastuni* and *babbu* (good, beautiful, stick and dumb). Even if the "b" occurs in the middle of the word the sound is pronounced as though it were a double consonant. This does not mean you pronounce the letter twice, it simply means that the vowel that precedes the double sound is shorter than normal. This will take some practice because English does not make much use of the double consonant sound. It does occur in compound words such as "bookkeeping" or "good day". The sound is made primarily by pausing slightly after the vowel that precedes the double consonant. Try pausing in pronouncing the following words: *à bbitu, sà bbatu, sù bbitu.* Now pronounce the words at nomal speed: *àbbitu, sàbbatu* and *sùbbitu* (suit, Saturday and right away). The pause will help you to pronounce double consonants which occur frequently and affect most sounds, except the *sci*, *gli*, and *gn* sounds. Practice with the following pairs: *Caru/carru; Vini/vinni; Nanna/nana; Spisa/spissu; Jattu/Jatu; Cottu/cotu; Ccani/cani; Assai/usai; Potti/poti; Viti/vitti.*

C

C has either a hard sound (k) as in *cani* (dog) or a soft sound (ch) as in *celu* (sky). If the "c" is followed by the vowels *"a," "o," "u"* or the letter *"h",* it has a hard sound as in the English consonant k. If the "c" is followed by the vowels "e" and "i", then the sound is pronounced as the English words *check* and *chin.* Thus, if we add the five vowel sounds of Sicilian *a, e, i, o, u,* to the "c" we will get the following sounds *ca, che, chi, co, cu.* Note how in order to obtain the had sounds of *che* and *chi* we placed an "h" between the "c" and the two vowels. If the h were absent, the two sounds would be pronounced with a soft "c": *ce* and *ci*. Pronounce the following words: *cani, chesa, china, cori, cuda* (dog, church, full, heart, tail). The "h", of course, was used to write the words *chesa* and *china.* The English "ch" is made by placing an *e* or *i* after the "c". If other vowels follow the *e* or *i* sometimes you will pronounce both of them as one sound, as in *cia, ciu*, or as separate vowels as in *ceusa.* Repeat the following words: *cessu, cinima, Ciullu, ciaula* (toilet, movie, Ciullu, crow).

The "c" in initial position is usually single, while in medial position it is usually double: for example: *chiavi, chiovu,* but *occhiu, specchiu* (key, nail, and eye, mirror). A peculiarity of the *parrata*, that is, the subdialect of Ragusa in the southeastern part of Sicily is that these same words are pronounced with a soft "c" as *chavee, chovoo, occhoo, spehcchoo.*

The letter "c" has also been used to reproduce a special sound of certain Sicilian words that are derived from Latin, words beginning with *fl,* such as *flumen* (river) or *fl*orem (flower), which in Sicilian became *ciumi* and *ciuri.* Specialists on the Sicilian language have been arguing for centuries on how to write this sound. Today you may see it written as *ciu* or *sciu*. Without going into the technical explanation of how the sound is made, you can come very close to it if you say "shoe" keeping your tongue well inside your mouth, instead of holding it between the teeth. A puff of air should come out of your mouth in pronouncing *ciumi, ciuri*. If the stress falls on the succeeding syllable, however, as in *ciusciàri*, the initial sound is made further back in the mouth and no air should escape. Repeat the following words: *ciocca, ciauru, ciariari, ciumara* (hen, smell, to smell, riverbed).

D

D is slightly different from the English "d". The d of "dog" or "dig" is more explosive than the Sicilian "d" of *dumani* or *dopu* where the "d" is pronounced with the tongue completely inside the mouth rather than between the teeth. This letter, depending on where you are in Sicily will be pronounced as an "r", as in the words *duminica/ruminica, dota/rota, nidu/niru, dici/rici* (Sunday, dowery, nest, says), and as a "t" in and around Messina in initial and in unstressed positions, as in *denti/tenti, diavulu/tiavulu* and *tebbidu/tebbitu,* (tooth, devil, tepid). When the "d" is followed by a vowel in unstressed position such as in *vidu, cridu* (I see, I believe), it changes to a "y" sound. In Sicilian the "y" sound is written with a "j". Thus *vidu, cridu* change to *viju, criju.*

Unlike Italian, the "d" can be pronounced as a double consonant even in initial positions, as in *ddimoniu, ddibbulizza, ddebbitu* (demon, weakness, debt), as well as in medial position as in *addumannari, addurmirisi, addunarisi* (to ask, to fall asleep, to notice). This double "dd" sound is not to be confused with the retroflex sound of *beddu, Turiddu* (beautiful and Turiddu) that we will describe shortly. In the first examples, *addumannari*, the double "dd" is made by shortening the preceding vowel and striking the bottom of your upper teeth with the tip of your tongue protruding slightly beyond them. Remember to pause after the initial vowel. In the following examples the double "dd" is pronounced as above: *addinucchiari, addisiari, addivintari, arridduciri* (to kneel, to yearn for, to become, to reduce). This is the same as the Italian sound *addormentarsi* (to fall asleep).

The d and the t followed by an r have a distinctive Sicilian sound, different from Italian. Such words as *ddrittu, draddraia* (straight, witch) and *trenu, tronu* (train, thunder) are pronounced with the tongue inside your mouth rather than between the teeth, as in the English "dry" and "train". The double dd of *Turiddu* is described in the next section.

Dd

Dd. The "dd" sound is made almost exactly as in such American English words as "caddy," daddy" "batty". Pronounce the following words and observe how the tongue curls a bit and then strikes the upper part of the palate: *beddu,* (beautiful) *liveddu* (level), *cuteddu* (knife), *purceddu* (pig), *agneddu* (lamb), *capiddi* (hair), *munzedda* (mounds), *Mungibbeddu* (Mt. Etna), *jaddina* (chicken), *jaddu* (rooster), *madduni* (brick, tile), *cavaddu* (horse), *nuddu* (no one). In certain parts of Sicily, primarily in the western part, the "dd" sound above is made by adding a slight trill to it, so that when the sounds are written they add an "r". In Trapani, for example, the words above will be pronounced *beddru, liveddru, cuteddru, purceddru, agneddru, capiddri, munzeddra, Mungibbeddru, jaddrina,* etc...

F

F. The "f" sound presents no difficulty whatsover. It is the same as the English f as in *fame, film*. Pronounce the following: *fami* (hunger), *filu* (thread), *feli* (bile), *fulinia* (cobweb), *fogghia* (leaf), *chiffari* (things to do), *affettu* (affection), *fuddittu* (sprite).

G

G. The "g" sound presents the same difficulties as the "c". G has either a hard sound (go) as in *gamma* or a soft sound (jet) as in *genti*. If the "g" is followed by the vowels *a, o, u,* or the letter *h,* it has a hard sound as in "go". Repeat the following: *gattu, gamma, gaddu, gaggia, ghiommaru* (cat, leg, rooster, cage, ball of thread). If the "g" is followed by the vowels *e* and *i,* then the sound is pronounced as the English "j" as in the following words: *raggiuni, giovani, gilusia, gebbia* (reason, young person, jealousy, water tank). In some *parrati* of central Sicily the initial hard "g" drops off and the five words above will be pronounced as *àttu, àmma, àddu, àggia, òmmaru*. The same words, however, will be pronounced as *jattu, jàmma, jaddu, jommaru* in eastern Sicily (Messina, Catania). The combination "g" plus "r" in such words as *granni, grossu, grutta* (big, large, cave) in many parts of Sicily will also lose the "g" and will be pronounced *ranni, rossu, rutta.*

The "gn" combination is similar to its Italian counterpart and to the Spanish "ñ" sound. It is equivalent to the sound of *canyon* or *onion*. Pronounce the following words: *castagna, vegnu, tigna, vigna, signali* (chestnut, I am coming, bald head, vineyard, signal). Differentiate between this sound and words like *Catania, ddimoniu, tistimoniu* (Catania, demon, witness).

Another sound peculiar to Romance languages that is written with a "gli" in Italian and with a "ll" in Spanish exists in Sicilian in certain areas, but for the majority of speakers on the island this sound has been replaced by "gghi". Thus, where Italian will have *famiglia, figlio, foglio, taglio, travagliare,* (Family, son, sheet of paper, cut, travail-work) Sicilian will have *famigghia, figghiu, fogghiu, tagghiu, travagghiari.*

H

H has no sound of its own. Its only purpose is to make a soft *c* or *g* into a hard *c* or *g. Cetu* (social rank) becomes *chetu* (quiet) by placing an h after the c. G*ettu* becomes *ghettu* by placing the h after the g.

J

The "j" in Sicilian is equivalent to the English "y". It is a consonant that is slowly disappearing and being replaced by the Italian vowel i. In the past, words such as *boja, noja, gioja* (executioner, boredom, joy) used to be written with a j. Today they are being replaced by the Italian "i" as in *boia, noia, gioia.* Nevertheless the j has a role to play and its pronunciation requires some attention. It occurs in words such as *jornu, jiri, jurnata, Japicu, jitu, jenniru, jardinu, jaddu* (day, to go, length of day, Jacob, finger, son-in-law, garden, rooster) etc... If pronounced separately or if it is preceded by an unstressed word the j in these words is simply equivalent to the English y. Thus the j of *jorna* preceded by an unstressed word such as *cincu* or *quattru* will be pronounced *cincu jorna, quattru jorna.* (five days, four days) But if the words beginning with "j" are preceded by monosyllables such as *tri* and *a,* the combination will be pronounced *trigghiorna, agghiurnata* (Three days, for the day) even though *jornu* is still written with a "j" . Before titles such as *San*, and *Don* as in *Japicu, Jachinu* the resulting sound would be *dongnabicu*, *dongnachinu.* Following the word *ogni* (every) as in *ogni jornu*, the combination would be pronounced *ognigghiornu* and in the area of Messina and province *ogningnornu.* A sentence that is written as *"a jiri a vidiri a don Jachinu"* (I have to go see Don Jachinu) would sound like *"agghiri avvidiri a donGnachinu."* In some parrati the "v" in stressed position may be pronounced as a "b". Thus a*vvidiri* could be pronounced as *abbidiri.*

L

The **L** presents no difficulty when it is in initial position. Thus the "l" of the following is the same as the English "love". *Lana, lena, linu, lona, luna, mulu, mali, meli.* The double "ll" exists in certain Gallo-Italic areas (Bronte, Maletto, Randazzo, S. Domenica) and in most of Sicily for words that have been borrowed from Italian such as *ballu, cristallu, ribbelli,* (dance, crystal, rebel), however, the double "ll" in most parts of Sicily became the retroflex sound "dd" we already discussed. Thus words that in Italian would be written as *collo, bellezza, cavallo, gallo* (neck, beauty, horse, rooster) in Sicilian became *coddu, biddizza, cavaddu* and *jaddu.*

The "l" followed by a *c*, an *m* or a *v* as in *falcu, calmu, salvu* (falcon, calm, safe) generally lose the "l" in favor of an "r", becoming *farcu, carmu, sarvu* in most parts of Sicily. The same words in the eastern part lose the "r" and double the consonant that follows as *faccu, cammu, savvu*, and in the area around Palermo, speakers will add a trailing "i" to the stressed syllable and pronounce the words *faiccu, caimmu, saivvu.*

M

The **M** does not present any difficulties for English speakers. It has the same sound as the "m" in *man, merit.* The "m" that follows a stressed vowel usually is pronounced double as in *càmmira, fìmmina, nùmmiru, cucùmmaru*, (room, woman, number, watermelon) etc... In Italian the combination *mb* is usually changed to *mm* in Sicilian as in the case of *gamba/jamma; piombo/chiummu; colomba/palumma* (leg, led, dove).

N

The **N** does not present any difficulties for English speakers. It is the same as the English "n" in *name.* Pronounce the following words: *Navi, ninna nanna, niuru, nudu, panuzzu* (Ship, lullaby, black, naked, bread). When the "n" is followed by a "d" in Italian, it generally changes to a double "n" in Sicilian, as in *rutunnu, munnu, funnu, quannu, munnizza* (round, world, bottom, when, garbage). The "d" sound is retained in a small area around Messina where such words would sound like *mundu, quandu, mundizza* etc...

The combination of *nv* of such words as *nvernu, nvidia, nvitu, cunventu* (winter, envy, invitation, convent) in most areas changes to *mmernu, mmidia, mmitu, cummentu* in the spoken language.

The combination **ng** merits special attention. Sicilian words such as *sangu, fangu, longu* (blood, mud, long) are not pronounced at all as their Italian counterparts *sangue, fango, lungo.* Nor are they pronounced as the English words "longer, finger". The Sicilian sound is closer to the *ng* of the English "Long Island" or "hanger" where the sound is made by withdrawing the tongue towards the back of the mouth. Pronounce these words: *rangu, sgangu, ngagghiari, ngratu, nfangatu* (rank, bunch, to catch, ingrate, muddy).

P

The **P** is similar to the English "p," however, it is not as explosive. Put your hand before your mouth and pronounce the words "pop" and "pipe". Your hand should feel a puff of air coming out of your mouth. Now pronounce the following Sicilian words: *pani, petra, pumu, papà* (bread, stone, apple, daddy). You should not have felt any air come out of your mouth, or at least not as much. Differentiate between the English and Sicilian "p" in pain/*pena*, poor/*pouru*, pidgeon/*picciuni*.

R

The **R** is trilled. It's pronounced by pointing the tip of the tongue toward the top of the upper front teeth. It can occur in medial position as in *soru, cori, amaru, scuru* (sister, heart, bitter, dark) and it's pronounced with a single trill. When double, the trill is stronger as it is in *carru, merru, ferru, guerra* (cart, blackbird, iron, war).

When it occurs in initial position, it is often doubled as in *rridiri, rragghiari, rraggiu, Rroma* (to laugh, to heehaw, ray, Rome). When the "r" is followed by another consonant in most parts of Sicily the "r" disappears and the following consonant is doubled, as in the following: *curpa/cuppa; mortu/mottu; corda/codda; porta/potta; curnutu/cunnutu* (fault, dead, cord, door, cuckold). In the area around Palermo, the same words will add a trailing "i" before the stressed vowel. Thus you will have *moittu, coidda, poitta, cuinnutu.*

S

S in Sicilian is like the English "s." In initial position and in medial position, it maintains the sound of the "s" as in Sam. Thus *sira, sali, sugnu, servu,* (salt, I am, servant) and *casa, spisa, stissu, vossia* (house, shopping, same, you) are all like the "s" in Sam. For double "s", apply the same rules as any double consonant, that is, pronounce the preceding vowel shorter. The "s" is pronounced like a "z" when it precedes a voiced consonant as in *sbulazzari* (to flutter), *sdintatu* (toothless) or *sminuzzari* (to break into small pieces) where the "b", "d" and the "m" are all voiced consonants. In the province of Palermo, "s" followed by a consonant will be be pronounced as the English phoneme "sh". Preceding voiceless consonants, the "s" will be like the "s" of *sight* as in *scappari, scippari, scola, spagu, stubbitu, stazioni* (to flee, to pull out, school, thread, stupid, station).

A group of words written with an "s" present the peculiarity of changing the "s" sound into the "sci" sound in the eastern part of Sicily, around Messina. The sound is like the "ciu" of *ciuri.* Compare *cammisa, bbasari, cirasa, fasola, cusiri* (shirt, kiss, cherry, bean, to sew) with *cammicia, bbaciari, faciola, cuciri.*

We ought to point out that when the *"s"* is combined with the phoneme *tr* or *dr* the result is akin to the English pronunciation of "shrill" "shroud". Recall the peculiar sound of *trenu, drittu* (train, straight). Adding an "s" will cause a whistling sound between the teeth. Pronounce the following words: *strittu, strata, finestra, mastru, strummulu, seggiasdraia* and *strammu* (tight, street, window, master, spinning top, rocking chair and strange). Here Sicilian differs markedly from Italian.

In the province of Palermo and Trapani, the s before a voiceless consonant such as the p or twill be pronounced as in the English "shush". The following words *spisa, spata, stidda* will be pronounced "shpisa, shpata, shtidda."

A mosaic of Roger II being crowned by God in Monreale.

T

The **T** is not the same as the English "t." It is not aspirated. The pronunciation of the expression *tutti i frutti,* which in American English sounds like *tudifrudi,* and *spaghetti,* which sounds more like *spaghedi,* clearly illustrates the difference. The "t" in Sicilian is formed by striking the upper front teeth with the tongue. Pronounce the following: *Tanu, timuri, stadda, stima, poti, potti, pattu, matina, muturi, carrettu.*

V

The **V** is primarily the same as the English "v" of *valiant.* Pronounce the following: *vinu, vinnigna, vita, vistina, vutti.* The "v" sometimes takes the place of the "b" in certain areas. Words such as *vutti, vucca, viviri, vinni* sometimes can be written and pronounced as *butti, bucca, biviri, binni.* Such dualities can give rise to misunderstandings as in the following dialogue between a judge and a defendant:
Judge—*To patri vivi?* Judge—Is your father alive?/ Does your father drink?
Defendant—*No, me patri litrìa.* —No, my father puts it away by liters.

Z

The **Z** is either equivalent to "tz" or "dz". In such words as *zeru, zabbara, zocculu*, it is a voiced consonant (dz) while in words like *zzappagghiuni, mazzu, azzioni, pazzu* it is a voiceless consonant (tz).

Phono-Syntactical Changes

When you pronounce words in a sentence each word has some effect on the words that follow. In this section we will examine some of the most important elements that can affect pronunciation.

The use of certain words results in the doubling of the initial consonant of the word that follows. Here are the most common words that cause the doubling:

The preposition *a.* "A Roma" (To Rome). Although "Roma" is written with a single "r", the combination will be pronounced "aRRoma". Similarly "a mia" (to me) *ammia*, "a tia" (to you) *attia*, and "a vui" (to you) would be written with a single consonant but pronounced double;

The verb *à* (has). In the phrase *Tu a ccapiri na cosa.* (You have to understand something) the "c" of "capiri" is pronounced double;

The words *ccà* and *ddà* (here, there). When combined with adverbs of place such as *sutta, fora, dintra,* (below, inside, outside) they become *ccassùtta, ddassùtta, ccaffòra, ddaffòra, ccaddìntra, ddaddìntra* (down here, down there...);

The interrogative *chi* (what). Questions such as "what are you doing, what are you saying, what did you see?" will be pronounced *Chiffai? Chiddici? Chivvidisti?* The same thing happens also in exclamations preceded by "chi" as in *Chi vvirgogna! (What a shame!) Chi ttistazza!* (What a head!)

The verb *è* (is) and the conjunction *e* (and). In such combination as *è ggranni, è bberu, è bbonu, io e ttu* (it's big, it's true, it's good, I and you);

The 3rd person of the present of the verbs *fari, stari, putiri,* and *jiri*; as in, *fa mmali, sta vvicinu, pò ttrasiri, va ffora* (it hurts, lives close by, may come in, goes out);

The third person of the past tense of *essiri, fu* (was) as in the expression *fu cchissa a rraggiuni* (that was the reason).

The preposition *pri, (pi)* (for)as in *pri mmia, pri mme matri* (for me, for my mother);

Other monosyllables such as *tri, sì, su, sta, nè*;

Doubling can occur also with two-syllable words such as *quacchi, ogni* (some, every) as in *quacchivvota, ogniffimmina* (some time, every woman); even accented two-syllable words can cause doubling such as *pirchì*, "*pirchì vvinisti?*" (Why did you come?).

Diphthongs

Although the diphthongs will present no difficulty in terms of their pronunciation, we recognize that because they can take place in so many different ways they offer additional obstacles to understanding. Students need to be aware that in some areas of Sicily words having stressed *e* and *o* can often give way to the formation of diphthongs, that is two vowels instead of the one they replace, pronounced as one sound. For example words such as *ferru* (iron) may be pronounced as *fierru*; *pettu* (chest) as *piettu; ventu* (wind) as *vientu*, while *corvu* (crow) may be pronounced as *cuorvu*. In some *parrati* this may become *cuarvu*; *porcu, puorcu* or *puarcu*. The diphthongs in some areas are reduced to a single sound that is something in between, for example *felu* for *filu* or *molu* for *mulu* where the *e* and the *o* have a mixed sound.

Such diphthongs regularly occur also in verbs affecting all persons except the first and second plural of the present tense. For example, the verb *circari* (to look for) and the verb *truvari* (to find) are normally conjugated as follows: *cercu, cerchi, cerca, circamu, circati, cercanu*. But in some areas where diphthongs occur it will conjugated as: *ciercu, cierchi, cerca, circamu, circati, cercanu*, while the verb *truvari* will have the normal conjugation as *trovu, trovi, trova, truvamu, truvati trovanu*. Where diphthongs occur, it will be *truovu, truovi, trova, truvamu, truvati, trovanu*.

Accents

Like Italian, Sicilian words are generally stressed on the next to the last syllable. *Amùri, picciriddu, armàli, cùrtu* (love, little boy, animal, short). When the stress falls on the last syllable, the accent is written. Sicilian uses only the grave accent. Thus *pirchì, pò, ddà, ccà* (why, can, there, here). In Sicilian, the accent is used also where the corresponding Italian word has a different stress. In Italian the verb "persuadère" (to persuade) has a stress on the next to the last *e*, where Sicilian "pirsuàdiri" the stress falls on the *a*. The third person plural endings of the imperfect are written with an accent*: avìanu, avèvanu, facìanu, liggìanu, jucàvanu, currèvanu*. This practice, however, is not uniform. Accents should be used to help the reader pronounce correctly. Sicilian also uses the circumflex accent to indicate that a contraction has taken place, that is, two elements have been fused together. Thus instead of writing "di lu" (of the) you may see *dû*; instead of "nta la" (in the) you may see *ntâ*, instead of "a lu" you may see *ô*.

There are other marks that affect the correct reading of texts such as the apostrophe and the aphaeresis. The apostrophe simply joins two words together by eliminating the vowel at the end of the first word as in *lu armali* (the animal) which becomes *l'armali*, *na acula* (an eagle) which becomes *n'acula*. The aphaeresis is also an apostrophe that indicates that an element has been left out of the word. The negative "nun" (not) drops the initial "n" and is replaced by an apostrophe. The same can be said of the preposition *in* where

The Tombs of Frederick II and his mother, Costance of Hauteville, in the Palermo Cathedral.

the "i" is replaced by the apostrophe. Sometimes words that were originally written *invidia, invitari,* and *invernu* in time lost the initial "i" and to indicate this many will write them with an apostrophe as follows *'nvidia, 'nvitari, 'nvernu.*

Intonation

The intonation of a sentence, in Italian or English, is an important element that adds significance to the statement. In Sicilian the intonation generally follows an undulating movement. Listen to the following sentence: *A signura Maria ìu a chesa stamatina.* (Maria went to church this morning) Notice how the voice rises and falls. Here is another utterance: *Me patri mi purtau a fera l'autru jornu.* (My father brought me to the fair the other day). When we are asking a question, however, the voice will rise at the end of the utterance. Here is an affirmative statement: *U prufissuri ci spiegau a lezzioni ê so studenti.* (The professor explained the lesson to his students). The same statement can become a question simply by changing the tone of the voice on pronouncing "ê so studenti?" : *U prufissuri ci spiegau a lezzioni* ***ê so studenti****?* Here is a statement followed by an exclamation mark: *Mizzica, quantu costa stu libru!* (Damn, this book is really expensive!) The voice will rise on pronouncing the first "i" of "mizzica" and dip when pronouncing the "o" of "costa". The same sentence read as a question: *Mizzica, quantu costa stu libru?* (Damn! How much does this book cost?) will pronounce "mizzica" as before but the the rest will dip toward the end. Generally If a question word such as "pirchì, "unni" "quannu" precedes the question the intonation will curve downward. *Pirchì vinisti?* (Why did you come?) If no question word is present the intonation will rise toward the end. *E' bedda Maria?* (Is Mary beautiful?) Although it's possible to change statements into questions by altering the intonation, often Sicilians will place the verb at the end of the question. Thus the following statement, *A signura Cuncetta havi a frevi.* (Cuncetta has a fever), can become a question by placing the verb at the end and changing the intonation upaward: *A signura Cuncetta a frevi havi?* or leaving the sentence as is and simply altering the intonation upwardly, *A signura Cuncetta havi a frevi?*

Part II

Giovanni Meli: The Sicilian Muse

Historical Background

Giovanni Meli (1740-1815) is undoubtedly the most accomplished poet who ever wrote in Sicilian, a language that had already distinguished itself, under Frederick II, as the first poetic idiom of Italy. While there has been considerable disagreement over Meli's specific place in the history of Italian literature (was he an Arcadian poet? How open was he to revolutionary ideas?), he is regarded today as one of the most important literary figures of his time. In spite of the fact that the use of his native language made his poetry nearly inaccessible to a majority of Italians, Meli occupies a place of prominence among Italian poets of the 18th century. Mario Apollonio goes even farther in his assessment of Meli by claiming that his is "among the purest and most lofty poetry in 18th century Europe."

Meli's European connection is easily demonstrable. While it is true that "the god of the poet was Sicily" (as Luigi Settembrini put it in his *Lezioni di Letteratura Italiana*) and that Meli was "the perfect Sicilian poet" (as his French translator Gustave Chetenet wrote in the preface to an anthology of his poems published in Paris in 1892), it would be erroneous to think of Meli as a "Sicilian poet" if by that we mean a person whose intellectual concerns were entirely of a regional or provincial nature. Indeed, as Giorgio Santangelo has shown, particularly in one of his last works (La "Siepe" Sicilia, Palermo: Flaccovio, 1985) as well as in his masterful introduction to Meli's *Opere* (Rizzoli: Milano, 1965), this Sicilian poet's spiritual world cannot be comprehended unless it is framed against the background of the history of ideas in Europe. Modern research has proved conclusively that Sicily, especially during the second half of the 18th century, was not the backward island completely cut off from civilization that thinkers such as G. Gentile had supposed it was. While Sicilian society was still in large part very conservative and backward-looking, a small group of intellectuals had started a dialogue not only with their counterparts on the Italian mainland, but also with those philosophers in France and in England whose works had created a new intellectual climate culminating in the French Revolution and the birth of the modern era. Bacon, Descartes, Leibnitz, Wolff and J.J. Rousseau were read avidly in Palermo. In 1728, at Messina, Tommaso Campailla had published a long poem in octaves entitled

The Trinacria from a decoration in the Palermo Cathedral

L'Adamo ovvero, Il mondo creato, a popularization of Renè Descartes' philosophical system, and Tommaso Natale in 1756 had tried to do the same thing for the next hegemonic philosophical system by writing a verse treatise entitled *La filosofia leibniziana.* Economic and social problems were the subject of many a study conducted with more modern techniques. Numerous treatises in physics, astronomy, agriculture, and volcanic phenomena, to name but a few of the many fields of interest, give evidence of the new spirit that animated the intellectuals of the island. Schools were opened, not to duplicate the work of the ecclesiastical institutions already in place, but to foster the creation of a new breed of educated persons. New methods of scientific investigation were being employed. Meli himself, who as we will see was a practicing physician and a chemistry professor, published a pamphlet describing the extraordinary effects of a spider's poison. The importance of Meli's contribution was not in the content of the pamphlet but rather in the manner in which he approached his investigation. His findings were based exclusively on the direct and verifiable observation of reality, without recourse to traditional explanations or unverifiable theories. This procedure — central to the modern scientific approach — reveals an important component of Meli's personality, that is, his lifelong belief in experience as the most reliable of teachers.

The lessons of the Enlightenment had not gone unheeded in Sicily. Diderot, Boileau, Voltaire, Fenelon, Young, Locke, Hume, Pope and other major writers were well-known in Palermo, albeit to a relatively small group of intellectuals and aristocrats.

The rule of two successive Viceroys offers us clear evidence of the spread of the principles of the Enlightenment: they were Domenico Caracciolo, Viceroy of Sicily from 1781 to 1786 and Francesco D'Aquino, Prince of Caramanico, who ruled the island from 1786 to 1795. Caracciolo, who had lived in Paris and had been nurtured on the ideas of the French "Lumieres," attempted during his short government to introduce a number of reforms designed to free Sicily of its feudal shackles and to bring it out of its backwardness. He sought (1) to restore the authority of the state over an aristocracy that had come to regard its feudal powers as divinely-given rights, (2) to revive the depressed economy of the island, and (3) to improve the lot of the poor classes. Caracciolo's actions scored some successes in curbing the power of the barons — one of his greatest was the abolition of the Inquisition in 1782-, however, the Viceroy's attempts at reforms eventually clashed with the Sicilian Parliament — the political arm of the Sicilian aristocracy — and he was forced to give up the fight returning to Naples as King Ferdinand IV's Minister of Foreign Affairs.

His successor, chosen by Caracciolo himself, though animated by the same antifeudalistic, enlightened principles, was a more realistic and prudent man who was able to win the support of the Sicilian barons, instituting a number of those reforms that had been the cause of the rift between Parliament and his predecessor. The Prince of Caramanico ruled Sicily for 19 years and was responsible for many important changes in the political, economic and social life of the island. In May of 1789, for example, even before the French legislators promulgated similar reforms, Francesco D'Aquino passed an ordinance abolishing slavery, guaranteeing personal freedoms, granting the right to a legal defense and civil equality of citizens, as we learn from Giuseppe Quatriglio, *Mille anni in Sicilia: dagli Arabi ai Borboni* (Palermo: Ediprint, 1985). His government continued to work towards a more liberal and progressive rule, even after the events of the French Revolution that were seen in Sicily as a tremendous threat to the established authority of the king. The events of France caused a harsh and repressive reaction in the island and many of the gains made by the masses were lost. The Jacobins were particularly feared. In fact, the name was synonymous with scoundrel and murderer.

The negative reaction to the French Revolution was not typical only of the monarchical forces within Sicily, which understandably could not embrace the republican ideals of the Jacobins with open arms, but also of the small group of intellectuals who considered themselves free thinkers, men who adhered to the principles of the Enlightenment, with the exception of the idea of revolution. Thinkers such as Francesco Paolo Di Blasi, who has been called "the only believer in the religion of the Enlightenment in 18th century Sicily" (Santangelo, *La "Siepe" Sicilia*, op. cit, p. 129) envisioned their reforms always within the frame of the Monarchy, seen as the only valid means through which they could be implemented. This belief was shared by the overwhelming majority of intellectuals and clergy. Another belief which acted as a damper on the spread of revolutionary republican ideas espoused by the French Revolution was the myth, among the intellectuals, of the "Sicilian nationhood," that is, of Sicily as an autonomous political entity that identified itself with its Parliament and with the feudal rights of its barons. The intellectuals' conviction that all reforms had to be channeled through the system, that is, maintaining the monarchy in place — which in turn would be a guarantee of the Sicilian nation's microcosmic feudal system — created strong negative sentiments toward any idea that threatened the political *status quo*: hence the antipathy towards the French, in which undoubtedly old memories of the Sicilian Vespers of 1282 played a part, and the sympathy towards the English system of reforms that eventually was responsible for the formulation of Lord Bentinck's Constitution, adopted by the Sicilian Parliament in 1812. One very important psychological attitude common among Sicilian intellectuals of Meli's time, which remains a constant point of reference even today, was their tendency to consider any new idea not deeply grounded on reason and on a solid appreciation of reality as utopian and delirious. A very strong vein of skepticism has always been the patrimony of Sicilians. This is probably why the philosophy of J. Locke, the founder of Empiricism, was found congenial by Sicilian intellectuals. His *Essay on Human Understanding* was widely read in Palermo. The writings of D. Hume were equally well-known, as well as those of the French thinkers who subscribed to Empiricism and further developed its tenets, namely Diderot, Voltaire, Condillac, D'Alembert and Helvetius. These philosophers, who exerted a strong influence on Meli, represent his European connection.

The Sicilian intellectuals' skepticism played an important role in shaping their reactions to political and social problems, and that role is best illustrated by considering their responses to the French Revolution. The Parisian events of 1789 found few supporters, if any, among Sicilian intellectuals. Most of them, including Meli, condemned them as an abomination. Sebastiano Ayala, to name but one of the many critics, defined it "a frightening and horrible monster," which had tried to play a hoax on people with the legislation of the rights of man (Santangelo, *La 'Siepe Sicilia*[11], p. 129). Their failure to understand the principles that had animated the reign of terror was equivalent to their failure to carry to their logical conclusions their assessments of Sicilian

A medallion of Giovanni Meli from the tomb in the Pantheon of great Sicilians, the Church of San Domenico in Palermo.

realities. The obstacles that stood in the way of a freer society, a fairer division of wealth and a better standard of living for the lower classes resided in large measure in the feudalistic institutions of Sicily. The intellectuals understood this. So did Caracciolo and D'Aquino, whose efforts were directed primarily against the barons. Belief in the myth of the "enlightened monarch" caused the intellectuals to fail to carry their assessment a step further, and embrace the republican ideals of the Jacobins which would have done away with the monarchy and its appendage (the feudal barons). They failed to go that far because the system had been in place for so long (since the 14th century) that any alternative, especially if it came from the outside, was viewed with suspicion. The task of overhauling the system, and undoubtedly it must have crossed their minds, would have appeared as totally beyond reality, a delirium. Their common sense, their widespread skepticism, their reliance on empirical data and the weight of four centuries of rigid feudal domination spoke eloquently on behalf of the *status quo* regarding political institutions. It is perhaps axiomatic that sane, sober-minded men are almost never found at the center of revolutions. The Sicilian intellectual of this time had his feet on solid ground, and relied on experience and history. A few visionaries at this juncture might have changed the course of Sicilian events. It could not be said, however, that these men wanted reforms with less intensity or that they felt the need to renew Sicilian society with any less urgency. Their desire to improve the standard of living of the poor classes was genuine. However, the means through which they chose to pursue their aims (through concessions granted by an enlightened monarchy) failed to take into account the greed of the barons and the self-interests of the many groups that would suffer economic losses through the introduction of those reforms. Their desires were bound to be thwarted and frustrated. In his longing to bring about reforms and his skepticism, Giovanni Meli was a product of his time, indeed, we may say that he was the perfect embodiment of the dichotomies that troubled the Sicilian intellectual of the second half of the 18th century and the beginning of the 19th century. The *Don Chisciotti e Sanciu Panza* is the meeting point between the principles of the Enlightenment and the ideals of a deeply conservative society.

His Life and Works:

Giovanni Meli was born in Palermo on March 6, 1740. His family was not wealthy. His father, Antonio, was a goldsmith; his mother Vincenza Torriquos, was of Spanish origin. Having received a traditional education (seven years in the Jesuits' Collegio Massimo, which he later characterized as worthless), he felt the need to study on his own. He began reading Latin and Italian classics as well as the authors of the French Encyclopedia when he was 16 years old. More at the urging of his mother than of his own volition, young Meli began attending the lectures of the most renowned physicians of his time at the Accademia degli Studi, which became the University of Palermo in 1805. His mother intended to prepare him for the medical profession in the hope that he might help alleviate the family's financial difficulties. While attending to his medical training, Meli devoted himself to writing verse in the manner of Metastasio, Rolli and Frugoni, the foremost representatives of the Arcadian movement in Italy. His facile pen earned him a place in several poetic academies which flourished in the capital. His first poetic season saw him writing entirely in Italian, but after the poem "La Ragione," (a compendium of his vast scientific and philosophical readings), Meli wrote primarily in Sicilian. The search for a more vivid linguistic medium with which to give expression to his inner world culminated in *La Fata Galanti*, (*The Gallant Fairy*), a Bernesque poem in eight cantos, written in octaves and inspired primarily by Ariosto's *Orlando Furioso*. *La Fata Galanti* was his first substantial experiment with an "Illustrious Sicilian" idiom. The poem was recited in 1761-2 at the meetings of the "Accademia della Galante Conversazione," and earned him the admiration of fellow poets, as well as the protection of the Prince of Campofranco who invited the "pueticchiu," as Meli referred to himself on account of his young age, to live as a member of his household.

Many of Meli's traits are contained in this poem: his penchant for philosophical and literary satire, his concern for social problems, his personal aspiration for a life of peace and tranquility in the bosom of mother nature, and his vocation as a painter of idyllic and bucolic scenes. Particularly important are the passages in which Meli, under the guidance of Fantasy, passes in review the most famous philosophical systems from Leibnitz' vantage point. Indeed, this part may be considered as a celebration of Leibnitz' deism. The poem is also important to understand the literary apprenticeship of the poet. In it he imagines that with the aid of his Fantasy he is visiting the shops of the greatest ancient and modern poets, whose wares are set on display for every one to compare. The largest and the most impressively decorated tents are those of Metastasio, Ariosto, Anacreon, Pindar and Homer, among many others. His dislike of Baroque poetry is made evident by the epithet he hurled against the 17th century. He called it "un seculu strammu" (a weird century) adding that it would have become mute if hyperbole and metaphor had been withdrawn from it. (Canto II, 34) Named medical officer for the town of Cinisi, (30 kms. from Palermo) Meli moved there in 1767. He had received his license to practice medicine in 1764. As was the custom of the time, he began wearing the typical short tunic with the collar of a clergyman and was called "Abbate" from that time onward, even though he did not receive Minor Orders until 1814, one year before his death. He remained in Cinisi for five years and it is there that he wrote part of *La Buccolica*, most of his Elegies, and *L'origini di lu munnu.*

The Origin of tile World, translated into English verse by the present writer, (New York: Arba Sicula, 1985), consists of 75 octaves written between 1768 and 1770. It was published in 1787 but it had circulated in manuscript form among Meli's friends since shortly after its completion. The satire represented Meli's contribution to the hotly debated philosophical issues revolving around the views of Vincenzo Miceli, a thinker from Monreale who had attempted to reconcile Spinoza's pantheism with Catholic theology. Meli, who regarded with skepticism any system that claimed absolute validity for itself, ridiculed Miceli and his followers likening them to "Aesop's blackbirds who dressed themselves with the feathers of other birds." (*Le Lettere di G. M.* ed. Giovanna Micali, Palermo: Trimarchi, 1919, p. 13). Miceli's adversaries in the controversy were not spared either. The poem, which F. De Sanctis and other critics praised as Meli's satirical masterpiece, — "a real jewel," as Francesco Orestano said, — is in reality a caricature of the various conjectures that man had advanced to explain the origin of the universe. Miceli's system corresponds with the final part of the poem in which Jove — who had been seeking the advice of his family of gods on how best to make the world and had listened patiently to their absurd notions — decides that he is the only substance that exists in the universe-void and, therefore, he is the world. He asks his children to dismember him so that his limbs could become nature. His thigh becomes

Italy, and his head, of course, becomes Sicily. With his usual, subtly ironic smile Meli concludes the poem:

> E certu ch'è un piaciri essiri tutti
> non chiù fangu, non petri, mancu crita;
> ma estenzioni, numeri produtti
> di l'eterna Sustanza ed infinita;
> ma s'iddu si ritira, ohimè! n'agghiutti;
> si movi un'anca, l'Italia è la zita;
> prigamu a Giovi cu tuttu lu ciatu,
> chi stassi sempri tisu e stinnicchiatu.

> It's certainly a pleasure for us all
> no longer to be mud or stones or clay,
> but numbers and extensions manufactured
> by the eternal, never-ending Substance.
> But if he should withdraw, or move a thigh,
> he'd swallow us; poor Italy would be quite lost!
> Let's pray with all our breath to Jove to stay
> forever stiff, upon the ground.

If Miceli's conjecture was the target of Meli's satire, all others are shown "in their weakness and absurdity." The biblical account is not mentioned for fear of the censors — a fear that was responsible also for the deletion of octaves 12-20 from the first edition of the work. Jove and his family are given in these octaves postures and speech that are less than godly, that is, in low burlesque style.

In this satire Meli poked fun at the materialists who denied the existence of the soul, will, and consciousness, and at the idealists who believed that only what exists in the mind is real. His satire, as Paolo Emiliani Giudici wrote, "is pungent without ferocity. He corrects but does not insult." (*Storia della letteratura italiana*, Firenze, 1857, p.15.) But it is inventive, delightful, earthy, humorous, fully charged with slyness at times bordering on the blasphemous. The opening line of the poem announces both the subject matter and the tone with which it is going to be treated: "Jeu cantu li murriti di li dei" (I sing of the tumescences of gods). To speak of the gods' swollen condition in preparation for the act of creation is an irreverent but also mischievous tone that is maintained throughout the poem, often with hilarious effects.

Before his departure for Cinisi, Meli had written four poems, one for each of the seasons. *La Buccolica* grew around these four poems. In the final edition of Meli's works *La Buccolica* contained two sonnets, five eclogues and ten idylls. The changing of the seasons was a very popular topic in the European literature of the 18th century. Thomson (The Seasons), Saint Lambert (Les Saisons), Gessner (Idyllen) as well as the Prince of Campofranco, Meli's protector, had been inspired by the same subject. The *Buccolica* has been regarded as Meli's masterpiece by most critics, especially by those who consider him an Arcadian poet. Attilio Momigliano regarded this volume as "the only genuine bucolic work that Italian literature has ever produced." (*Storia della letteratura italiana*, Messina-Milano, 1958, p. 346) Generally speaking, the collection may be considered a celebration of love, seen as a primordial and regenerating force in the world. Love is the dominant theme. Its celebration is interwoven with the changing of the seasons: delicate and tender hues in the spring; harsh and violent tones in the summer to reflect the harshness of the Sicilian sun; in autumn, feelings of warmth and melancholia permeate the poems, replaced by coldness and fear and dark forebodings in winter. The *Buccolica* should not be seen as just another volume of Arcadian poetry in which shepherds and nymphs are shown gamboling amorously in an effort to escape the corrupt and tumultuous world of the city. Meli's education as a scientist and the lessons of the Enlightenment allowed him to look at the world with attitudes that were unknown to the poets of Arcadia. Meli brought to his poetry a greater sincerity and a fresher imagination which revived and rekindled the old and worn-out clichés of the shepherd-loving poets of the previous age. Whereas the poets of Arcadia had sung of a return to the simplicity of nature as a reaction against the eccentricities and convolutedness of the Baroque age, Meli's return to nature was predicated on a fresher reappraisal, not only of nature as a wise, benevolent, and providing mother, but also of the innate qualities of man which by nature tended toward what was good. If man were freed of the corrupting influences of the cities, happiness would still be found in the bosom of Mother Nature. In such attitudes, of course, one can recognize J. J, Rousseau's pervasive influence on Meli. Rousseau's works, perhaps more than those of any other author, have left an indelible mark on Meli's opus.

The first sonnet, which serves as an introduction to the collection and is emblematic of Meli's lifelong aspiration to live in peace and quiet in harmonious communion with nature, opens on a grandiose vista of Sicilian landscapes. The poet addresses the mountains of Sicily, its meadows, crystalline lakes, silvery waterfalls, dark caves and barren countryside as though they were living and pulsating creatures that inspire tenderness as well as apprehension, and asks them to welcome him to their midst. While nature is presented in its dual realities as threatening and welcoming, the poet characterizes himself as "l'amico di la paci e di la quieti." (The friend of peace and of tranquility). The search for such rare moments of communion between man and nature constituted Meli's lifelong struggle, and represents the nucleus out of which, according to Giorgio Santangelo, he derived his most original poetry. (See the Introduction to Meli's *Opere*, op. cit.)

Since the poems in the *Buccolica* were written at different stages of Meli's career — in the second edition of 1814 six more poems were added — the work may be regarded as a compendium of the most pervasive and time-resistant traits that contributed to Meli's poetic personality. The open character of the collection which permitted Meli to add poems makes it possible for us to see the evolution of the poet through the years. In fact, the addition of the six poems to the 1814 edition allows us to see how Meli's concern for social and economic issues became stronger with the passing of time. Given his wide reading and considering the intellectual climate of the times, it is not surprising that his poems should contain strong social commentary on the plight of the poor classes, and particularly on the plight of agriculture in the island. Social justice, economic fairness, an end to the abuses of one class against another, greater rewards for the peasants who alone are the producers of the wealth of nations, are themes that will return even more insistently in the *Don Chisciotti e Sanciu Panza*.

Coursing through many of the poems of the *Buccolica* there is a sense of restlessness and dissatisfaction with the world that Arcadians probably never felt. Meli's attitudes toward the world and the scope of his concerns foreshadow the Romantic Movement. There is a sense of skepticism in some of the poems that critics have regarded as pre-Leopardian. Typical of this vein is "Polemuni's lament" which Meli probably wrote in a moment of despair during his sojourn in Cinisi. It is the story of a man who has lost everything, his love, his boat, his friends — who sits by the sea complaining about his bitter fate. In his touching soliloquy he questions the very meaning of life. The waves themselves are moved by his complaint, so much so that they try to intercede with Destiny and when their prayers are unanswered, they grow mountainous and stormy and fall upon Polemuni swallowing him. Meli's comment is:

> "Pri l'infelici e li disgraziati
> qualchi vota è pietà si l'ammazzati."
> "For wretched and unhappy human beings
> sometimes to kill them is much more humane".

The same pessimism is present in the three Elegies written in Cinisi, entitled "Lu chiantu d'Eraclitu" (The Crying of Heraclitus) and "Su lu stissu suggettu" (On the Same Subject). It is not difficult to see why many critics have seen in these works a precursor of Leopardi. We need to read but a short passage of the "The Crying of Heraclitus" to realize how Meli and Leopardi were kindred spirits, as G.A. Cesareo wrote:

> Miseru! In quali abissu penetrasti!
> cu respitrari l'auri di la vita!
> Aho quantu car l'essiri cumprasti!
> Cumplessu miserabili di crita,
> unni regna la barabar incertizza,
> chi spargi di vilenu ogni feritas.
> E chist è l'omu? Ahi neti, ahi stupidizza
> assurbiti di mia sinu a lu nomu,
> o canciaimi in ciumi d'amarizza.
> C'è lagrimi chi bastanu pri l'omu?

> Ah wretched man! In what abyss you fell
> by breathing in this atmosphere of life!
> How dearly you have paid just to exist!
> O worthless mixture of the humblest clay
> where barbarous uncertainty's supreme,
> spreading its poison over every sore!
> And this is man? Ah, stupid nothingness,
> absorb my being and my name as well!
> Have we sufficient tears to weep for man?

Another poem in which Meli expressed his bitterly skeptical views about life is "Lu specchiu di lu disingannu, o sia la cugghiuniata" (The Mirror of Disillusionment, that is, the Mockery") recited originally during the days of Carnival in the home of Baron Lombardo in 1779. In a volume of Meli's poetry, published in 1783, this poem had the title of "Eraclito," confirming the thematic thread I have been following. The poem was published in Pisa in 1805. This work is a systematic destruction of all those values and qualities that man holds dearest. One by one, the myths that man lives by are revealed as nothing but a hoax, a great mockery. Luigi Pirandello, who knew the work of his fellow Sicilian very well — as I have shown elsewhere — (See my "Pirandello: Don Quijote or Don Chisciotti?" in the present volume) objected strongly to the tag of "Sincere Arcadian" which critics such as Zendrini and Carducci had pinned on Meli. In his essay on "Umorismo," Pirandello spoke of Meli as a humorist:

"Isn't there veritable humor in much of Meli's poetry? To demonstrate it we need only quote "La Cutuliata": Tic tic. . . what was it? Mockery!" Quoting from memory, Pirandello got the title wrong and substituted "cutuliata" for "cugghiuniata." The playwright was, however, very accurate as to the contents of the poem. Indeed, it is a perfect embodiment of the "sentimento del contrario" with which Pirandello defined his concept of humor. I suspect the playwright owes much more to Meli than has been so far acknowledged, for the Palermitan poet, in this and in many of his other works, fulfills most of the requirements of a Pirandellian humorist. As a humorist, Meli proceeds to peel away all of the delusions, all of the intellectual fabrications of man to leave him naked and alone in a godless and mocking universe. The "little demon" which Pirandello held responsible for breaking up every image to show its opposite, that "special function of reflection" which allowed the Pirandellian humorist to see the two faces of a coin, the surface and what is beneath the surface, must have been at work in Meli too. To show the depth of Meli's skepticism as well as his humoristic approach I will quote the entire poem, translated here for the first time into English:

Oh! vera inclita matri di li Dei,
basi e sustegnu di l'illustri eroi,
scinni, ti prego, ntra li versi mei,
Cugghiuniata, cu li grazii toi.
Pri tia sunnu spassi li nichei,
u spusu abbrazza li figghi non soi,
a summa di li cosi è in tia appujata,
e 'un si rispira chi cugghiuniata.

Oh! ch'è beddu lu munnu cuncirtatu,
oh! chi machina immenza, oh! chi stupuri,
l'omu! Oh poi l'omu è privilegiatu,
ogni cosa è criata in so favuri.
Benissimu. Vossia ha chiacchiariatu?
Vossia mi dica: Nn'ha avutu duluri?
Vicchiaia, camurria, nn'ha mai pruvata?
Provi e poi vija. s'è cugghiuniata.

Oh la gran primavera, oh! comu ridi
fra ciuri ed ervi la campagna tutta!
L'estati ohimè, lu caudu nni ocidi.

La terra ciacca, ogni riconca è asciutta;
l'autunnu poi di frutti nni providi;
l'invernu nni sequestra a stari sutta;
'nzumma di beni e mali crapiata,
passau l'annu: chi fu? Cugghiuniata!

Oh! ch'è beddu lu mari, oh! l'orizzonti
comu vagu si pinci ntra l'alburi!
Eccu lu carru chi guidau Fetonti!
Eccu la bedda stidda di l'amuri!...
Ohimè si turba! Ohimè! comu su pronti
li turbini, chi apportanu l'orruri,
ohimè, comu di ventu un rufuluni
la navi s'agghiuttìu! Cugghiuniuni!

è prena, figghia, e l'omu picchiannu
nasci, poi fa lu cuntu, poi si smamma,
poi cuva, poi valori e ogn'autru affannu,
di poi va sulu e dici pappa e mamma,
poi crisci e va li donni assicutannu;
sica, viaggia, acquista; già la gamma
vacilla, e vecchiu, mori e in tri assaccuni
la scena già finìu, cugghiuniuni!

Oh! Chi bedda picciotta! Oh ch'è sciacquata!
Oh chi sangu! Oh chi vezzi! Oh chi attrattiva!
Ah! mi la vogghiu teniri abbrazzata,
ah! lu so alitu stissu mi ravviva:
mettiti bona, figghia nzuccarata,
proi ssu labbru... Apri ssi cosci Oh viva!
Moviti, stringi... Oh estasi biata!
Ticchi, ticchi, finìu... Cugghiuniata!

Chi pezzu d'omu bonu! Chiesa e casa,
criditimi na pagghia nun ci pisa,
ogni santuzza chi vidi la vasa
e 'un si la tocca chi cu la cammisa
Ah mariolu, è fatta già la vasa,

avi chiù impieghi mmanu ch' 'un ci pisa
e l'orfana e la vidua c'è affidata,
la chiù chi frutta è sta cugghiuniata!

Cugghiunia Furtuna, chi a l'avaru
pri sua felicità mustra un tesoru.
Natura cugghiunia, chi a lu capraru
prumittennu ci va l'età di l'oru.
Cugghiunia lu cori, ch'avi caru
posti, ricchizzi, dignità e decoru;
su sfilocchi di cutra a chiddi dati,
chi vonnu essiri chiù cugghiuniati.

Si dunca cugghiunianu l'aria e lu mari
e la natura e tutti l'elementi,
oh! nobil'arti di cugghiuniari,
oh! eterna e prima liggi di li genti,
oh! eroi di dui culuri chi a purtari
la vinisti a sti spiaggi espressamenti,
tu lu Cunfuciu si, tu lu Maumettu,
tu vera stidda, tu profeta elettu.

Sarà, sarà a li seculi futuri
sagr'un Cugghiuni to supra l'altari:
Dall'arsa zona, e dall'ursa minuri
d'unni Febu tramunta, e d'unni appari
lu pilligrinu Cugghiuniaturi
virrà stancu lu votu a sodisfari
notannu di lu tempiu a li lati
tra brunzi e marmi li Cugghiuniati.

The Mirror of Disillusionment, that is, the Mockery

True worthy mother of the godly race,
of heroes of renown, base and support,
descend upon my verse with all your grace,
descend, o Mockery, you I exhort!
Because of you a groom may yet embrace
children of others: woes for you are sport.

The sum of things is in your custody,
and nothing else exists but Mockery!

The world's arranged in such a lovely way!
What wondrous thing is man! What complex brain!
And man is privileged in every way!
All things have been created for his gain!
Oh, very well! Now that you've had your say,
please tell me, Sir: have you felt any pain,
known gonorrhea and old age? You'll see,
when you have tried them, if it's Mockery!

Oh, how the fields do smile in time of spring,
with grasses and with flowers everywhere!
Alas, the summer kills us with its sting,
the ground's completely cracked, each pool is bare;
The autumn then her fruit for us does bring,
but winter keeps us in its frigid snare.
With good things and with bad, then, finally,
the year elapsed. What was it? Mockery!

How lovely is the sea! Oh, how at dawn
horizon's rim is painted with delight!
The chariot behold of Phaeton!
Behold, the lovely star of love's in sight!
Alas, the weather's changed. How quickly spawn
the whirlwinds that leave horror in their flight.
Alas, that sudden burst of wind at sea
swallowed a ship! Oh, what great Mockery!

She's pregnant, she gives birth, and wailing, man
is born. He stammers, then he's weaned, anon
cuts his first teeth; small pox comes next, and then,
come woes of every kind; he walks alone,
says wawa, mommy; women chases when
he's grown; he travels, roams, and earns his own;
his leg is weak, he's old, the comedy
is over in three gasps: what Mockery!

Oh, what a pretty lass! What prodigy!
What spirit and what charm! What winning way!
Oh, how her very breath rekindles me!
Oh, how I want her in my arms to stay!
Oh, sugarcoated child, do lie with me!
Give me your lips. . . your thighs expose. . . hurray!
Strive now. . . hold tight. . O wondrous ecstasy!
In-out. . . in-out. . . It's over: Mockery!

What a fine man! All church and home he is!
Believe me, feathers do not weigh him down.
He kisses every female saint he sees,
and he won't touch himself but through a gown.
The scoundrel's busy with conspiracies.
He handles everything without a frown.
He's made of orphans, widows a trustee,
but all his scheming ends in Mockery!

Thus fortune mocks all avaricious men,
by showing treasures as true happiness;
and nature mocks all simple shepherds when
to bring the Golden Age she does profess;
Alas, the heart is mocking you again,
when it holds dear decorum, wealth, success,
and pride. These are pall threads against those stocked
who want to be, alas, more greatly mocked!

If then the air is mocking us, the sea,
nature, and elements of every kind,
O truly noble art of Mockery,
O first eternal law of all mankind,
O hero of two shades who purposely
came to our shore to give it to our kind,
Confucius and Mohammed, too, you are,
the chosen prophet, and the truest star.

In future centuries, upon a shrine
one of your balls will be a holy sight.

From where Apollo rises and declines,
from Minor Bear and from the parched-out site,
will come the weary Mocker peregrine
to realize a vow he made: to write
along the temple's walls, within a frieze
of marble and of bronze, his Mockeries.

Throughout Meli's poetic career seldom did such bitterness become so pervasive and all encompassing. However, it would be entirely wrong to think of Meli as a lugubrious and bitter man. Indeed, the picture that emerges from a reading of his work is rather the opposite, so much so that Meli on several occasions felt the need to caution the reader not to be misled by his apparent joviality and amiability. A sonnet which was to be a preface to the 1814 edition of his *Opere* addressed itself to the contrast between appearances and reality. In this poem Meli warns the reader who should happen to read his playful rhymes not to be deceived into thinking him a happy man:

"How wrong can human judgment be! Not always
are one's true feelings in a song expressed!"

Meli succeeded in masking his serious temperament with an outgoing personality. According to Agostino Gallo, his friend and first biographer, Meli was affable and witty, humble and generous with his friends and with everyone. (It seems that he was at times even too embarrassed to ask for his physician's fees). The image that best characterizes Meli is perhaps the one that he himself created. He compared himself to an oyster, always attached to the rock where it was born, bearing on its back the vehemence of the waves and storms.

Meli was endowed with a very rich imagination and it was this virtue that enabled him to accept the difficulties of life. He used his imagination to escape into the world of poetry, the world of artistic creation. His verses, even the most bitter, were equivalent to a cathartic release. His muse was a safe harbor for his storm-tossed sail. She liberated him "from the corrupt valley and brought him into the bosom of nature," as he wrote in the ode "A la Musa."

The happiest season of Meli's life began when he returned from Cinisi to Palermo. Dr. Gianconte, a well-known physician, having to travel abroad, invited Meli to take over his medical practice. Thus dawned a period of great success: loves, honor and money were his to enjoy. Already famous, Meli became the favorite of Palermitan aristocracy. The ladies of the nobility vied to have him as a guest at their elegant parties. The most celebrated gallant and erotic odes, written for the likes of Baroness Martinez, Duchess Lucia Migliaccio, the Marquise Regiovanni, Lady Marianna Mantegna and others, belong to this period. In these poems he sang the beauties of women, that half of the human race without whom he could not live, as he was to say to a monk who had invited him to live in a cloister in his mature years. His consummate artistry and absolute command of his linguistic medium contributed to the creation of the most delicate, erotic odes of his time. In a rarefied atmosphere of sighs and restrained sensuality, of words that are whispered more than spoken, the poet celebrated various parts of the beloved's figure -"Lu labbru," (The Lips)" Li capiddi," (The Hair); "La vuci," (The Voice); "La vucca," (The Mouth); and "L'occhi," (The Eyes) to name a few of his most famous poems. These topics were hardly original and belonged to a rich tradition dating back to the Sicilian School of poetry and culminating with the Arcadian movement, but Meli, whose language shed here the coarseness of every day speech, contributed to renewing the imagery of Arcadia and making it appear fresh and new. Typical of Meli's ability was the ode "Lu labbru" created around the worn-out clichè of the beloved's lips storing the sweetest honey. Meli succeeded in giving it a new loveliness and delicacy by using diminutives and a complex pattern of rhyme. This ode, translated into German by J. Herder, bears the curious distinction, according to R. Wis, (See Santangelo op. cit., Vol. I, p. 338) of being the first Italian poem to be translated into Finnish:

Equally famous is "L'occhi," (The Eyes) inspired by Lucia Migliaccio, Duchess of Floridia, who was to become the morganatic wife of King Ferdinand, and with whom the poet may have had a romantic interlude. W. Goethe, who visited Palermo in 1787, liked the poem so much he translated the first eight lines into German, entitling it "Sizilianisches Lied" (Sicilian Song).

Dimmi, dimmi, apuzza nica:
unni vai cussi matinu?
Nun c'è cima chi arrussica
di lu munti a nui vicinu;

Trema ancora, ancora luci
la ruggiada ntra li prati:
duna accura nun ti arruci
l'ali d'oru dilicati!

Tell me, tell me buzzing bee,
what so early do you seek?
There's no redness yet appearing
on the nearby mountain peak.

And along the field the dew
is aglow, still quivering.
Oh, take care you do not wet
your most dainty golden wing.

Li ciuriddi durmigghiusi ntra li virdi soi buttuni stannu ancora stritti e chiusi cu li testi a pinnuluni.	Pretty flowers, sleepy-eyed, are still snug and tightly closed in their verdant buds abiding all with heads that droop and doze.
Ma tu voli e fai caminu! Dimmi, dimmi, apuzza nica, unni vai cussi matinu? Cerchi meli? E s'iddu è chissu	But your gentle wing is weary, yet you fly, in air you streak. Tell me, tell me, buzzing bee what so early do you seek?
chiudi l'ali e 'un ti straccari; ti lu 'nzignu un locu fissu, unni ai sempri chi sucari: lu conusci lu miu amuri,	If 'tis honey you desire fold your wings, strive no more. I will show you one sure realm where you'll find enough to store.
Nici mia di l'occhi beddi? Ntra ddi labbri c'è un sapuri na ducizza chi mai speddi; ntra lu labbru culuritu	Don't you know my love, my Nici, Nici with the lovely eyes? On her lips such flavor rests 'tis of sweetness a great prize.
ntra la labbru culuritu di lu caru amatu beni c'e lu me li chiù squisitu: suca, sucalu, ca veni.	On the lips incarnadine of my own beloved Joy there's a honey most divine. Kiss them sweetly and enjoy.

Poems such as these, whose validity rests on the poet's technical abilities, on the musicality of their rhythm, on the allusiveness of the message, and the apparent simplicity of the language, which carries instead the weight of long literary tradition, are a challenge to any translator.

Ucchiuzzi niuri si taliati faciti cadin casi e citati; jeu, muru debuli di petri e taiu, cunsidiratilu si allura caju! Sia arti maggica,	Dear Raven's eyes, if you look coy, houses and cities you will destroy. I'm but a wall of stone and sand, if I should crumble please understand. It may be magic

- sia naturali,
in vui risplendinu
biddizzi tali,
chi tutti 'nzemmula
cumponnu un ciarmu
capaci a smoviri
lu stissu marmu.
A tanta grazia
ssa vavaredda
quannu si situa
menza a vanedda,
Chi, veru martiri
di lu disiu
cadi in deliquiu
lu cori miu!
Si siti languidi,
ucchiuzzi cari,
cui ci pò reggiri?
cui ci pò stari?
Mi veni un piulu,
chi m'assutterra,
l'alma si spiccica,
lu senziu sferra.
Poi cui pò esprimiri
lu vostru risu,
ucchiuzzi amabili,
s'e un paradisu?
Lu pettu s'aggita,
lu sangu vugghi,
su tuttu spinguli,
su tuttu avugghi.
Ma quantu lagrimi,
ucchiuzzi amati,
ma quantu spasimi
ca mi custati?
Ajàti lastima
di lu miu statu:
vaja, riditimi,
ca su sanatu!

or nature's way,
but many beauties
you do array,
and all together
they form a charm
that my defenses
can all disarm.
Such winning graces
have your bright eyes
when they conspire
in playful guise
that a true martyr
from its desire
this heart so wretched
may soon expire.
If you are languid,
dear gentle eyes,
who can continue,
who can just gaze?
Such woe I suffer
it makes me groan,
gone is my reason,
my soul's undone.
And then who's able,
enchanting eyes,
to show your laughter?
It's paradise.
My pressure rises
and my head spins.
I am all needles,
I am all pins.
How many tears,
beloved eyes,
must I still weep?
How many sighs?
For my sad state
to pity yield.
Come now, start smiling,
and I'll be healed!

"La vucca" (The Mouth) is a little jewel in which Meli has staged a silent drama whose characters are the beloved's most attractive features: her hair, her eyes, her eyebrows. The poet has, however, a great weakness for the mouth on which his gaze rests longingly, causing the eyes to feel a tinge of jealousy and resentment:

Ssi capiddi e biunni trizzi su jardini di biddizzi, cussì vaghi, cussì rari, chi li pari nun ci sù	Oh, those braids of golden hair are a garden sweet and fair, they're so beauteous and rare none comparison will dare.
Ma la vucca cu li fini soi dintuzzi alabastrini, trizzi d'oru, chi abbagliati, pirdunati, è bedda chiù;	But the mouth with eburnine, pearly teeth so neat, so fine, Golden Braids that all outshine, please don't mind, 'tis more divine.
Nun lu negua, amati gighia, siti beddi a meravigghia; siti beddi a signu tali chi l'uguali nun ci sù.	My dear brows, I can't deny you're as lovely as the sky, you're so lovely to the eye, all who see you simply sigh.
Ma la vucca 'nzuccarata quannu parra, quannu ciata, gigghia beddi, gigghia amati, pirdunati, è bedda chiù.	But the mouth's a sugar beet when she opens it to greet, lovely brows that love entreat, please forgive me, 'tis more sweet.
Occhi, in vui fa pompa Amuri di l'immensu so valuri, vostri moti, vostri sguradi ciammi e dardi d'iddu sù.	Love has chosen you, dear eyes, just to flaunt his greatest prize. All your actions, all your sighs represent his flames, his guise.
Ma la vucca, quannu duci s'apri e dmoduula la vuci, occhii...ah vui mi taliati!... Pirdunati, 'un parru chiù.	But the mouth I so adore when her words begin to pour. Lovely eyes, why do you stare? Please forbear...I'll say no more.

The sensuality that exudes from these poems and from many of the others in the collection, goes beyond the Arcadian poets' exercises with their Venuses and little Cupids floating in the air. In reading these poems one feels the longing of the poet to touch the beloved tresses, to linger with a kiss on her skin, to caress her. In terms of inventiveness, freshness of images, and technical ability, these Melian poems can stand side by side with those of such masters as Chiabrera, Rolli, Frugoni and Metastasio.

It is undoubtedly symptomatic of Meli's divided self that at the same time that he was composing his Anacreontic odes, he was also writing his Satire, Capitoli and Epigrammi. As a physician who had access to the homes of the aristocracy, and as a celebrated poet, Meli had first hand knowledge of how the wealthy lived. He also saw how the poor people of Palermo lived, and his enlightened sense of justice was offended. In satires such as "La Moda" (Fashions), "Lu Cagghiostrisimu" (Cagliostrism), and "Lu Cafeaos," (The Coffeehouse) he chastised the wealthy for their vanity, their endless intrigues, their fatuous love affairs, and their corruption. But the attitudes that prevail in these poems are not those of an ardent zealot. Meli himself stated in "Lu Cafeaos" that he had always been a "friend to man" and that he had never written out of spite, "but only to warn him when he went astray." Meli was never moved by personal animosity against any one. His attitudes toward man, in the satires and elsewhere in his opus, are those of one who understands the nature of delusions, who laughs and feels compassion at the same time. He was not a true satirist. Indeed, as Pirandello insightfully saw, he was a humorist, as we will see more precisely when we discuss his *Don Chisciotti e Sanciu Panza*.

But when the sufferings became too strong, when the injustices of the world became too unbearable and he was no longer able to laugh at man's folly, Meli offered this advice: give yourself to the god Bacchus. Oblivion can't be far behind. This Dionysian vein cannot be ignored in Meli. The praises of wine was a literary subject of great popularity in the 18th century (See for example F. Redi's "Bacco in Toscana," and in Sicily Domenico Tempio's "Ditirammu" and Giuseppe Leonardi's "Cuntu supra di lu vinu"). Meli himself sang of it on various occasions: "Li Baccanti," "Innu a Baccu," "In lodi di lu vinu," and in a long episode of the *Don Chisciotti e Sanciu Panza*. But the poem in which, according to Alessio Di Giovanni, he reached "the pinnacle of his expressive powers," (*La vita e l'opera di G. M.,* Firenze, 1934) was his "Ditirammu: Sarudda," the most famous drinking song in Sicily which, according to Lorenzo Marinese, is still recited at weddings and parties in Palermo (*Poesie di G. M.*, Messina, 1973, p. 1). In this song Meli has temporarily forsaken the whispering of his erotic odes to grovel in a tavern together with some less than elegant drinking companions whose names — Andrew the flop, Tommy the blind, Lame Tony, Crazy Joe and Con-man Blaise — are hardly reassuring. The leader of this little group of drunkards is Sarudda who functions as Meli's alter ego, especially when he chastises the old Palermo for its corruption and pretenses as a city of glamour when in fact it is morally and economically bankrupt, and when he sings the curative powers of Sicilian wines. Particularly hilarious is Sarudda's, and Meli's, listing of the illnesses that wine can cure. Sarudda's attitudes reflect Meli's characteristic stance when confronted with things that he could neither change nor control in any way. After his denunciation of the city's ills, Sarudda resorts to wine to drown his frustrations: "To the devil with such melancholic thoughts," he exclaims, promising himself to live like monks who sing and dance and eat with their heads inside a sack. Sarudda-Meli, at times, may have sought to drown his awareness of the evils of the world in wine-caused oblivion.

The "Ditirammu" is a volcanic eruption of sounds and concepts which go from learned reflections to mere games of associations and word play. Its immediate impression on the reader is of an explosion of sounds that wane only to begin again in infernal cacophony. The meter is very irregular; lines of various lengths are placed one after another at random. Rhyme is irregularly distributed throughout the poem, both internally and externally, together with assonances and consonances that contribute to giving the poem its irrepressible sense of motion and energy. What follows is a rendition of the beginning of the poem:

Sarudda, Andria lu sdatu e Masi l'orvu Ninazzu lu sciancatu,
Peppi lu foddi e Brasi galiotu
ficiru ranciu tutti a taci maci
ntra la reggia taverna di Bravascu,
purtannu tirrimotu ad ogni ciascu.

E doppu aviri sculatu li vutti,
allegri tutti misiru a sotari
ed abballari pri li strati strati,
rumpennu 'nvitriati
ntra l'acqua e la rimarra, sbrizziannu
tutti ddi genti chi jìanu 'ncuntrannu.
E intantu appressu d'iddi
cucchieri cu stafferi,
decani cu lacchè
ci jìanu dappressu, facennuci olè.

All'urtimata poi determinaru
di jiri ad un fistinu
d'un so vicinu, chi s'avìa a 'nguaggiari,

e avìa a pigghiari a Betta la caiorda,
figghia bastarda di fra Decu e Narda;
l'occhi micciusi, la facciazza lorda,
la vucca a funcia, la frunti a cucchiara,
guercia, la varvarottu a cazzalora,
lu nasu a brogna, la facci di pala,
porca, lagnusa, tinta, macadura,
sdiserrama, 'mprisusa, micidara.

Lu zitu era lu celebri ziu Roccu,
ch'era divotu assai di lu diu Baccu:
nudu, mortu di fami, tintu e liccu;
e notti e jornu facia lu sbirlaccu.

Eranu chisti a tavula assittati
cu li so amici li chiù cunfidati;
ntra l'autri cunvitati
c'era assittata a punta di buffetta
Catarina la Niura,
Narda Caccia-diavuli
Bittazza la linguta
Ancila attizza-liti
E Rosa Sfincia 'Ntossica mariti.

Eranu junti a la secunna posa,
cioè si stava allura stimpagnannu
lu secunnu varrili,
chera chiddu di dudici 'ncannila
ben sirratu,
imnvicchiatu,
accutturatu,
e pri dittu di chiddi ch'annu pratica,
era appuntu secunnu la prammatica.

Sarudda, Andrew the flop, and Tom the blind,
Lame Tony, Crazy Joe, and Con-man Blaise
had eaten chow, all paying their own ways,
inside the royal tavern of Bravascu

creating wild turmoil with every flask.
And after they had drained the barrels
dry all mighty "high"
they all began to leap
and dance and bump each other in the street,
jumping in pools of water and in mud,
and splashing every "bud"
they chanced to meet.
Behind them grew a crowd
of children and young men,
porters, supporters of chairs,
deacons and lackeys with beacons,
cheering them on, with cries most loud.

At last they all agreed to join the feast
of their fast friend
who was engaged to wed Narda,
brother Degu's bastard daughter
whose name was Lizabeth, the slob:
Watery eyes had she, an ugly dirty face,
a mushroom mouth; her forehead was spoon-like.
Half blind, her chin was a protruding ledge.
A flat pug nose, a shovel for a face,
she was a slimy, grimy, mean old wench,
lazy and crazy, murderous and whining.

The groom was the most famous
uncle Ruckus
who was devoted to the old god Bacchus.
Dying of hunger, poor, mean and voracious
he led a most ungracious bum's existence.
These folk were sitting at the banquet table,
together with their closest friends and kin.
Among the other guests,
sitting right at the table's edge
were Catherine, black-skin,
Devils-chasing Narda,
Ugly Beth with wagging tongue,

Rose Dumpling who choked husbands for a song.

They'd reached the second stage,
that is, they had uncorked the second barrel,
the one that cost a pretty penny,
which had been gauged, correctly aged,
to shine on any stage,
and which to hear men who should know
was made according to the rules of law.

The "Ditirammu" was written at about the same time as the episode in the Don Chisciotti in which a young man, suffering from a case of unrequited love, received from a wise old man of the town the same advice Sarudda dispenses freely: drown your sorrows in wine. It can make a happy man even of the most miserable of beings. The two works, as well as the last major project, *Favuli morali, (Moral Fables)* which we will now discuss in order to consider the Don Chisciotti more carefully later, were born out of the same substratum of pessimism. Indeed, the disappointments of his later years took a toll on Meli. His pessimism grew even more bitter towards the end of his life. His *Favuli morali*, 89 fables written in verse, are an embodiment of his lifelong search for wisdom. In them he celebrated the wisdom of the animals who live according to their natural instincts, taking care of themselves without harming others. Man is portrayed as less wise than animals because civilization has corrupted him. The concepts of goodness and honesty are praised over talents and ability. Meli's fables are not the biting work of a stern moralist. Yet they remain sufficiently barbed to burst many balloons of hypocrisy (The Bat and the Mouse), of vanity (The Crow and the Parrot), of ingratitude (the Mouse and the Hedgehog), and of ambition (The Dogs and the Statue). Meli denounced the exploitation of the poor classes by the rich and powerful (The Boar and the Corsican Dog), the corruption of the governing class (The Realm of the Foxes), and such evils as malice, cunning and deceit. He seems to have had an obsession with cats whom he regarded as the symbol of deceit, representing men who are able to disguise their emotions and intentions through pleasing manners and appearances. In "La Surcia e li surciteddi" (The Mother Mouse and her Young) the mother teaches her young mice to differentiate amongst animals. The mice had seen an enormous horse in a stable which had appeared to them as a fearful monster, and a purring, sweet-looking cat. The mother, utterly terrified by the risk her young had run, tells them to:

Di tutti l'animali che ci sunnu,
chistu è lu chiù terribili; nun cridi
nè cridiri lu pò cui nun a munnu!
A sti cudduzzi torti 'un dari fidi;
guardati di st'aspetti mansueti;
l'occhiu è calatu, però nun ti sbidi!
Chisti sù sanguinarii, inquieti,
crudi, avari, manciuni, spietati,
tradituri, latruni, ed indiscreti.

Among all beasts he's the most troublesdome,
the worst on earth. The truth you can't believe
unless you've learned of life a minimum.
Dont trust such hypocrites! Don't be naive!
Of such tame looks and manners be on guard!
Their eyes seem closed, but they all things perceive.
They are bloodthirsty, restless, and rock hard,
traitorous, thieving, heartless, indiscreet.
selfish and greeedy and without regard..

According to F. Biondolillo ("Meli favolista" in *Studi su G.M. nel secondo centenario della nascita*, (1740-1940) Palermo 1942, p. 181) this tale is much more lively in Meli's rendition than in La Fontaine's original formulation. Meli's fable is more successful in capturing the mother's terror of the cat through the use of interjections, exclamations and cries of fear. In addition, Meli's substitution of a horse for the original rooster as the fear-evoking but harmless animal seems more appropriate, considering the disparity of sizes involved.

In another fable (XIV) the cat is made the symbol of egotism and self interest. In a blacksmith's shop a cat sleeps through the continued and loud hammering only to awaken upon hearing the sound of smacking lips and dishes. Meli comments discreetly and with his familiar smile:

Perciò lu scrusciu di li labbri e di piatti
basta pri arrisbigghiari omini e gatti.
Therefore the noise that lips and dishes make
is strong enough to wake both cats and men.

Meli's satire, as I've said, is never biting, because he does not condemn from the ivory tower of moral righteousness. His fables are an act of condemnation as well as an act of acceptance of the shortcomings of man. The prevailing attitude is the one displayed in the justly famous tale of the mouse gone astray:

> Un surciteddu di testa sbintata
> avia pigghiatu la via di l'acitu
> e faceva na vita scialacquata
> cu l'amiciuni di lu so partitu.
> Lu ziu circau di tirarlu a bona strata
> ma zappau a l'acqua pirchi era attrivitu
> e dicchiù la saimi avia liccatu
> di taverni e zàgati peritu.
> Finalmente mucidda fici luca;
> iddu grida; Ziu ziu cu dogghia interna;
> so ziu pri lu rammaricu si suca;
> Poi dici, "Lu to casu mi costerna,
> ma ora mi cerchi? chiaccu chi t'affuga?
> Scutta pi quannu jisti a la taverna."

> A little mouse who heedless was and brash
> had gone the way of wine to vinegar
> and lived a life of pleasures with great dash,
> together with some pals who were his par.
> His uncle tried to save him from the crash,
> but dug in water, for he'd gone too far;
> what's more, the taste of lard had made him rash,
> expert on many a tavern and sweet jar.
> But Kitty finally caught up with him.
> "Uncle, oh, uncle!" cried he from each limb.
> His uncle with regret was quite oppressed,
> and therefore said: "Your case makes me distressed,
> but, may you hang, just now you come my way?
> The price for going to the taverns, pay!"

As was the case for the *Buccolica, L'origini di lu munnu, "Ditirammu. Sarudda"*, each of which found admirers who claimed that it was Meli's masterpiece, The *Favuli Morali* has also evoked critical appraisals that qualify it as the work in which the poet expressed his inner world in a more complete way. Francesco Biondolillo is one such critic. In an article entitled "Meli favolista," in *Studi su*

G.M.... op. cit. p.181, Biondolillo acknowledged Meli's considerable lyrical, bucolic and satiric gifts, but he concluded that "Meli as a fabulist was a lot greater both because in the brevity of the tale he was best able to engage his inventive and imaginative powers, and because behind the screen of the fable he was best able to express his soul and his thoughts, coloring the one and the other with the grace and wit proper to his temperament." (My translation).

Meli's presumed timidity need not be considered a major factor in the choice of the fable as a means of expression. He devoted the last years of his life to this genre not only because it was growing in popularity and in critical esteem, but because he saw it as an effective tool for reaching a wider audience composed of different social classes. As Gisella Padovani pointed out in an unpublished article entitled "L'itinerario culturale di G. Meli," the poet had intended his fables to exercise an influence on Sicilian society similar to that performed by Addison's *Spectator* on British society, that is, a democratizing influence, which by offering entertainment and wisdom to all classes would have a leveling effect on the differences among them.

These remarks point to the difficulty in classifying and categorizing Meli. His interests were many and he expressed his inner world in different ways. Who is to say that one aspect was more important than another? Perhaps it would be better to let the multifaceted poet speak to his audience through his many voices. Those voices are present in all their modulations in a work neglected for too long. I am referring to the *Don Chisciotti e Sanciu Panza,* his most ambitious project, a mock-heroic poem of 12 cantos written between 1785 and 1786 and published for the first time in 1787.

The *Don Chisciotti e Sanciu Panza:*

My decision to translate this work was based primarily on the simple fact that I had enjoyed the poem immensely. While reading it at night it was not uncommon to hear myself laughing inwardly and sometimes outwardly, often loudly. Meli's inventiveness, his ability to keep me interested in the novel adventures of his *Don Chisciotti and Sanciu Panza*, the freshness of his language (undoubtedly the use of the Sicilian language, which is my native tongue, had a great deal to do with my enjoyment since I recognized in Meli's use of it situations and realities long forgotten), his subtle irony, the vividness of his descriptions of Sicilian nature, the wisdom of a natural philosopher, and his typical Sicilian skepticism seemed congenial to my soul. In reading the poem I revisited Sicily in my mind, I saw old friends, uttered epithets of mockery and joy: in short, I experienced many epiphanies.

My translation is in a sense a vote of confidence in Meli, for I believe, with G.A. Borgese, that his work deserves to be read and studied more. But it is also a vote of confidence in the *Don Chisciotti e Sanciu Panza*, a poem that reflects, perhaps more fully than any other of his works, the author's personality and the conflicts of his time. From this point of view, this Sicilian Don Chisciotti can be studied from a number of perspectives: as an historical document embodying the dynamic relationship between the ideas of the Enlightenment and the deeply conservative ideals of tradition-bound Sicilian society; as a record of social customs and traditions of a society that until recently had not changed appreciably; as an important moment in the struggle between social classes; and as a literary work of considerable scope and depth which shares in a tradition having deep roots in the Italian spirit and which has produced such poets as Pulci, Ariosto, Tassoni, and Berni, to name but a few of the best known. Let us now look at the genesis of the poem. Why did Meli choose the two characters of Don Quijote and Sancho Panza?

While the motivations for creating poetry are seldom clear cut or readily apparent, we may be certain that when Giovanni Meli conceived his ambitious project he was well aware of the possible risks involved in the choice. Undoubtedly the two characters — living symbols of the opposing forces within man — fulfilled deep-seated psychological needs of the Sicilian poet. Meli knew very well that his work would be judged from the perspective of the Cervantian masterpiece. His selection of the Spanish characters was an open invitation to compare the two works. In retrospection, Meli's choice may have to be considered an act of hubris punished by silence, neglect and often unjust dismissal of his poem. Those critics who have measured the Sicilian Don Chisciotti by his Spanish counterpart, (Emiliani Giudici, Settembrini, De Sanctis and Cesareo) that is, who have regarded him as a mere continuation or extension of the *Don Quijote* — an imitation of an inimitable work — have done a great disservice to Meli and have failed to understand his goals. Meli was too consummate an artist not to have realized that imitation was doomed to failure from the beginning. His Don Chisciotti was conceived in a different manner and had different goals to pursue on his return to earth. While the Sicilian knight had the same physiognomy as his predecessor, he lived in a different time and spoke with a different voice. The character of Sancho Panza underwent an even greater metamorphosis, the most obvious manifestation of which was his elevation to the rank of his master. The Sicilian poem is entitled *Don Chisciotti e Sanciu Panza*. The Spanish novel was entitled *El ingenioso hidalgo Don Quijote de la Mancha*. Sancho's name did not appear in it. This shifting of emphasis is in reality more important than it seems, as we shall see shortly. The two works must not be seen as an original and an imitation, but rather as two different manifestations of the same archetype. Don Quijote and Sancho Panza, as Bakhtin noted, constitute an archetypal couple: an inseparable and separate union of opposites. Don Quijote could not exist alone, as Cervantes learned after his hero's first solo adventure. Miguel De Unamuno, commenting on Don Quijote's acquisition of Sancho as his squire, said:

> "Now Don Quijote is complete. He had need of Sancho. He needed him so as to be able to talk, that is, to think aloud with frankness and listen to the sound of his own voice in the world." (From Our Lord *Don Quixote*, Bollingen Series LXXXV, - 3 Princeton: Princeton Univ. Press 1967, pp. 53-54)

We have been conditioned to think of Sancho Panza as an extension of Don Quijote, an appendage, an embodiment of the knight's less developed psychological components. In fact, this complementary role of Sancho may be nothing more than a bias of Cervantes' own peculiar psychological and philosophical attitudes, or perhaps a bias of the critics who have considered the archetypal couple: a natural reaction, since in every couple there must be a dominant aspect, "un maggior corno," as Dante said referring to that "greater horn" of the flames engulfing that other archetypal couple of Ulysses and Diomedes in Canto XXVI of the *Inferno*. Unanumo considered Don Quijote the dominant half of the couple. But neither Unamuno's nor Cervantes' need to be the sole viable interpretations of the archetype.

Archetypes are experienced in a manner that is not independent of the psychological conditions present in the person. As we know, archetypes are always polyvalent and their contents are never static, fixed or unchangeable. Indeed, their contents are fluid, contradictory and blurred, — a feature that manifests itself even after the couple has been projected onto two separate identities. Is there not a bit of Don Quijote in Sancho Panza and vice versa? In fact, we might ask whether Sancho in Cervantes' novel is not more "Quijotic" that Don Quijote himself: knowingly, he chooses to follow a madman in search of glory while Don Quijote follows his own inner call. Thus when a poet experiences an archetype he does so through all those personal factors that make up his distinctive self. The contents of the archetype being, however, fluid, he is apt to rearrange the proportions assigned to each half of the couple to fit his needs.

Meli, in this context, need not be seen as an imitator of Cervantes, but rather as a poet in whom the archetype was activated. Don Chisciotti and Sanciu Panza were as alive in Meli as they had been in Cervantes. In addition to the psychological resonance that the couple had for Meli, he may also have been following a long literary tradition that can still be heard at Sicilian festivals as Bakhtin reported. I am referring to another manifestation of the same archetype which takes the form of a poetic dispute between two antagonistic points of view voiced by such couples as father and son, old man and young man; I was present at a reading of such a dispute written in Sicilian octaves in Brooklyn one night in November 1984. Two poets expressed opposite views on life that might be characterized as realism versus imagination; rationalism versus irrationalism; or idealism versus materialism.

What we need to do at this point is to see how the archetype manifested itself in Meli. In 1813, twenty-six years after the Don Chisciotti had been published, Meli added an epilogue, 56 octaves entitled the "Vision" in which he imagined that Sanciu had appeared to him one night to thank him and to relate his last adventures. In these octaves Meli addressed himself to the poem's objectives. In octave 40 Sanciu expresses a judgment on Cervantes that we can use to reconstruct Meli's poetics. Sanciu said:

Scervantes, chi pritisi sbarbicari
lu pregiudiziu dominanti allura
di l'erranti bravura militari,
non conuscìa di l'omu la natura,
chi tra lu mezzu nun ci sa marciari;
pigghia sempri un estremu chi l'oscura;
e si da chistu si distacca e sposta,
sauta e rumpi a l'estrema parti opposta.

Cervantes, who intended to uproot
the dominant delusion of his time-
the martial prowess of the Errant Knights-
man's very nature did not understand.
Man cannot take the middle of the road.
He chooses an extreme that humbles him.
If from this point he parts and steps aside,
he jumps completely to the other side.

Sanciu's chastisement of Cervantes for his failure to understand that man is incapable of walking in the middle of the road, always tending towards what is exaggerated, lacking judiciousness and measure, may be an incomplete statement of Meli's philosophical attitudes, but it is sufficient to identify the parameters of those attitudes. Meli's lifelong concern — as De Sanctis himself in a famous essay was able to identify — was a search for wisdom. (See his *Saggi critici*, vol 3, Bari: Laterza, rpt. 1965) Throughout his poetry the Aristotelian principle of moderation is constantly praised. Happiness, if such a thing exists, consists of never allowing our own desires to exceed the boundaries of our means to attain them. Meli always exalts the wisdom of common sense, of the middle-of-the-road-approach to life. In Canto III, octave 5, he speaks through his Don Chisciotti on behalf of moderation:

> Chiù chi si voli, chiù si pati, amici.
> Lu riccu stissu, si la sbrigghia cedi
> a li proprii disii, oh chi cuntrastu!
> Martiriu ci adddiventa lu so fastu.

> "The more you want, the more you suffer, friends.
> And if the rich themselves gave a free rein
> to their desires, what conflicts would there be!
> Their pomp would soon become sheer agony."

Meli's philosophical attitudes were those of an empiricist. He believed that all knowledge was made possible by the senses. He had great admiration for Bacon whom he called the Columbus of modern philosophy - and for men such as Galilei and Telesio. He trusted only in the laws of nature. These components of Meli's personality were embodied by Sanciu, the man who cared only for what was "present tense," who believed only what he saw with his own eyes and touched with his own hands.

William James' typological study of opposites can be utilized here to give an approximation of Meli's philosophical stance as it emerges from his writings. James tabulated the qualities that belong to the two types of philosophers as follows:

> "Tender minded vs tough-minded; Rationalistic (going by principles) vs Empiricist (going by facts); Intellectualistic vs Sensationalistic; Idealistic vs Materialistic; Optimistic vs Pessimistic; Religious vs Irreligious; Monistic vs Pluralistic; Dogmatical vs Skeptical." *(Pragmatism: A New Name for Some Old Ways of Thinking,* London and N.Y., 1911, pp. 10 ff).

The attributes that are listed in second position constitute a very close approximation of Meli's predominant attitudes, displayed with varying degrees of conviction throughout his career. Such preeminence need not be considered exclusive of the qualities described in first position.

Meli's reaction to the Cervantian masterpiece become predictable now that we have identified certain constants in his personality. For a man who believed in everything that is tangible, real, rational, materialistic and commonsensical, Cervantes' Don Quijote had to appear as an exaggeration, a risible combination of foolishness and virtue. Meli, as he stated in the Vision (octave 46), believed he was the first man to understand the true moral lesson contained in the Don Quijote. The character of Don Quijote for him was a diamond mounted in a lead setting. A true philosopher would appreciate his many virtues because he would know how to distinguish the wheat from the chaff. The tragic flaw in Don Quijote's character was an inability to gauge his powers *vis à vis* the task at hand, that is, his projects always involved greater powers than he possessed which in the Melian universe was a recipe for unhappiness. Meli's Sanciu wrote on Don Chisciotti's tombstone:

La cinniri ch'è sutta sta balata
fu spogghia d'un Eroi di desideriu;
chi mai sappi cunsari na 'nzalata,
non ostanti pritisi in tonu seriu
di cunsari lu munnu.

The dust that lies beneath this slab of stone
is what remains of one who would be hero,
who never knew how to prepare a salad
and yet presumed in all sincerity
he could repair the world. (XII, 97)

Sanciu, the pragmatist, the empiricist, the man who abided by the facts rather than by universal principles, was a personality more congenial to Meli than was his master. And it is for this reason that Meli emphasized the character of Sanciu in his work, making him the hero, ascribing to him the highest wisdom that suffering and experience, the greatest teachers, could impart.

In this sense, the archetype of the antithetical couple was experienced by Meli in a different manner. The fact that Sanciu became for Meli the "maggior corno" that is, the dominant half of the couple, represents a shifting of the components to suit Meli's psychological and philosophical stance toward the world. This rearrangement was Meli's peculiar and unique reaction to the archetype, brought about by all those psychological, historical and sociological factors that contributed to making him the man he was. Meli, to use a term dear to Unamuno, would seem to be proponent of Sanchopanzism. The difference between Meli and Cervantes was that the scale containing the two halves of the archetype was weighted more on the side of skepticism for the Sicilian poet. Although skepticism was a predominant attitude in him, it cannot be said that he was incapable of being moved by optimism. Nor would it be true to say that his empiricist's attitudes prevented him from harboring idealistic beliefs. Indeed, the poet was continuously torn between these two divergent attitudes throughout his life. In fact, this is the most evident characteristic of his poetry.

As an enlightened man who believed in the dignity of human beings and as a physician who saw how the different classes of Sicily lived (there were primarily the rich and the poor without any middle classes) Meli fervently longed to see the suffering of peasants and shepherds alleviated. He believed in and advocated many reforms designed to bring Sicily out of its backwardness. In 1801 he wrote a treatise entitled "Riflessioni sullo stato presente del Regno di Sicilia intorno alla agricoltura e alla pastorizia" (Reflections on the Present State of Agriculture and Stock-Breeding in the Kingdom of Sicily) in which the poverty, sickness and malnutrition of the poor people of Sicily were deplored most bitterly. Many of the points contained in the treatise had already been made in the *Don Chisciotti e Sanciu Panza.*

The fact that he joined the movement of the Masons reflected his commitment to humanitarian and social ideals. As we know, this international organization was guided by philanthropic objectives. It is significant that Meli became a member of this organization sometimes between 1781 and 1785, that is, at the time when the fervor for reforms was at its highest thanks to the political action of the enlightened viceroy Domenico Caracciolo. (See Eugenio di Carlo, "Spigolature Meliane," in *Studi su G.M....* op. cit., p.432)

Meli's social ideals are clearly expressed throughout the work. We need no special lens to see where Meli's heart was. The rich, the powerful, and the titled are constantly denigrated, while the peasants, the shepherds — in short those who are the producers of wealth — are exalted. Social justice, an end to the perennial exploitation of the working classes by the parasitic noblemen, the right of every person to work, the establishment of an international tribunal to settle cases, the abolition of wars, were ideas to which Meli subscribed wholeheartedly, and are the ideals which animate his Don Chisciotti. (See Don Chisciotti's agenda for social reforms carved on a tree trunk. Also, see notes to Canto XII, octaves 60-67).

Thus Meli can be defined as an empiricist with idealistic tendencies, a realist with a penchant for dreaming, a skeptical man who harbored optimistic views, a man who relied on facts but tended to be governed by principles. The *Don Chisciotti and Sanciu Panza* was an embodiment of such a conflict. In a letter written in 1804 to Filippo Rehfues, he described the conflict in vivid terms. He confirmed that his lifelong preoccupation had been "to think of the most plausible ways to arrange and order the society of men so that the just would not be overcome by the unjust, the honest would find ways of living without being oppressed or humbled, virtue would be given the consideration due to it, and the laws would not be used for vile trafficking, which by employing countless loafers, charlatans and delinquents is ruinous for the state and for the individual as well, and prevents those who are entrusted with the administration of those laws from freeing themselves from the yoke of such parasites. But then, realizing my humble condition as a private and the imbecility of my spirit, I would consider myself completely mad, promising myself I would no longer venture beyond the sphere of my desires or thoughts: a moment after, having moved away from such resolutions, I would return to my first deliriums, then I'd see the errors of my ways and I'd repent again. Now this state of perpetual contradiction with myself prompted me to mask with the allegory of Don Chisciotti e Sanciu the periods of my deliriums and the lucid intervals of good sense." (*Le Lettere*, op. cit. p. 130) (My translation.)

If on the one hand Meli fervently hoped to redeem the poor people of Sicily, on the other side he felt that all efforts were inevitably futile. His humanitarian ideals -embodied by Don Chisciotti- conflicted externally with the attitudes of an entrenched and intransigent nobility, unwilling to give up any of its privileges and, internally, with that realistic, skeptical part of himself that considered the task of changing the social fabric of the island a foolish and hopeless attempt. In Don Chisciotti Meli projected his yearnings for human justice, liberty and a more equitable division of wealth among the peoples of the world. But, at the same time, these yearnings had to be represented as the dreams of a delirious fool. Sanciu Panza, on the other hand, represented Meli's own skeptical attitudes toward Don Chisciotti's deliriums.

In the "Vision", Meli explained that he had meant his own Don Chisciotti as a satire against the charlatans and pseudo-scientists who were too quick to propose reforms without any experience and understanding of the problems of Sicily. Meli's assertions, written 27 years after the completion of the work and after many disillusions, family squabbles, and constant struggling to make ends meet, need not be taken as the whole truth. Much had happened in those 27 years. Between the moments of Don Chisciotti's deliriums of 1785-6 and 1813 there was, as we read in "Il buon gusto in Sicilia: G. Meli tra Arcadia e Riformismo," (*II '700. Storia e testi*, vol VI, Bari: Laterza, p. 387) "the disillusionment of history embodied by the apparent failure of those principles fostered by the French Revolution — even if Meli never was favorably disposed towards the events in France or the Jacobins — there was Lord Bentinck's Constitution of 1812, there was the traditional Misogallism of Sicilian history". (My translation.) Thus, for a man who in the end had come to regard the search for happiness on earth as an eternal joke, "una trizziata eterna," as he wrote in a letter to his friend F. Nascè, to admit that he may have nurtured illusory longings for human justice may have been too painful: hence the cynical attitude regarding the pseudo-scientists looms larger, and obscures the other objectives of the poem. Furthermore, satire implies an overcoming of conflicts, a superior view, a condemnation from above, a distance between subject and author. Such distancing does not appear to have taken place. There is one moment in the *Don Chisciotti e Sanciu Panza* in which this is clearly manifested. In Canto VII, Don Chisciotti, having mistaken a rock for an enormous whale, jumped inside a cave, thinking it the throat of the leviathan, and began to swing his sword against it. After a while he was almost ready to admit his blunder but he saw a rivulet of blood on the ground. He rejoiced because the blood was proof that he had been fighting a whale, but in fact, in the heat of the battle against the rocks he had injured himself without realizing it. Meli has a fit of anger at his hero's foolishness and inability to see reality, and addresses him directly:

"Minnali, di chi gudi?
"Ah, silly man! Why are you pleased?

A satirist would have found a more elegant and indirect form of chastisement.

Why the vehemence, why the passion? I believe with Francesco Guglielmino ("II pensiero del Meli nel "Don Chisciotti" in *Studi su G. M. ...* op. cit. p.. 76) that Meli was berating and chastising himself for his deliriums. Too much emotion was invested in the epithet. Meli here was experiencing the same feelings he had when he wrote the already cited letter to Rehfues.

The *Don Chisciotti e Sanciu Panza* is a humoristic poem in the Pirandellian sense, that is, as an embodiment of the "sentimento del contrario." Meli embodies the Janus figure within himself. Each of the two heroes is the embodiment of opposite tendencies. Indeed, each hero contains within himself his own contrary, the other side of the coin. Don Chisciotti is a humoristic character. Sanciu described him well when in Canto V, 28, he said:

Cu tuttu ciò patìa d'un certu mali
ch'essennu 'nterra si cridìa a li celi;
mendicu, si crideva un signurazzu;
dijunu saziu, 'nzumma era un gran pazzu".

"A certain malady possessed him, though:
Being on earth, he thought he was in heaven;
Being a beggar he believed he was a lord;
Not having eaten, full. In short: out of his gourd!"

Don Chisciotti was a "would be hero," a fruiting tree that could never produce a fig or a pear; his good intentions were always undermined by his faulty reading of the physical evidence before him. His senses were constantly deceiving him. In Canto III we can observe how Don Chisciotti slipped from a recounting of Aristotelian ethics to the insane mouthing of some Arcadian gibberish. (See notes Canto III, 10) Don Chisciotti was himself the negation of his desires. His death was a perfect embodiment of the humoristic mode. The man who presumed to set straight the world died of hernia while attempting to straighten an old and odd-shaped rowan tree. His death was more quijotic than that of his predecessor who, as you recall, died in his own bed in a very peaceful way after recovering his senses.

Sanciu too was created in a humoristic way. Whereas Don Chisciotti was a mass of undigested learning, a conglomeration of unassimilated notions without a unifying principle, Sanciu was an ignorant man who grew to become a natural philosopher, another Aesop, the fabulist whom Meli admired most of all. Experience and suffering changed him from a poor illiterate peasant into a highly esteemed, wise and prudent man. This metamorphosis is but one of the most obvious humoristic touches.

Critics have attempted to associate Meli with one or the other of his characters. The truth is that Meli was both Don Chisciotti and Sanciu Panza and it would not be too difficult to identify those utterances that Meli would have acknowledged as his own. If one were to separate the sane utterances of Don Chisciotti from those that are patently insane, one would have a compendium of Melian wisdom. Canto III is probably the most abundant in such utterances. But they are also numerous in Canto IV and in Canto XII, and elsewhere. And Sanciu, too, is Meli. Indeed he represents the prevailing attitude within the poet. He is, as we have seen, the "tabula rasa" that experience and the example of Don Chisciotti have filled. He is the empiricist, the sensationalist, the skeptic, the man who does not believe in witches, and the materialist who believes in the need to work.

It is symptomatic that it is Sanciu and not Don Chisciotti who returns after his death. He is the Melian hero. In the battle between idealism and materialism the latter won. Sanciu who had suffered during his life on earth was rewarded by being allowed to enter the Elysian Fields to spend his time with the greatest philosophers, enjoying the vision of truth, while his master because of his extravagance was condemned to capture the wind with a net for six months and to stay in the Elysium for the other six. Sanciu, in fact, was made the object of an apotheosis. His good heart, his virtuous poverty, his hard work, and his wisdom, gained through long suffering, raised him to a state of bliss.

A word about the translation. Meli's language is difficult to classify. As Salvatore Santangelo wrote in his study *(La lingua del Meli*; Palermo: Palumbo Editore, 1941, p. 36). "Taken as a whole, Meli's language, like that of every prolific and complex author, is something fluctuating and heterogeneous, on which no judgment can be pronounced." (My translation.) A work of the size of the *Don Chisciotti and Sanciu Panza*, reproduces in a microcosm the linguistic physiognomy of the poet and defies any attempts to categorize it. Some generalizations can be formulated, however. While Meli may have intended to create an "illustrious Sicilian," the result of his efforts was a mixture of the literary idiom of Italy, that is, Tuscan, especially in its Arcadian tradition, and of Sicilian. The interrelationship between these two components represents an essential feature of Meli's language. This interrelationship may be articulated along an axis that includes a highly literary Tuscan (a direct quotation from Petrarch, for example), passing through a line or expression that is structurally Tuscan but with Sicilian superimposed on it. A third point of the axis might consist of "illustrious Sicilian," that is, purified from its local Palermitan dress and distilled from a variety of idioms spoken in Sicily, and finally there might be a line or expression which comes from the everyday jargon of the streets. I have tried to reproduce such sliding along the axis wherever possible. In the case of the Petrarchan line quoted by Don Chisciotti, in Canto I, "un bel morir tutta la vita onora," I tried to differentiate it from its linguistic environs by introducing a term that would be recognized as more archaic than the rest. Thus the line became "a worthy death brings honor to thy life," in which the adjective "thy" is charged with the task of signaling its literariness and more archaic nature. Consonant with the tone of the original which obtains comic relief by mixing a highly dignified language with popular speech, I have tried to maintain the same combination in English, allowing myself to slide in the direction of archaic terms or slang, according to the situation.

Mindful of his promise to employ the trumpet and the bagpipe, "to avoid the monotony for which many famous poems have been indicted," (see note to Canto I, 3) Meli adopted a variety of styles in the *Don Chisciotti e Sanciu Panza*. This poem is a microcosm of the Melian opus for it contains examples of his multifaceted personality. We find beautiful lyrical passages descriptive of nature that remind the reader of the *Buccolica*; erotic and gallant passages that bring to mind the delicate touches of his odes of love (Sanciu's description of Dulcinea's beauty, Canto IV, 43-45); fight scenes of irrepressible energy and wit (the fight between Don Chisciotti and Sanciu, Canto V, or Don Chisciotti's struggle with the pack of dogs, Canto II, or Don Chisciotti's struggle with the three weird characters, Canto X), scenes of pathos and suffering (the description of Don Chisciotti's death, Canto XII), and scenes in which Meli's technical poetic virtuosity is displayed (such as the peasant's love song, written as a parody and with feminine rhymes throughout. In these octaves (Canto VII) I felt that an idea of the poet's virtuosity had to be conveyed in the English version and I introduced an uncommon rhyme scheme in my translation to counterbalance Meli's use of "rime sdrucciole" (feminine rhymes). The paucity of feminine rhymes in English convinced me not to attempt a more precise correspondence.

Describing one's translation runs the risk of becoming a confession of sins, minor and major, committed knowingly and unknowingly. Translating poetry into poetry is, as Dryden once said, an act of sympathy. In my own case, I think it was something more than that. I felt like an advocate pleading a special case: Giovanni Meli's poetry as the embodiment of an aspect of the Sicilian soul. My work is done. Let now the jury's verdict decide whether my pleading has been successful.

On Translating Giovanni Meli's Poetry

Translation studies have not as yet developed a comprehensive theory of the processes of translation that can be utilized as a tool of description as well as of prescription.[1] For this reason I will not discuss its theoretical and philosophical aspects. Instead I will focus my attention primarily on the actual problems posed by the translation of some of Giovanni Meli's works as a way of illustrating some of the problems translators meet when they are asked to translate from one language into another. I think Ivan Fonagy summed up the status of translation studies very well when he introduced his discussion of the translation of certain every day phrases with the following remarks:

"If we knew everything we know, I would not be able to talk to you about a problem that is resolved a hundred times an hour during a simultaneous translation. Fortunately for us linguists there is a considerable distance between practical competence and theoretical competence." (Se si sapesse tutto ciò che si sa, non potrei parlarvi oggi di un problema risolto cento volte all'ora durante una traduzione simultanea. Fortunatamente per noi linguisti, c'è una considerevole distanza tra la competenza pratica e la competenza teorica)".[2]

In addition to the chasm that exists between theoretical and practical competence another reason for avoiding getting too deeply involved with the philosophical problems raised by translation is the fact that translators are in general very pragmatic, intent on solving specific problems that arise out of the texts they are translating. Indeed, while all translators seek the optimal solution to their difficulties, one finds that they generally opt for the Minimax Strategy, that is, when confronted by a series of possible renderings for an expression or word, they choose the one that offers the maximum effect with the minimum of effort.[3]

My translation of Meli's ambitious mock heroic poem, *The Don Chisciotti and Sanciu Panza,* required about four years to complete, precisely twice as long as it took Meli to write his poem, a fact from which several conclusions can be drawn:

1) that Meli was a more accomplished poet than I am,

2) that he had a lot more experience with the technical aspects of writing poetry, and

3) that he was not handicapped by an existing text, as his translator was.[4] At any rate, translating over 8600 lines into iambic pentameter with the seventh and eighth lines of each octave rhymed can be trying on any translator. The problems posed by the text are enormous and require a great deal of ingenuity and creativity from the translator.

What follows is a summary of the processes that went into the translation of the work. The first problem I had to solve was the choice of language and the meter. Meli's idiom is difficult to classify. Because of its length, the work reproduces the linguistic physiognomy of the poet in all its varieties. Meli wanted to create an illustrious Sicilian [5] The result of his efforts was a mixture of the literary language of Italy, that is, Tuscan in its Arcadian formulation and of Sicilian. The interrelationship between these two components represents an essential feature of Meli's language.

In my English rendition I tried to maintain a language that is dignified without being archaic. Consonant with the tone of the original l which obtains comic relief by mixing a highly dignified language with popular speech, I tried to keep the same combination, allowing myself to slide in the direction of archaic terms or slang, depending on the requirements of the situation. Meli often quotes entire lines from Dante, Petrarch, Ariosto and others. Different strategies could be have been adopted in such cases. The lines in question could have been left in the original language, for example. I chose to translate them. But it had to be made clear that the lines had been quotations from other sources, because in the original the reader would immediately grasp the change of tone and diction of the quoted lines in comparison with the author's text. So, in my rendition I had to signal that such a change had occurred. Putting quotation marks alone would not have been sufficient. Therefore, I had to find a different solution. Let's look at two examples: Don Chisciotti in trying to encourage the frightened Sanciu to undertake an adventure exhorts him by quoting a line from Petrarch: *un bel morir tutta la vita onora.*[6] In order to differentiate this line from its linguistic environs, I introduced a term that would be recognized as more archaic/poetic than the text in which it is found. Thus the line became, *A worthy death brings honor to thy life,* in which the possessive adjective *thy* is charged with the task of signalling its literariness since *thy* and *thou* are normally not used in the translation. Another Petrarchan reminiscence, *Povera e nuda vai, Filosofia?* was translated with a similar procedure: *Philosophy, thou goest naked and forlorn!*

The choice of meter was relatively simple: the iambic pentameter was a natural choice. It is the most common and most natural narrative meter in English. The rhyme, however, was not part of the original plan In fact, I had translated the first two cantos before I decided to rhyme the final couplet of each octave. As I went on translating, it became increasingly clear to me that Meli had placed particular emphasis on the final couplet. He seemed to have elaborated them with greater care than the other rhymes, because they served as a link between each octave and as an incentive to the reader to continue. I felt that in order to do justice to Meli, my final couplets had to be as striking as I could make them, without departing too much from the original, of course. It became a kind of competition, in a way. A few examples will do:

Si chiddu si riscalda, chista adduma,
viduva è mecciu astutatu chi fuma.

If he was kindled, she was set on fire.
A widow is a flameless, smoky pyre.

ci avìa dittu un oraculu indovinu:
«Fuiri l'acqua e unirisi a lu vinu! ».

This did an Oracle far him divine:
«Beware of water, but make friend with wine! ».

e chiddi ch"un si quadranu a sta scola,
nu li quatta lu ferru ni la mola.

and he who will not profit from this school,
no matter what, will always be a fool.

In connection with the rhyme, special problems were posed by Meli's technical virtuosity in Canto VII. Here Meli introduced the song of a peasant-turned poet during a lull in the adventures of Don Chisciotti and Sanciu. It is a parody of a love song, similar in nature to those that Ruzante wrote in imitation of Petrarch.[8] A peasant who writes in an apparently awkward style a poem that is in reality a considerable *tour de force* of technical and prosodical abilities. In all, the peasant-poet sings seven octaves, almost exclusively rhymed with feminine endings, which vary only in the accented vowel: *iviri, òviri; àuli, èvuli;* and *àniu, iniu,* as in the following octave:

La curatola bedda pri cui smàniu
chidda ch'avi di mia lu predomìniu
punci comu na macchia di piràinu
ed apporta la frevi e lu sdil1ìniu;
un vermi mi ficcati dintra lu cràniu
pri cui mi criju juntu all'estermìniu.
Ma ohimè, ch'è dura chiù di rùvulu,
ed eu n'abbampu comu cosunùvulu.

Although I did not attempt duplicate the rhyme scheme, because English is poor in feminine rhymes, I felt it necessary to raise the level of difficulty in my translation, and I chose an unusual but manageable rhyme scheme: AAABBBCC, which mimics the Sicilian *àniu, iniu* with the English *ine,* and *ane:*

The steward's lovely lass far whom l pine,
the one who's mistress of this heart of mine,
stings me as though she were a porcupine,
giving me fever, driving me insane.
She stuck a worm inside my sorry brain
which makes me think I've reached the last domain.
Alas, she s even harder than an oak
and l am just consumed like burning coke.

The parodic element underscored by the feminine rhyme is present in the English version in the too facile rhyme of£ *"pine"* with *"mine"* in which the inversion, *this heart of mine* signals on purpose the peasant-poet's inexperience and lack of sophistication. Naturally, translators know that perfect equivalence, intended as synonymity, cannot be achieved.[9]

What are some specific problems posed by translating from the Sicilian? I think the problems are basically the same as those encountered in translating from any Romance language. Generally speaking, linguists recognize two main sources of difficulties in translation: those that arise from the inevitable linguistic differences between the source language and the target language and those that arise from the cultural differences that exist between the two.[10] The distinction is not quite so clear cut, far as Lotman said: *"No language can exist unless it is steeped in the context of culture; and no culture can exist which does not have at its center, the structure of a natural language".11* Naturally, at this level, even translating such words as *butter* into another language poses almost insurmountable problems. In fact, *butter* and the Italian *burro* are not exactly equivalent. In Italy *burro* is used differently, carries different connotations and even looks and tastes differently.[12]

For the sake of brevity, I will begin with a few problems of a linguistic nature, that is, with problems arising from the different structures of Sicilian and English. In my translation of Meli's *Favuli morali,* published in 1988, a number of linguistic structures posed serious difficulties and challenged what little ingenuity I possess. The difficulties were also magnified by my choice to translate the fables with the same rhyme scheme as the Sicilian.[13] In addition, there were specific problems of a different nature. One example will be sufficient to make the point. In the third fable of the collection, "L'Aquila e lu Reiddu," Meli plays with the word *Reiddu,* the name of a tiny bird, common in Sicily. In English, this little bird is known as a kinglet. The fable relates how, having to elect a new king, birds decided to test the candidates' intelligence and qualities. Eagles, being the most powerful, pushed for a test of strength and it was agreed that the new king would be the bird that flew the highest. Naturally, the eagle flew higher than all other birds and thinking it had won the test, came down to earth to claim victory. But without the eagle's knowledge, a tiny kinglet had stowed away on top of the eagle's head, and technically had flown highest. Thus the kinglet was declared the winner, far, as the birds said, talent and intelligence should be prized above brute strength in a civilized society:

Chist'aquila a li stiddi sinni va,
e 'n vidennusi oceddi a lu so latu,
ritorna gluriusa e dici: "Olà!
sù Re, pirchì chiù in aùtu aju vulatu";
m'addunannusi l'autri di chiddu
ch'aveva in testa, gridanu: "Re iddu!"

This eagle flew so high it reached the stars,
and when he saw there was no one abreast,
with pride he flew down saying: "There you are!
I'm now your King-Elect. I flew the highest!"
The others, noticing the bird-vedette
just pointed straight at him and cried: "King-let!"

Of course, the play on words between the actual name of the bird, *reiddu* and the *re iddu* which is equivalent to saying *he is the king, not you!* is lost. I

An original illustration of Don Chisciotti practicing his fighting skills on Sanciu Panza by Beppe Vesco. From G. Meli, *Don Chisciotti and Sanciu Panza,* (New York: Legas 2003).

had to resort to a play of a different nature between "King-Elect" and "Kinglet" which offers a less demonstrative image but which retains some of the playfulness of the verbal game.

Less serious problems were posed by Meli's fondness for coining epithets in Sicilian by combining nouns and one or two suffixes, as in *armalunazzu,* which is a combination of *armali,* (animal) *uni,* the suffix for *large* and *azzu,* the pejorative suffix for *ugly* or *dumb.* Since English does not have the same structural system of accretion, various combinations of adjectives and nouns render the Sicilian fairly accurately. *Armalunazzu* became in my version *You big dumb ox!* Similar problems were posed by a series of names invented by Meli for a group of devils. In Canto IX, a magician called a council of devils to advise him on the best way to seduce women. The names that Meli gave to his devils obviously were intended as humorous. At times, they are simple strings of echoing sounds, such as *Ciciamiciacia,* and in this case I let the sound be my guide as well, transcribing the names phonetically as *Chèecha-meechàcha;* in other cases, the names were a combination of meaning- of phonemes, and here I translated them: *Carrittigghiu* became *Little Cart; Smargiazzu, Loud Mouth; Tizzuni, Burned-out-Log; Vurpigghiuni, Great Sly Fox; Catapocchiu* and *Pisca a Funnu* became respectively *Gotchatite* and *Goflyakite,* to accommodate the need of the rhyme.

In the same canto, Meli invented other names of knights with parodic intents. The names were meant to convey nobility and a certain chivalric pomposity to impress Don Chisciotti: *Scumpiu Pimpannacchiu* which became *Scabby Pimpernel; Sbru/ / a-Simula* was rendered with *Puffin Bran;* and *Lu Gran Caddozzu di la Transilvania* which was rendered with *The Noble Cheez o/ Transylvania.*

As regards difficulties arising out of culturally-determined differences between Sicilian and English, the list is endless. I will give only a few of the most troublesome cases from the *Don Chisciotti and Sanciu Panza* and tram the *Favuli morali.* At the end of Canto I, Don Chisciotti sees fires in the ears of Ronzinanti and Sanciu's donkey and, convinced that the animals are actually harboring witches in their bodies, he-heroically strikes at them, killing the animals as well. When Sanciu saw his dead donkey the next morning and was told that it had been a witch, He was torn between compassion for his dead "friend" and anger for having been betrayed by the hypocritical donkey, and he exclaimed in frustration:

"Parivi un coddu tortu, un Marabbutu!
E tu eri bonu, lu beccu curnutu?"

The problems here .are many. To begin with, the Sicilian expression «coddu tortu» signifies a hypocritical being, someone who is crooked, devious in nature, not straightforward. The noun *Marabbutu* refers to a Mohammedan holy man who is also regarded as insincere and crafty. Translating the first line literally, *You seemed to be a crooked neck, a Marabout,* simply would not do, far *crooked neck* in English does not suggest hypocrisy. At best, it might suggest a birth defect! And the noun *Marabout* would mean exactly the opposite of the Sicilian. In fact, the *Living Webster Encyclopedic Dictionary o/ the English Language* defines *Marabout* as a Mohammedan holy man, honored, and revered, holding great influence in religious and secular affairs. Contrary to what the term means in Sicilian, *Marabout* carries positive connotations in English. After several different versions, the two lines were rendered with:

You were a Pharisee, a hypocrite!
A worthy ass, indeed! A dumb misfit!»

The substitution of *Pharisee* far *Marabout* seemed perfectly legitimate because it means for an American of today what the term *Marabout* meant far the Sicilian of the 18th century. Another example of what Catford would designate as culturally untranslatable comes to mid when Meli uses the expression *liccannusi la sarda.*[14] In the context, Meli was arguing that a smart father who wanted to see his patrimony grow should leave it to a son who will increase it by living frugally and making every penny count. The line in question is: E *l'accrisci liccannusi la sarda.* Obviously, contemporary Americans would find *licking a sardine* a strange behavior, if not a distasteful one. In Sicily, however, where sardines are plentiful and cheap, they used to be considered staple for the poor. Therefore, eating sardines, or better, licking them, which conveys the idea of making it feed many mouths, came to mean, *to live frugally, to make little go a long way,* etc... Thus the line was translated with the following:

... to guard and to increase
by living on plain bread and goatherd's cheese.

In Canto IX, the magician to whom I referred earlier, addressed his audience, to ask them advice on how to seduce women. When he finished his harangue, the hall began buzzing with the devils' comments and Meli's adds with his typical sly humor:

Dissi e un oscuru ciarmuliu s'intisi
'ntra tutta d'Accademia curnuta».

Meli, of course, was playing with the double meaning of *curnutu.* On the one hand he was referring to the normal attribute ascribed to devils, that is, the fact that they have horns; on the other, he was underlining the fact that devils are *sly, mean,* and *wretched.* The comic effect, however, is provided by a third and most common meaning of *curnutu,* that is, *cuckold,* even though technically it could not be applied to devils because they have no wives. The two lines were rendered with:

He spoke and a dark whispering was heard
to rise among that horned Academy.

Instead of *horned* I had toyed with *horny,* whose primary meaning is today *eager far a sexual encounter,* but I had to abandon it because the stress would have fallen on the wrong syllable and because it would have added something that was not in the spirit of Meli's line. The various meanings of *curnutu* had to be given in a note.

Another example of *cultural untranslatability:* Meli refers to a Sicilian delicacy known as *sfingi* which consists of a smalI semicircle of thin dough filled with a number of ingredients *(ricotta,* usualIy) which is deep- fried and covered with sugar afterwards. The two lines in question somewhat equivalent to the Christian *dictum, he who is without sin, let him cast the first stone!* are

Illustration from the *Don Chisciotti and Sanciu Panza* by Beppe Vesco

"ma la quaddara ch'a fattu li sfingi
po' diri a la padedda: tu mi tinci?"

and they were rendered with

But can the skillet where the fish was fried
of greaseness the pan accuse and chide?

I will mention one other type of difficulty encountered by all inexperienced translators, which is what I was when I began translating Meli's *Origini di lu munu.*[15] I am referring to the trap set by *faux amis,* by words, that is, derived from the same root which have evolved differently in the two cultures, and which mean different things in the two languages. We already saw two such words in *Marabbutu* and Marabout. The list is endless and the problem extremely serious and challenging to all translators, even the most experienced ones. This book deals especially with this problems and will be very helpful to any would be translator in avoiding the trap. The examples I will provide here could be multiplied endlessly. I will start with a few examples from the Don Chisciotti and Sanciu Panza: When Don Chisciotti died, Sanciu carved the following inscription on his tomb stone:

La cinniri ch'è sutta sta balata
fu spogghia d'un eroi di desideriu».

My first rendition was:

The dust that lies beneath this slab of stone
is what remains of a hero of desire.»

of course, in Sicilian un *eroi di desideriu* refers to Don Chisciotti's yearning to be a hero, in his imagination. My first version made Don Chisciotti appear as a hero in whom sexual desire had heroic proportions! The second line, therefore, was changed to read:

is what remains of one who would be hero.»

In Canto VI, frustrated by his difficult and harsh life, Sanciu, complained:

ma la mia vita e la mia morti foru
o cucini carnali oppuru soru.

My first version of the couplet had been:

My life and death, however, must have been
either two sisters or just carnal kin.

It took several readings to make me realize that I had transformed an innocent relationship between first cousins or blood relatives *(cucini carnali)* into some kind of incestuous affair. The second line was changed to read: "either two sisters, or just kith and kin".

Needless to say, it is not unlikely that many more such cases will be discovered by sharp-eyed critics or by me. Translators are notoriously critical of one another and of themselves. That's why describing one's translation runs the risk o£ becoming a confession of sins, minor and major, committed knowingly and unknowingly. In conclusion, translating poetry is, as Dryden said, an act of sympathy. In my own case, I think it was something more than that. I felt like an advocate pleading a special case: Giovanni Meli's poetry as the embodiment of the Sicilian soul. My work is done. Let now the jury's verdict decide whether my pleading has been successful.

Notes

1. See the conclusion of S. Bassnett-McGuire's book *Translation Studies,* London and New York, Methuen, 1980, for a brief and illuminating look at the state of the art.
2. I. Fonagy, *Il traduttore e il problema degli enunciati legati,* in *Processi traduttivi: teorie, ed applicazioni,* Atti del Seminario su *La traduzione,* Brescia, 19-20 novembre 1981, Brescia, Editrice La Scuola, 1982, p. 143.
3. Bassnett-McGuire, *op. cit.,* p. 37.
4. The *Don Chisciotti e Sanciu Panza* was written between 1785 and 1787. lt was published in 1787. Translating with meter and with rhyme is like entering into a double bondage, as A. Lefevere said in his *Translating Poetry, Seven Strategies and a Blueprint,* Amsterdam, Van Gorcum, 1975. Naturally, a greater mastery of the technical aspects of the craft will allow the translator more freedom and flexibility in translating.
5. For an analysis of Giovanni Meli's poetic language, see S. Santangelo, *La lingua del Meli,* Palermo, Palumbo, 1941, and G. Santangelo's introduction to Meli's *Opere,* Milano, Rizzoli, 1968. See also the introduction to my translation of the *Don Chisciotti e Sanciu Panza.*
6. F. Petrarca, *Canzoniere,* Canzone 207, 65.
7. Ivi, Sonnet VII.
8. See P. Possiedi and G. Cipolla, "Ruzante's Petrarchan Canzoni'; a paper read at the Renaissance Venice Symposium, Hofstra University, 1980. Using the technique of the peasant- turned-poet, Ruzante translated several Petrarchan canzoni into Pavan dialect, rendering unrecognizable such famous poems as *Chiare, fresche e dolci acque* (Canzone 23) and *Quando il soave mio fido conforto* (Canzone 359), until we chanced to discover their derivative nature.
9. The problem of equivalence has been studied tram many perspectives. See the interesting discussion of it in A. Popovics, *A Dictionary for the Analysis of Literary Translation,* Edmonton, Alberta, University of Alberta, 1976; and E. Nida and Ch.R. Taber, *The Theory and Practice of Translation,* Leiden, E.J. Brill, 1982.
10. J .C. Catford, in his *Linguistic Theory of Translation: an Essay on Applied Linguistics,* London, Oxford University Press, 1965, distinguished two types of untranslatability: linguistic and cultural. See Bassnett-McGuire's refutation of some of Catford's distinctions in *Translation Studies,* p. 32.
11. J. Lotman and B.A. Uspensky, «On the Semiotic Mechanism of Culture», in *New Literary History,* IX(2), 1978, pp. 211-32.
12. Personally I subscribe to Georges Mounin's well taken position that translation is a dialectic process that can be accomplished and, in fact, is accomplished as a matter of routine:

Translation may always start with the clearest situation, the most concrete messages, the most elementary universals. But as it involves che consideration of a language in its entirety, together with its most subjective messages, through an examination of common situations and a multiplication of contacts that need clarifying, then there is no doubt that communication through translation can never be completely finished, which also demonstrates that it is never wholly impossible either, *Les problèmes théoriques de la traduction,* Paris, Gallimard, 1963, p. 279.

13. The difficulties with trying to maintain the same meter and rhyme scheme of the Source Language text are well known. In the translation of the *Favuli morali,* 89 verse fables written in a variety of meters, ranging from hendecasyllabic verse to septenaries, and rhyme schemes that include even "terza rima", I felt that rhyming was absolutely essential to retain the flavor of the originals.

15, See Giovanni Meli, *The Origin of the World,* translated into English verse, with an Introduction and Notes by G. Cipolla, New York, Arba Sicula, 1985.

Pirandello's Poetics of the Labyrinth

At a press conference held in Buenos Aires, as a reply to a jour nalist who had enquired about the genesis of his play *Così è (se vi pare)*, Luigi Pirandello said what follows:

> "Ecco un sogno: vidi in esso un cortile profondo e senza uscita e da questa immagine paurosa nacque il *Così è (se vi pare)*".
>
> "I had a dream: and in it I saw a deep courtyard without an exit and from this frightening image the *It is so (if you think so)* was born."

This statement is interesting for several reasons, but primarily for what it reveals about the relationship between the unconscious and the creative act in Pirandello. Let us briefly consider the remembrance of this oneiric event. Evidently it was a nightmare, recalled long after it had occurred, which had sunk deep roots in the writer's unconscious. Inasmuch as a considerable amount of emotion accompanied the revisiting of the dream, its nightmarish character was still present. The sense of fear that accompanied the vision of the courtyard has not vanished completely. The courtyard remained "frightening" for two essential reasons: its depth, which can be interpreted both as an extension from a high place to a low place that is, in the direction of the center, the crypt where the mysteries are, the unconscious and an absence of light, as a place of darkness and of abyssal void; the other disquieting and anguish-causing aspect is the absence of a way out of the courtyard.

It would be interesting to make a brief comparison between the description of the dream and a statement of a similar nature, but very different in reality, made on the same subject. I am referring to a sentence which describes his state of mind at the time of writing of *Così è (se vi pare)* written by Pirandello to his son Stefano on the 17th of April 1916:

> "Scavo, scavo. . . Mi sono ridotto in un pozzo da cui non riesco a trarmi fuori. Del resto perché trarmene? Ora più che mai la vita mi sembra una buffa e pazza fantasmagoria.[2]
>
> "I keep on digging. . . and I have backed myself into a well from which I cannot get out. On the other hand, why try to get out? Now

Pirandello standing in front of the temple of Concordia in Agrigento.

more than ever, life seems to me a funny and mad phantasmagoria."

It's evident that the dream referred to in Buenos Aires was the revision of the prevailing state of mind expressed in the letter. The image of the deep courtyard and of the well without an exit are identical from a psychological point of view. There is, however, a substantial difference between the two images that can furnish us with some interesting data to help us arrive at a definition of Pirandello's poetics. While in the second statement the answer to the Argentinian journalist Pirandello had put some distance between himself and the image, in the image of the well, he is still involved in the anguish-causing and uncertain action of digging. When looking at the deep courtyard Pirandello is already a humoristic writer, for, as we know from the essay on *Umorismo*, the distinguishing feature of this manner of writing concerns the position of the writer. A writer who is truly a humorist, is always outside the field of observation.

In remembering the courtyard, Pirandello made use of his famous inverted binoculars, moving the image away from him and reducing its psychological weight.[3] With the image of the well, however, he was describing a precise historical moment, not yet viewed through his "Philosophy of distance," that is, through that typical instrument of humor that interprets according to a corrected and distanced perspective. Pirandello was not a spectator, but an actor, directly involved in the desperate act of finding a way out. Indeed, one might even say that, like Dante's Lucifer who, by freezing the waters of Cocytus with the beating of his wings, was at once victim and instrument of his own punishment, Pirandello was a victim of his own cognitive action. With his continuous and feverish searching, he had dug his way into a well without an exit. It was his cognitive action that confined him to the infernal regions where certainty did not exist, where darkness reigned supreme. The Pirandellian striving was not directed towards the heavens, that is, towards a religious presence, but towards the depths of the being, toward the black darkness of the unconscious where instead of finding some illumination, the glimmer of some ray of clarity, he found a darkness ever more dense and impenetrable. Instead of finding a torch with which to restore faith in the existence of truth, he found the confirmation that life was nothing but a funny and mad phantasmagoria, a clowning, a puppet show, ("pupazzata ") or to say it with words dear to the great Giovanni Meli, whom Pirandello admired as a humorist, "una trizziata eterna" (an eternal joke.)[4] The image of the well was, therefore, not a casual remembrance, an insignificant detail, but it represented a vital aspect of his philosophical and artistic attitude, as we shall see momentarily. I would like to consider here two statements which I consider important for the discussion at hand: the first one goes back to 1886, when Pirandello was 20 years old, and the second was uttered in 1936, the year of Pirandello's death. The first one makes it abundantly clear that the well and the courtyard represent for him an image of the unconscious which must be explored through meditation:

> "La meditazione è l'abisso nero, popolato di foschi fantasmi, custodito dallo sconforto disperato. Un raggio di sole non vi penetra mai e il desiderio di averlo ti sprofonda sempre nelle tenebre dense (. . .) E' una sete inestinguibile, un furore ostinato, ma il nero ti abbevera, la immensità silenziosa ti agghiaccia."[5]
>
> "Meditation is the dark abyss, peopled by sombre ghosts, guarded by a desperate discouragement. A ray of light never penetrates into it and the yearning to have it drives you into the dense darkness (. . .) It is an inextinguishable thirst, an obstinate fury, but the darkness sates your thirst, the silent immensity freezes you." (my translation)

The second quotation is not a description of the effects that the contact with the unconscious produces in Pirandello, but rather the statement of a program not only for the future, but more precisely for the past: a kind of artistic testament written at the point of death. Again Pirandello recalls the dark abyss:

> "Nietzsche diceva che i Greci alzavano bianche statue contro il nero abisso per nasconderlo. Io le scrollo, invece, per rivelarlo." [6]
>
> "Nietzsche said that the Greeks raised white statues against the black abyss in order to hide it. On the contrary, I shake them to reveal it."

Pirandello's literary production had as an objective the razing of these Nietzschean white statues: the myths, the illusory constructions that men use in order to go on living Pirandellian humor is nothing other than this continuous razing of the white statues, intended to destroy them, and with them, the illusory constructions, and to show the black abyss in its satisfying and paralyzing essence. The descent into hell, the continuous revisiting of the unconscious is the foundation of the Pirandellian impasse. The contact with the unconscious gives Pirandello a breath of life, as water does to a thirsty and dry plant, but the immense silence, that is, his inability to channel the just received vitality in other directions, that is, in alternative ways of living, paralyzes him, freezes him into a situation that is stagnant, immobile, in fact, without exit. The only possible activity seems to be moving in the hope of finding a glimmer of light and finding oneself ever more deeply immersed into the dense darkness. In this universe without light, Pirandello has only one consolation: Art:

> "Fra tante apparenze, fra tanti sogni ed illusioni che formano il labirinto della vita, una ve n'è che riscatta con pregi suoi propri tutti i difetti delle altre cose: l'arte."[7]
>
> "Among so many appearances, among so many dreams and illusions which form the labyrinth of life, there is one which makes up with its own worth for the defects of the other things: Art."

Going back now to the images of the courtyard and the well with which I began, it seems to me that a metaphor of Pirandellian poetics can be discerned in the arc that goes from the writing of the letter to his son and the memory of the nightmare, a metaphor that can be defined in an inevitably reductive and preliminary way as a journey which departing from a perturbing vision, loses its obsessive character as it is transformed into art. The act of writing represents a unique way of exorcizing the traumatizing and anguish-causing visions that rise out of Pirandello's unconscious.

At this point, let us see how this transformation of oneiric materials into artistic constructions occurs. The image that I have avoided so far and which represents the Pirandellian impasse in an emblematic way is that of the labyrinth. The deep courtyard, the well without an exit, the dark abyss, the search for a way out, entanglements and imprisonment, as well as the contact with the "numinosum" are all componential elements of the labyrinth, variations on a ground theme, as we have already seen.[8] We could talk at length about the appropriateness of this image for the

Pirandellian opus, but for the moment, I will suggest that the play *Così è (se vi pare)* born out of a labyrinthine vision, is constructed in accordance with a labyrinthine structure.[9] In other words, Pirandello, following his labyrinthine vision, built a true labyrinth, going out of it to look at it from the outside to see how it was constructed and to reduce the paralyzing psychological resonance.

The plot of *Così è (se vi pare)* "è una gran diavoleria" (a great piece of devilry) according to Pirandello himself.[10] In order to understand that we are dealing with a structure constructed on paper through elaborate and extremely lucid plans, it will be necessary to review the two versions of the truth on which the drama hinges. As we know, the three acts are built around the attempts by a group of bourgeois people to discover the identity of a person: the wife of a bureaucrat who recently arrived to town, a certain Mr. Ponza, accompanied by a little old woman named Frola, his mother-in-law. The play revolves around the people's attempt to discover if Mr. Ponza's wife is Mrs. Frola's daughter, as she maintains, or whether she is the bureaucrat's second wife, as he claims. Mrs. Frola says that her son-in-law with his violent and excessive love had threatened the health of his young and fragile wife so much that she, together with her doctors, had been forced to take her from him and put her in a clinic to recover. Mr. Ponza believed that his wife had died, and when she was brought back to him once again in good health, he insisted that his wife was dead. Finally his doctors and friends convinced him to accept her by having a second marriage performed. Mrs. Frola, however, is convinced that her son-in-law understood that his second wife is in reality one and the same person, but being very passionate and egotistical, wants his wife's love all for himself. He does not allow the mother-in-law to have a close relationship with his wife, insisting that mother and daughter talk to each other from far away. Furthermore, afraid that he might lose her again, Mr. Ponza keeps his wife locked up, forcing her to act as though she were somebody else, and forcing his mother-in-law to feign madness.

Mr. Ponza, on the other hand, offers a different and opposing version of the truth. He maintains that Mrs. Frola's daughter died four years before and that sorrow for her death had driven Mrs. Frola insane. Two years afterwards, having remarried, Mr. Ponza passed before Mr. Frola's house and was seen by her in the company of his new wife. Mrs. Frola imagined she was seeing her daughter alive and with this thought in mind immediately regained her health. She behaved in a rational and sane way. The only clue to her former madness was that she would not accept her daughter's death. Therefore, in order to keep her behaving sanely, Mr. Ponza was forced to take many precautions, one of which was keeping his mother-in-law from coming too close to his wife. The old woman could discover that the wife was not her daughter precipitating another crisis and madness. Thus, what was regarded as an act of egotism by Mrs. Frola, is, in Mr. Ponza's version, an act of caring and generosity.

I have left out other aspects of the two versions, but even in this shortened form it is clear that Pirandello had to study the two versions very carefully. It order to reach his goal, he had to construct two perfectly parallel and yet opposite versions of the same story: an emblematic humoristic construction.

The two versions can be represented with a graph in the shape of a dovetail, so that the two interpretations of reality are wedged into each other, occupying a perfectly parallel space but without ever touching. The story that Mrs. Frola related is nothing more than a tracing of Mr. Ponza's, and viceversa. If we place on a page a series of dovetails we would obtain a drawing in the form of a zigzag or a labyrinth. As we know, one of the methods of constructing labyrinths is to place squares or rectangles within other squares or rectangles and then proceed to erase parts of the lines of the corridors. We can also substitute another type of labyrinth, shaped like a spiral to this right-angled labyrinth, and imagine its sinuous lines as the two versions of the story. In a labyrinth that has one center which consequently can be reduced to a spiral, two persons walking in two different corridors can meet only in the center.

The drama of *Così e (se vi pare)* represents a complete circuit for every act: a vain attempt to arrive at the truth The three acts of the play represent in reality, three labyrinths which possess, like all mazes, the capacity to deceive the seekers into believing that they are near the center when in fact they are far away. Each intervention of the two characters, which has the temporary effect of convincing the curious bourgeois of accepting one of the versions as true, corresponds to an illusory approaching of the objective. Pirandello, like a humoristic Ariadne, leads the curious bourgeois, and the spectators as well, through the uncertain maze, razing as he goes the white statues of certainty to show the black abyss of relativity. That we are dealing with a labyrinthine procedure is self-evident. Plato, in his *Eutidemo* had described the essence of this labyrinth:

> "We arrived to the kingly art. We were trying to see if this art were capable of producing happiness. But at this point we found ourselves as in a labyrinth, and when we thought we had reached our goal, when the circuit had been completed, we found ourselves again, as we

had been at the beginning of our investigation as far away from the conclusion, exactly as when we had begun to seek."[11]

Plato's definition, a fitting and appropriate description of the structure of the Pirandellian drama, focuses upon an important component of the humoristic attitude. Plato had not approached the kingly art with any preconception or bias. Pirandello, instead began his investigation to demonstrate an idea of his, that there are no absolute truths, and that only the black abyss exists which reflects upon itself as in a mirror.

The labyrinth is not the only structure on which *Così è (se vi pare)* is built, but represents a metaphor of Pirandellian poetics. The labyrinth is the perfect oxymoron which opposes the chaos of its tortuous and dark corridors to the geometric precision of its external forms; in the precision of its external order it embraces being, form and the tendency to become fixed; in its internal confusion, it embraces the constant becoming, the uninterrupted flowing of life. To the clarity of its external form, already identified in the lucid and unexceptionable intellectual construction of the plot, Pirandello counterposes the chaos of relativity; the clear structure of the drama is made to convey uncertainty and existential doubts.

The character who represents the authorial voice, the "raisonneur," the philosopher Laudisi, plays an important role which will permit us to widen our perspective on Pirandello's art. As we know, Laudisi tries to convince the characters that their insistence in discovering the truth at all costs is cruel and useless. Unable to do so, Laudisi underscores the others' failures by laughing in amusement and desperation. At the end of each act, the curtain falls on Laudisi's laughter, and this underlines the play's circularity. Laudisi is, in fact, reminiscent of another emblematic laughing figure that represents an essential part of Pirandellian poetics. I am referring to a figure described by Pirandello at the beginning of the volume of short stones *Erma Bifronte*:

> "Io vedo qualcosa come un labirinto, nel quale la nostra anima vaga per interminabili vie che si intersecano, e dal quale essa non riesce a trovare una via d'uscita. E in questo labirinto, io vedo un'erma bifronte la quale da una faccia ride e dall'altra piange, anzi la faccia che ride, ride dell'altra che piange." [12]
>
> "I see something like a labyrinth in which our soul wanders through interminable streets which cross one another, and from which she is never able to find a way out. And in this labyrinth, I see a two-faced Hermes who laughs from one face and weeps from the other, in

fact the face that's laughing is laughing at the weeping face."

The Janus figure is the emblem of Pirandellian humor. Laudisi is its dramatic expression. Laudisi, doomed to uncertainty in a labyrinthine space, laughs and cries about his own destiny. Before the darkness, his laughter represents the desperation and the nostalgia of the light, the desire to "solve" the knots of the universe and the condemnation to fail. Laudisi is the god of the labyrinth, but, at the same time, he is one of its victims. In this context, the scene in front of the mirror in which we witness the disintegration of his personality into the many different Laudisi's of which it is composed, is symptomatic of the procedure I am describing.

Given the labyrinth as the existential space in which the Pirandellian characters move, the mirror could not have been absent. The mirror reflects the psychological significance of the original myth which saw Theseus in mortal combat against the Minotaur. The two beings were sons of the same father. The god Poseidon showed himself to Pasiphae as a beautiful white bull and from their union the Minotaur was born. The Athenian hero, in addition to being the son of king Aegeus, also claimed the spiritual paternity of the god of the sea. The struggle within the labyrinth was a duel between brothers, and therefore, between two aspects of the same individual, between consciousness and the unconscious, between a man and his image reflected in a looking glass. That's why mirrors were often placed at the center of the mazes: they represent the duel with the Other.[13]

Pirandello once again reveals himself as a destroyer of myths. If in the original myth the labyrinth had been a place of initiation that had allowed Theseus to assimilate the psychic forces of the Minotaur, becoming a man, a being changed by the labyrinthine experience, in the Pirandellian context, the labyrinth and the mirror which represents it embody elements that are dispersive and destructive. The Pirandellian character who confronts himself with the image reflected in a mirror begins to doubt his own identity, and loses the battle with the Other in a bewildering multiplication of perspectives and polyvalent images.

Looking at himself in the mirror, Laudisi feels transported by the endless flux of becoming. And here we could introduce a long parenthesis to demonstrate how emblematic a situation this is, but it will be sufficient to refer to the novel *Uno, nessuno e centomila*, whose protagonist is an almost pathological embodiment of the Pirandellian tendency to see the world as a place of constriction in which the only movement possible is circular. It is not a coincidence that the labyrinthine journey of Vitangelo Moscarda begins before a mirror. Like Laudisi, who recognizes only a part of himself in the reflected image, Moscarda begins to lose his own consistency as a unique being in a polyperspective game of identity which culminates with the total dissolution of his ego. Moscarda annihilates himself completely, sacrificing his being, understood as a thinking individuality, in favor of a pantheistic happiness which measures itself to the beat of the universe. And it certainly is not another coincidence that the chapter in which the initial splitting of the personality occurs is entitled "Il filo di Arianna," (" Ariadne's Thread "). If in the original myth that thread had brought Theseus to a joining of the forces of the ego and the unconscious, and had made it possible for him to become a new man, in the Pirandellian context, Ariadne is one of those white statues that the author feels he must raze to the ground to show the void behind it. Ariadne does not lead to illumination, nor to the union with the vital center of the being, but to dispersion and to non-being.

Most Pirandellian characters, from Mattia Pascal to Laudisi, from Henry IV to Moscarda, move against such a background. Driven by the desperate need to find a way out of problematic situations, his characters enter one avenue after another until, like rats in a maze, they go insane or let themselves die. The labyrinth-anthill, whose exit has been plugged-up like a game by a cruel child, is their inalterable condition.

Pirandello's characters, however, do not become lost in labyrinthine castles, or in enormous libraries, as happens for Kafkian and Borgesian characters, not could it be said that the physical environment in which he places them have a labyrinthine nature, as in the case, for example, in Robbe-Grillet's labyrinth-city in the novel *Dans le labyrinthe.* The labyrinth in which Pirandello's characters are immersed is rather a metaphor of the chaos in the world, of the existential prison of modern man, and of the dichotomy between the need of the characters for absolute coherence in a world that presents itself as absolutely incoherent.

The use of the image in Pirandello has an historical value inasmuch as it represents the break with the Positivism of the preceding generations. Ours is the century of the labyrinth. Modern man, as Nietzsche announced, is a labyrinth. While this is not the place to review the history of the image, we can say that it has flourished in three epochs: the Fourteenth, Seventeenth and the Twentieth centuries, and that its preoccupation of modern man is due primarily to the reaction against Positivism. When the last euphoric beliefs of Positivism crumbled, and the last illusion of Rationalism exposed, when Faith died, twentieth century man found himself impotent, surrounded by mystery, and without God. The labyrinth became an image of the shiftless wanderings of modern man.[14]

I don't think it is a coincidence that the labyrinth occupies such an important role in the works of the major opponents of Positivism in Italy: Gabriele D'Annunzio and Luigi Pirandello. The tendency towards the labyrinth one of the few points of contact between these two writers reflects different perspectives, however. While for D'Annunzio the labyrinth is an emblem of the difficulties that his Superman faces and overcomes, for Pirandello, who did not yield to the dictates of Idealism, it is one more proof of the relativity of truth and of the inconsistency of being. Pirandello does not share D'Annunzio's "heroic" attitude; the labyrinth interests him as an image which fits well with his pessimistic and antiheroic conception of the world.[15]

It is not surprising that Pirandello's preoccupation with this image began with his debut as a young poet. Gosta Anderson in his *Arte e teoria: studi sulla poetica del giovane Pirandello*, pointed out that:

> "Dissidio interno, pensieri slegati, disgregarnento, discordia di voci, eterno labirinto, sciocche illusioni sono alcune parole centrali con le quali il P. in questi anni (1890—1900) cerca di interpretare una sua intima esperienza di tormento, che egli vede riflessa nei suoi contemporanei."[16]
>
> "Internal struggle, loose thoughts, disintegration, discordant voices, eternal labyrinths, silly illusions are a few central words with which Pirandello in these years (1890-1900) attempts to interpret his own intimate experience of torment which he sees reflected in his contemporaries."

Leaving aside the poems of *Mal giocondo* and *Pasqua di Gea*, which contain numerous labyrinthine images, we can say that Pirandello's preoccupation with the image manifests itself in a series of poems he had intended to publish under the heading of *The Labyrinth*. The volume was supposed to contain six chapters, divided by an "Intermezzo." The poems which were to be included in the volume were published separately in newspapers and magazines and appear now in Volume VI of his *Opere* as "Poesie varie".[17] It is interesting to note that the poems Pirandello himself defined as "labyrinthine" do not contain themes that are different from those of the poems found in other collections. These poems hinge on the image of the "way," which I studied elsewhere as a labyrinthine image, on the impossibility of escaping from the entanglements of life, on the sense of being lost in the world, and of not knowing where to go.[18]

Typically, Pirandello expresses the same concerns in some in the essays written at about the same time. Many phrases of the essay "Arte e coscienza d'oggi" (1893), reappear almost *verbatim*, with the addition of an occasional rhyme, in the poem "La via" published two years later:

> "Simuliamo con una ceria boria discreta indifferenza per tutto ciò che non sappiamo, e che pure in fondo vorremmo sapere, e ci sentiamo come smarriti, anzi sperduti in un cieco e immenso labirinto circondato tutt'intorno da un mistero impenetrabile. Di vie ce ne sono tante, quale sarà la vera? Va di qua e di la la gente in fretta, e ognuno ha l'aria di capirci qualcosa: tanto che certe volte qualcuno di noi si arresta colpito da un grave dubbio e si domanda: Ch'io sia solo a non capire nulla?" [19]
>
> "We simulate with a certain haughtiness a discrete indifference for everything we do not know, and that we really would like to know, and we feel bewildered, indeed, lost in a blind and immense labyrinth surrounded all around by an impenetrable mystery. There are so many avenues, which is the right one? People hastily scurry from here to there in a hurry, and everybody seems to understand something about it: so much so that sometimes a few of us stop overcome by a grave doubt, and ask ourselves: could it be that I am the only one who does not understand anything?"

A similar pattern is present in the essay "Il momento." The references to the labyrinth as an underground tunnel in which man is condemned to wander endlessly return in the poem "Esame," published shortly afterward as well as in *II fu Mattia Pascal,* and in "Ciaula scopre la luna"[20]:

> "Lampi di saggezza pratica! Poi si ricade nel buio e nel silenzio, che noi ostinatamente ci affanniamo ad animare coi lumi del nostro ragionamento e col grido della nostra lotta. Ahimè, il grido resta senz'eco, e i lumi non trovan aria e si spengono, come fiaccole in profondi sotterranei. S'aggira ognuno sotto un vario inganno; e noi credendo di lottare contro gli altri, non ci accorgiamo di lottare contro noi stessi."[21]
>
> "Flashes of practical wisdom! Then we fall back into the darkness and silence which we obstinately try to bring to life with the torches of our reasoning and with the scream of our struggle. Alas, the scream remains without an echo, and the torches find no air and go out, like torches in deep tunnels. We all wander about deluded by a different

deceit; and believing we are fighting against others, do not notice that we are struggling against ourselves."

The fascination that this image exercised on Pirandello's imagination is reflected by the fact that it appeared in different contexts. In the poem "Romanzi" it referred to man's difficulty in reaching his objective; in "Allegre" and in the short story "La Patente," it referred to the sky which became an eternal mystery, a labyrinth in which man was condemned to get lost; the withering of faith, in the poem "Torna Gesù," causes the wandering in the darkness of the labyrinth. Even the future has Daedalic connotations inasmuch as it holds in store for him nothing more than:

"un'ombra vana
un inganno mutevole, una meta
che quanto più t'accosti, s'allontana . . .
donde non puoi far più ritorno mai." [22]

a vain shadow, .
a mutable trap, an objective
which moves away, as soon as you approach. . .
from which you can never return.

In the early poems and essays, the labyrinth is therefore an important component of the pessimistic vision to which Pirandello remained faithful even in the last years of his life.[23] The presence of the image in the essays, because it is born out of a reasoned and conscious judgment, reflects the philosophical attitude toward life that did not change much throughout his career. Therefore, the labyrinth, whose presence in the Pirandellian opus is massive, remained a constant point of reference, a guiding principle through which Pirandello articulated his art.

It is not really surprising to find it even in expressions which appear, at least on the surface, to have so little psychological significance as to be considered phatic. In the play *Quando si è qualcuno*, I found an interesting play on words which is a propos and instructive. Tito, the son of the protagonist without a name, refuses to call Delago by his proper name. The name was the pseudonym under which his father published a volume of poetry of enormous success, a fact of which the son was not aware. He insists on calling him Dedalo (Daedalus). When his sister points this out to him, "Ma facci caso!, Dici sempre Dedalo!" (Please, pay attention! You always call him Dedalo!) Tito replies that he does it on purpose.

Tito wants to express his disdain for Delago because he considers him a usurper of the fame that justly belongs to his father. The substitution of Dedalo for Delago is dictated by the obvious similarity between the two names and rises out of a desire to strike his father's adversary by doing violence to his name. Dedalo and Delago have nothing in common. The former is an archetypal figure of the genial architect, the latter is a lyric poet of the new generation. A parallel based on analogous situations, at least as far as Tito is concerned, must be excluded. At this point of the drama, he lacks the necessary data to formulate such a parallel. He, in fact, is not aware of the psychological problems besetting his father, and above all else, he does not know that Delago is the alter ego of the old poet. These two pieces of information are essential to establish an analogy between the old poet laureate and the new one.

The association between the two names occurs within Pirandello. We have here a case in which the playwright did not bother to justify it in the context of the character. If for Tito the association remains at a phonic level, for Pirandello it is valid also on the level of signification. As we know, the play contains obvious autobiographical resonance. Pirandello saw himself in the poet without a name who having reached success, considers himself a prisoner of the Form that he struggled so hard to attain. He is the great poet laureate whose words are sculpted in stone, who can no longer act freely and spontaneously. Everything he has written, as well as everything that others have said of him, has concretized around an inalterable image of him which denies him the freedom to be different. To escape from this spiritual death, the old poet writes a book of verses which reveals an unknown aspect of his personality, and publishes it under the pseudonym of Delago. The poet quickly becomes the idol of the new generation, the new voice of poetry. For the old poet, and for Pirandello, Delago is the symbol of the man who has succeeded in escaping from the entanglement of Form. The parallel that Tito could not have established, is made by Pirandello. It is no longer a case of a play on words based on their similarity, but also, and more significantly, a juxtaposition of analogous situations: Daedalus, in fact, was not only the genial architect who built the Cretan labyrinth, but he was the first, together with his son Icarus, to escape from its meandering pathways. And, he was the one who gave Ariadne the ball of thread which allowed Theseus to retrace his way out of the "inremeabilis error" after slaying the Minotaur. Daedalus was the conqueror of the labyrinth. Delago's victory against the labyrinthine fixity of Form is comparable to Daedalus' victory.

Another reference to Delago which precedes the point we have been discussing confirms that the labyrinth was active in the mind of the playwright. I am referring to the scene in which a group of admirers of the new idol goes looking for him at Pietro's house. Together with Natascia and Veroccia, Pietro does not want to reveal the true identity of Delago and does his best to confuse his interlocutors, as in the following exchange:

NATASCIA. E allora è qua. Cercatelo!
PIETRO. Eh, già nascosto, a mia insaputa!
VEROCCIA. (Guardando***) Come in un disegno per bambini! "Trovare Delago! "[24]
NATASCIA. Then he is here! Look for him!
PIETRO. Of course, hidden, without my knowledge!
VEROCCIA. (Looking at ***) Like a drawing for children! "Find Delago!"

The drawing to which Veronica refers is something we have all seen: a series of lines which intersect one another and which after a tortuous journey lead into the center where the treasure is located, in this case, "Delago." The drawing is obviously another labyrinth. The association between Delago and the labyrinth confirms that the reference to Daedalus was suggested by a "labyrinthine" interpretation of the problem of the old poet. It would be ridiculous to think that Pirandello, generally very careful in establishing textual correspondences, did not remember the two images. The fact that Pirandello saw Delago inside a labyrinth, albeit in a children's game, clearly coincides with the symbolic nature of the escape artist, underscored by the parallel with Daedalus. It may be said then that the playwright considered the plight of his old poet, and incidentally of himself, as an exitless labyrinth, confirmed by the conclusion of the play when the old poet rejects Delago and literally becomes a statue of himself.

In conclusion, it must be said that Pirandello's reconnoitering of the underground tunnels of life was an exploration conducted without the help of Ariadne, and therefore without development or illumination, but nearly always on the border of madness and suicide. Pirandello did what the late Italo Calvino proposed when in 1962, in "La sfida al labirinto" he stated that the best attitude to adopt in finding a way out of the labyrinth-literature was to attempt decode it, even though such an exercise might mean nothing more than going from one labyrinth into another .[25] Ariadne's crown of lights was always beyond Pirandello's reach. By writing labyrinths, however, he defended himself against their paralyzing influence. Writing was what saved him: "La vita o si scrive o si vive! "[26] Life is either written or lived. The labyrinth was his realm. It was not for naught that he identified himself as the son of chaos, born under the shade of a labyrinthine forest near Girgenti:

> "Io dunque sono figlio del caos, e non allegoricamente, ma in giusta misura, perché sono nato in una nostra campagna, che trovasi presso un intricato bosco, denominato in forma dialettale, Cavusu dagli abitanti di Girgenti." [27]
>
> "Therefore, I am a son of chaos, and not only in an allegorical sense, but in true measure because I was born in a property of ours, located near an entangled forest that the inhabitants of Girgenti call chaos in dialect."

NOTES

1. Quoted by Gaspare Giudice in "L'ambiguità dei *Sei personaggi in cerca d'autore,*" in Atti del congresso internazionale di studi pirandelliani ," Venezia, 1961, p. 396
2. Ibid.
3. I am referring, of course, to the manner with which Dr. Fileno, a character in "La tragedia di un personaggio," succeeds in alleviating, indeed, in eliminating unpleasant feelings and events of the moment by projecting into the past and reducing their psychological effect on him.
4. Pirandello knew the work of Giovanni Meli very well. See the chapter on "Pirandello: Don Quijote or Don Chisciotti?" in this volume. Originally published in *Quaderni d'italianistica*, vol. VI, 1, pp. 111-16.
5. "Lettere ai familiari," a cura di S. D'Amico, in *Terzo Programma*, 1961, no. 3.
6. G. Cavacchioli, "Introduzione a Pirandello, in *Termini*, 1936, pp. 22-3.
7. Quoted by Gino Cucchetti in "Assoluto e relativo in Pirandello," in *Atti del congresso internazionale di studi pirandelliani*, p. 361.
8. See my "A Psychological Interpretation of the Myth of Theseus," in *Labyrinth: Studies on an Archetype*, New York and Ottawa: Legas, 1987
9. The bibliography on the labyrinth is very large. See my *Labyrinth: Studies on an Archetype*, New York and Ottawa: Legas, 1987.
10. Gaspare Giudice, *Pirandello: a Biography*, translated by Alastair Hamilton, London: Oxford University Press, 1975, p. 110.
11. Paolo Santarcangeli, *Il libro dei labirinti*, Firenze: Vallecchi Editore, 1967, p. 118.
12. *Novelle per un anno*, Milano: Mondadori.
13. Santarcangeli, pp. 195-202.
14. The image of the labyrinth is part and parcel of the modern world. In literature, in art, in the cinema, in the theater, we are bombarded with labyrinthine images...For a study of the the labyrinth as symbol of mannerism in art and in literature, see the following two volumes by René Gustav Hocke: *Die Welt als Labyrinth: Manier und Manie in der Europaichen Kunst*, (Hamburg, 1957), and *Il manierismo nella letteratura*. (Milano: il Saggiatore, 1965).

15. For a study of the labyrinth in D'Annunzio see, Emerigo Giachery, *Variazione su un tema d'annunziano: Il labirinto*, (Roma: Fratelli Palombi,1964).
16. Stockholm: Almquist and Wiskell, 1966, p. 89.
17. We don't know why Pirandello did not publish the volume as he had intended. It's possible that he could not complete the project, already announced in *La zampogna* (1901) for financial and family problems (the failure of his father's sulphur mines, his wife's illness) or by other literary interests (the novels *L'esclusa, Il turno,* and *Il fu Mattia Pascal* were written from 1901 to 1904.)
18. See Chapter 2, "Labyrinthine Imagery in Petrarch" in my *Labyrinth: Studies on an Archetype*, New York and Ottawa: Legas, 1987
19. *Saggi. poesie e scritti vari*, p. 900.
20. The labyrinthine character of Mattia Pascal's experience is self evident. His life is a continuous attempt to escape from unbearable situations. Each escape proves to be illusory, until he is forced to admit that outside the entanglements of society there is the void. His is a circular journey, dotted with deviations dictated by circumstances. There are several references to the labyrinth and to labyrinthine imagery in *Il fu Mattia Pascal*, particularly in the protagonist's encounter with Anselmo Paleari, the expert on the world that is beyond this life. One example will suffice:
"Perché? Ma non possiamo comprendere la vita, se noi in qualche modo non ci spieghiamo la morte! Il criterio direttivo delle nostre azioni, il filo per uscire da questo labirinto, il lume, insomma signor Meis, il lume dovrà venirci di la, dalla morte. Col buio che ci fa? Buio? Buio per Lei! Provi ad accendervi una lampadina di fede con l'olio dell'anima. Se questa lampadina manca, noi ci aggiriamo qua, nella vita, come tanti ciechi con tutta la luce elettrica che abbiamo inventato." (Milano: Mondadori, 1969) p. 121.
"Why? But we can't understand life if we don't try to explain death. The guiding criterion of our action, the thread to escape from the labyrinth, the torch, Mr. Meis, the light will have to come to us from there, from death. With all the darkness that's there? Darkness? Darkness for you! Try to light a lamp of faith with the oil of the soul. If this lamp is lacking, we wander here in life like many blind men in spite of the electricity we invented."
The similarity between this passage and the passage from the essay "Esame" is self evident.
21. *Saggi*, p. 911.
22. Ibid.
23. Pirandello remained always faithful to his early intuitions. There are no sudden changes in his attitudes towards life and in his art. The themes contained in his early poetry continue to be important throughout his career.
24. (Milano: Oscar Mondadori, 1969), p. 29. 25. *Il Menabò*, no. 5, (1962), p. 95.
26. *Saggi*, p. 1298.

Pirandello: Don Quijote or Don Chisciotti?

In the last paragraph of Chapter V of his famous essay on *Umorismo* (1908), while analyzing the differences between so true a hero as El Cid and Cervantes' unlikely candidate Don Quijote, Luigi Pirandello suffered an interesting mental lapse (not entirely due to the haste with which the book was supposedly written), which has escaped the attention of the critics. Let us read the paragraph in question:

> Ma Don Quijote? Coraggio a tutta prova, animo nobilissimo, fiamma di fede; ma quel coraggio non gli frutta che volgari bastonate; quella nobiltà d' animo è una follia; quella fiamma di fede è un misero stoppaccio che egli si ostina a tenere acceso, povero pallone mal fatto e rappezzato, che non riesce a pigliar vento, che sogna di lanciarsi a combattere con le nuvole, nelle quali vede giganti e mostri, e va intanto terra terra, incespicando in tutti gli sterpi e gli stecchi e gli spuntoni, che ne fanno strazio, miseramente.[1]

I am not concerned with the significance of Don Quijote in the context of Pirandellian humor. For the moment, I am primarily interested in Pirandello's characterization of the Knight of La Mancha. The part that deals with Don Quijote's personal traits, i.e., his great courage, the nobility of his soul, his unshakable faith in the codes of chivalry, his madness, the opposition between nobility of ideals and blindness in the face of reality, present no difficulties of any kind. They are the traits that one normally. associates with Don Quijote. However, when Pirandello refers to specific events in the life of the Knight, a problem arises. In the paragraph quoted, two such events are mentioned. The first one, "quel coraggio non gli frutta che volgari bastonate," while remaining general enough to be a cliché of quijotism, is anchored firmly onto an actual event in the life of the Spanish hidalgo. It is a Quijotian as well as Quijotic event, that is, an event described by Cervantes in his novel, as well as an event that obeys the rules of behavior under which Quijote operates. The episode from which the remark was derived can be easily identified. It is the episode (Part I, Chapter IV) in which Don Quijote receives a merciless beating at the hands of a young muleteer. It will be recalled that the Knight

An oil painting of Don Chisciotti by Beppe Vesco.

had demanded from a group of merchants traveling in a caravan that they acknowledge Dulcinea's superior beauty in comparison with all other women. When the merchants refused, Don Quijote threatened mayhem and began a murderous charge against them. Unfortunately, Rocinante stumbled and the Knight landed on the ground, where he remained, unable to move because of his heavy armor, becoming thus an easy adversary to the muleteer. Pirandello's comment is, therefore, an accurate assessment of the event.

As we continue reading the paragraph, we note that Pirandello's words have become highly metaphorical and do not seem to refer to the text of the *Quijote.* Certainly, when the playwright refers to a "badly made and patched up balloon that cannot catch the wind," no one would associate such an image with the Cervantian text. However, when Pirandello begins to describe the dream to wage a battle against the clouds in which the Knight sees giants and monsters as he runs on the ground bumping into all sorts of obstacles that tear his flesh to pieces, the passage cannot be dismissed as an extended metaphor of Quijotic behavior. We realize that we are dealing with another specific episode from the life of the Spanish hidalgo. The description is far too precise to be a simple metaphor. The playwright's attention is focused on an event that seems to unfold right before his eyes. He follows the Knight as he discerns giants and monsters in the clouds, he sees him falling and rising again, he recognizes the exact nature of the obstacles thwarting the progress of the Knight ("Sterpi, stecchi e spuntoni.") and he observes with a lingering glance how his flesh is being torn wretchedly. Such a detailed description would not have occurred, it seems to me, unless the author were following in his mind's eye a specific episode. And this is where the difficulty lies. Where did this episode take place in the Cervantian novel?

My attempts to find the event that may have been the matrix for Pirandello's account have been fruitless. There is nothing even remotely similar to the episode just described in the *Don Quijote.* The Knight fights against windmills; he has an encounter with some wineskins; he fights against a Basque, but there is no episode in which the knight engages or dreams of engaging in a battle against giant-hiding clouds. There is a reference to a cloud in which the magician Freston travels, but it is only a passing image that remains undeveloped.

The question that must be answered is: "Where does the episode come from, if it's not of Cervantian derivation?" Presumably, Pirandello could have invented a new episode. After all, just a few pages preceding the quotation with which we began, the playwright asserted categorically not only the independence of the character from the author who created it but the reader's right to imagine any given character in situations which had not occurred even to the author:

> Quando un poeta riesce veramente a dar vita a una sua creatura, questa vive indipendentemente dal suo autore. Tanto che noi possiamo immaginarla in altre situazioni in cui l'autore non pensò di collocarla, e vederla agire secondo le intime leggi della sua propria vita, leggi che neanche l'autore avrebbe potuto violare.[2]

In order to create a new episode, Pirandello would have had to remain faithful to the inner laws of behavior under which Don Quijote operated. The episode that we are examining is eminently Quijotic. Indeed, Pirandello's obeisance to the rules of Cervantian imagination is probably responsible for critics' failure to notice that the episode does not exist in the Cervantian novel, in spite of the fact that many scholars well acquainted with the *Don Quijote* must have been puzzled by their inability to locate it in the context of the novel.

At this point, I would like to suggest a scenario that could clarify the situation. The episode under discussing was not invented by Pirandello. It was derived from a poem of a fellow Sicilian of another century, whose work Pirandello seemed to know quite well.[3] I am referring to Giovanni Meli (1740-1815), the most accomplished poet who ever wrote in Sicilian. The Pirandellian description is in reality a condensation of a very long episode (almost 30 octaves) from Meli's ambitious mock epic, *Don Chisciotti e Sanciu Panza,* a poem of twelve cantos and a "Vision," written in Sicilian "ottava rima," between 1785 and 1786.[4] In the Sicilian poem, the archetypal couple of Don Chisciotti and Sanciu Panza retain their ancient physiognomies but express a different poetic sensibility as well as changed political, economic, and social conditions.

There can be very little doubt that Pirandello was actually thinking of the Melian episode when he wrote the paragraph in question. For the sake of brevity, let us compare the two accounts. In Canto V of the *Don Chisciotti e Sanciu Panza,* the Knight was startled from a moment of pensiveness by the sudden appearance of a giant running across the side of a mountain:

Quann' eccu un gran giganti smisuratu
chi pri dda costa rapidu curria.

When there appeared a huge and boundless giant
running in haste along the mountain side.

Canto V, 49:

(This excerpt and those that follow are my translations)

Immediately he called Sanciu to bring him his armor, but the squire, realizing quickly that the "giant" was only a reflection of a cloud passing overhead, began pondering the misery of man who frets needlessly and without cause:

Si cirnemu e si jamu esaminannu
li causi di li coluri e li rissi
truvamu chi sti mostri e sti giganti
sunnu nuvuli ed umbri tutti quanti.

If we but sift and carefully examine
the causes of all tantrums and of wrathful acts,
we'll find such monsters and such giants are
nothing but empty shadows and dark clouds.

Canto V, 52:

The giants and the monsters named here are the same as the ones Pirandello recalled. Don Chisciotti did not listen to his squire's advice because he claimed to have more experience with evil things and with the various disguises employed by witches. Thus he began a mad chase after the "giant":

Eccu s'abbia versu lu giganti,
e mustrannu ch'è mastru di la guerra,
isa lu scutu di la testa avanti:
ora s'inquarta, ora si abbassa a terra,
ora stenni lu vrazzu fulminanti. . . .

Behold! He started moving toward the giant
and showing he was master of warfare,
he raised his armor high before his head.
At first he parried, then he bent to the ground.
Then he extended his most dreadful arm. . . .

Canto V, 55:

While Don Chisciotti thought that he had discovered the weakness in the giant's defense, a fly flew into one of his eyes to seek refuge there from the pursuit of a horse fly that had. . . amorous intentions. The Knight was forced to halt the chase for a moment but as soon as he was rid of the fly, he resumed his race against the clouds. In his haste to catch up with the giant, Don Chisciotti is utterly mindless of the obstacles that stand in his way. Such a determination has predictable consequences:

Quantu voti cadiu, quanti s'alzau
Quantu contusioni in vrazza e rini,
Quantu macchi e piraini affruntau. . .
Quantu voti la carni si sfardau,
Quantu sangu chiuviacci da li vini. . . .

So many times he fell and rose again
so many bruises on his arms and sides,
so many thorns and brambles did he face,
so many times his flesh was torn apart,
and so much blood rained out of his poor veins!

Canto V, 63:

Finally the Knight caught up with the giant, so he thought, and struck him with a mighty blow. In reality his sword hit a large rock sending pieces of it all over the Mediterranean Sea.

The correspondences between Meli's episode and Pirandello's brief description could not be more precise. The only variant is represented by Pirandello's reference to Don Chisciotti's dreaming of waging a battle against clouds. This detail may seem insignificant, but it may have been the catalytic agent which activated the recollection of the Melian episode. Pirandello had probably intended to give another example of Quijotic behavior. In fact, the sentence, "sogna di lanciarsi a combattere contro nuvole . . . "is vague enough to be a cliché of Quijotism. At this point, in Pirandello's mind Don Quijote was not fighting against any specific cloud, but rather "clouds" in a general sense, that is, insubstantial things, ghosts of his imagination, shadows. However, the image of the clouds as a possible antagonist of Don Quijote probably triggered the recollection of the Melian episode which Pirandello proceeded to describe accurately and very likely without realizing that a superimposition of images from two different sources had occurred.

It is difficult to say whether Pirandello may have realized, at some later time, the unconscious substitution. It cannot be denied, however, that the mental lapse which permitted the intrusion of a Melian adventure in a Cervantian context, actually occurred. This can be seen as another affirmation of Pirandello's high regard for the work of his fellow Sicilian with whom he shared not only his native idiom but a common attitude toward the world and toward writing which can be summed up in one word: "Umorismo."

NOTES

1 *Saggi, poesie, scritti vrii,* Vol. V (Milano: Mondadori, 1960) p. 104. 2 ibid., p. 101.

3 In his essay on "Umorismo," Pirandello devoted a short paragraph to Giovanni Meli during the discussion of Italian humorists. The paragraph clearly demonstrates not only Pirandello's knowledge of Meli's work, but also his acquaintance with the critical literature on his fellow Sicilian as can be seen in his dismissal of G. Carducci's characterization of Meli's poetry as "arcadia superiore," and in expressing an original view of the Sicilian Abbot as a humorist: "Sul serio poi l' Arcoleo crede che nella nostra letteratura dialettale non ci sia altro che spirito comico? Egli è siciliano e certamente ha letto il Meli, e sa quanto sia ingiusto il giudizio di 'Arcadia superiore' dato della poesia di lui, che non fu sonata soltanto su la zampogna pastorale, ma ebbe anche tutte le corde della lira e si espresse in tulle le forme. Non c'è vero e proprio umorismo in tanta parte della poesia del Meli? Basterebbe citare soltanto 'La cutuliata' per dimostrarlo!
Tic tic . . . chi fu? Cutuliata." (Op. cit., p. 117) It is interesting to point out that Pirandello was relying on his memory for the title and for the line he quoted, both of which are incorrectly given. The correct title of the poem is "Lu specchiu di lu disingannu o sia la cugghiuniata" and the line in question reads "ticchi ticchi, finiu . . . cugghiuniata." The poem, however, is a perfect embodiment of Pirandello's definition of humor as "sentimento del contrario." You may read the complete English text of this poem in my translation of Meli's *Moral Fables and Other Poems*, Legas, 2003.

4 This mock epic, which deserves greater recognition, was translated into English verse by the present author with the title *Don Chisciotti and Sanciu Panza*. The first edition was published by Legas in 1987 with an ample introduction and notes by Gaetano Cipolla. A revised edition was published in 2003. A good portion of Canto I appeared in *Italian Quarterly* in 1984. The quotations from the Don Chisciotti come from *Opere, a* cura di Giorgio Santangelo, Vol. II (Milano: Rizzoli, 1968).

Nino Martoglio

Nino Martoglio is universally acclaimed in Sicily as a figure larger than life. He excelled in many activities and by the time he died at the age of fifty, he was one of the most famous Sicilians of his times. His reputation was based primarily on his activities as a promoter of Sicilian language poetry and theater, theatrical entrepreneur, playwright, and poet.

A caricature of Nino Martoglio by T. Roxas

Martoglio was born in Belpasso, a small town about 15 kilometers from Catania on December 3, 1870. His father, Luigi, was a teacher and a journalist. His mother, Vincenza Zappalà Aradas, was an elementary school teacher. His parents separated when Nino was very young. He lived with his mother for whom he had a special attachment reflected in many of his poems. He wrote two poems for his father but he excluded them from his *Centona.* As a youngster , Martoglio was restless and changed schools several times. He finally, enrolled in a nautical school in Catania and after serving as crewman for four years he received a license as a ship's captain. Like his father who had founded a newspaper, *La gazzetta di Catania*, Martoglio founded a political and literary weekly journal, naming it *D'Artagnan,* after the famous character from *The Three Musketeers* of A. Dumas and published it for fifteen years, from 1889 to 1904. He achieved fame for his humorous sonnets and for the biting satire with which he attacked the pomposity and corruption of his fellow *Catanesi.* While his biting criticism endeared him to most of the people of Catania, for whom Martoglio had a special affection, it caused him a number of problem. He was forced to fight duels with twenty-one men whose psyches he had bruised, risking injury and death. The *D'Artagnan* was written entirely or nearly by Martoglio under various pseudonyms. Of the many characters that he created, his Don Procopio Ballaccheri stood out. Ballaccheri, known as the "Ciciruni di Catania" (The Cicero of Catania) appeared as the main character of *La Divina Commedia di Don Procopio Ballaccheri,* which Martoglio serialized in his *D'Artagnan.* This satirical work written in Sicilian was recently published as a book by Salvatore Calleri. Ballaccheri was to be the model for *Oronzo E. Marginati*, which satirist Luigi Locatelli created for *Il Travaso delle idee,* the most famous satiric journal in Italy.

His contributions to the development of a Sicilian-language theatre are of paramount importance. His activities in this field justify the claim made for him by critics that he was the real founder of the Sicilian theater not only for his important contributions as a theatrical producer, director of theatrical companies and enthusiastic promoter but also for the numerous plays that he wrote in Sicilian. In addition to his own direct contribution, Martoglio was instrumental in getting some of the most important Sicilian writers of his time to write for the theater. He was able to convince a number of eminent writers such as Luigi Capuana, Giovanni Verga, Federico De Roberto, P. Maria Rosso di San Secondo and Luigi Pirandello to collaborate with him in creating a lively repertoire of Sicilian plays that became the vehicles for the three theatrical companies that he formed throughout his career. Indeed, the world owes Martoglio a debt of gratitude for it was he who convinced his friend Luigi Pirandello to devote his considerable talent to the theater and in particular to the use of the Sicilian language. Martoglio and Pirandello collaborated in writing two plays in Sicilian: *A Vilanza* (The Scale) and *Cappiddazzu paga tuttu* (Cappiddazzu pays for everything), both written in 1917.

As a playwright Martoglio authored some of the most memorable Sicilian plays of all time, creating unforgettable characters such as Messer Rapa of *I civitoti in pretura,* Don Procopio Ballaccheri of *U contra* and Mastru Austinu Miciaciu of *San Giuvanni decullatu* and Don Cola Duscio of *L'aria del continente,* a play that was recently translated and adapted for the American stage by Lou Cutell and Tino Trischitta with the title *The*

Sicilian Bachelor. In his relatively brief career he wrote numerous plays, and staged them with such success that they may be considered classics of the Sicilian theater. His plays shine a light on the varied and colorful life of the Sicilians of his time. He was at his best when he portrayed the peculiar and characteristic traits of his people: whether he was describing the foibles of his ignorant and illiterate inhabitants of the Civita section of Catania (*I civitoti in pretura*) as they come into contact with the other world outside that speaks Italian, an unintelligible language, or describing the peculiarities and eccentricities of that bizarre shoemaker, Austinu Miciaciu (*San Giuvanni decullatu*), who kept praying to his saint to make his wife's tongue fall out of her mouth, or describing the ironic fate of Don Cola Duscio (*L'aria del continente*). This is one of his most famous plays and it represents in an emblematic way Martoglio's gift for character creation. Don Cola Duscio is a wealthy landowner who considers himself more open-minded than his highly provincial and backward-thinking Sicilian compatriots. Having spent six months in Rome to undergo an appendicitis operation, he fell for the charms of an enticing cabaret performer named Milla Milord, who claims to be the daughter of an army colonel and a countess, and decided to take her back to Sicily to marry her. The arrival of the young attractive woman in town evokes the anger of Cola's authoritarian sister and the amorous interests of a number of Cola's acquaintances and relatives. The men who meet her become infatuated with Milla who coily encourages them while Don Cola, to show that he is above such provincial feelings as jealousy and possessiveness, behaves in a non-Sicilian way, displaying the attitudes of an enlightened "man of spirit" who has outgrown everything that smacks of Sicilianness. His sister, however, who did not welcome the "northern" interloper into her house, in collaboration with the local Police Delegate, finds out that Milla Milord is in reality an orphan and a greedy adventuress who is out to get Don Cola's money. That is not all. The humoristic high point of the play comes when the poor Don Cola learns that Milla Milord is actually a Sicilian herself and what's more from a small town in the center of Sicily, Carrapipi (Valguarnera Caropepe). She turns out ot be everything he was trying to avoid. While he wanted to marry an emancipated and modern woman from the north he was about the marry a "Carrapipana" that is, someone who for him represents the epitome of Sicilianness. Once the shock and disillusionment wear off, Don Cola Duscio resumes wearing his typical Sicilian clothes, puts on his "scuzzetta" (the typical cap worn by a Sicilian burgisi) and unceremoniously bids good riddance to his paramour, who regales him with a few chosen epithets in Sicilian as she leaves. The character of Don Cola is clearly made of the same humoristic paste from which Pirandello fashioned some of the characters of his own *Pensaci Giacomino* and *La Giara.*

While most of Martoglio's plays enjoyed much success when they were performed, *L'aria del continente* and *San Giuvanni decullatu* stand out. Martoglio was especially proud of their success. In a letter to Francesco De Felice, he said that the *San Giuvanni decullatu,* had been performed 2000 times in eleven years and had earned him the sum of 170.000 Lire.

San Giuvanni decullatu, written in 1908, became the "piece de resistance" of the actor Angelo Musco who apparently contributed to its success not only with his extraordinary acting abilities, but also his input in writing some scenes. The play does not have a compelling dramatic structure, but it makes up for that with very lively dialogue, peppered with continuous verbal gags and comic repartees that an actor such as Musco exploited in a marvelous way. The *deus ex machina* is undoubtedly Mastro Austinu Miciaciu, a tyrannical shoemaker who has a boundless devotion to the image of the beheaded St. John, referred to in the title. Austinu talks to the icon, keeps a lighted lamp before it and expects it to perform miracles for him. The most fervently begged for miracle is, as stated earlier, that the Saint should cause his cantankerous wife to lose her tongue. A good deal of the comic effect of the play derives from Mastro Austinu's use, rather misuse, of the Sicilian/Italian language and from the imaginative verbal exchanges with his wife. Having served in the military in the north of Italy, he considers himself above the people of his neighborhood. In fact, throughout the second and third acts he pretends to be a retired professor to appear to be of a higher social class than a simple shoemaker. This gives rise to comic misunderstandings, as for example when his son-in-law says he is a "prufissuri di lingue" which can be understood as "professor of languages/tongues". Naturally Mastro Austino understands "tongues" and he adds "già, sissignori, mintemu,

The great actor Angelo Musco who starred in many of Martoglio's plays

nasi...mussi" (yes, indeed, let's say noses... mouths". When the Secretary wants to know if the languages he taught were "vive or morte,"(dead or living), not having a clue as to what he meant, he replies somewhat embarassed "Well, according to the season, alive, dead or convalescing!" Through Mastro Austino, Martoglio uses a technique that is present in all his artistic production which consists of having characters trying to speak an undigested and poorly assimilated Italian language. The comic effect is guaranteed as when Mastro Austino wants to tell the others that Araziu u Lampiunariu is trying to murder him, he screams "mi voli suicidari!"misusing "suicidio" for "omicidio". The play is a verbal *tour de force* engaged primarily in surface humor with little concern for adding depth to individual characters. Mastro Austino, for example, in spite of the fact that he dominates the play, embodies many contradictory characteristics. He is domineering and cowardly, very knowledgable about his profession but ignorant about other things, lovable at times but a boor at other times. As for the miracle that Mastro Austino was praying for, it finally occurs. During his daughter's wedding celebration and following another spirited fight with his wife, completely disgusted by the saint's lack of concern for his wishes, Mastro Austino extinguished the candles before St. John's icon. At that point, his wife, while devouring candies, bites her tongue so badly it nearly falls out. She is no longer able to talk and Mastro Austino Miciacio hails the event as the miracle he had sought.

Luigi Pirandello, 1934 Nobel Prize for literature

If Mastro Austino can dominate the scene, making up for his limited knowledge with a quick wit, Don Procopio Ballaccheri, the main character of *U contra*, is a veritable intellectual among the ignorant people of the Civita section—one of the poorest neighboorhoods—of Catania. As the name Ballaccheri suggests, Don Procopio is a man who tells tall tales, someone who speaks in a way that no one understands. The problem is not so much that he uses terms that are unintelligible. The problem is that the people of the Civita section only understand Sicilian and when they hear Italian words they associate them with Sicilian words that have a similar sound, creating, of course, the usual comic relief. At the beginning of the play a woman complains that a someone at the Town Hall had expropriated a bucket of figs "pri ordini di l'incenuu!" (by order of the naive). Naturally, she does not understand who or what the "incenuu" could be. We have to wait for Don Procopio to find out that the figs had been confiscated because the authorities feared that a cholera outbreak was caused by eating fruit. "Incenuu" was her understanding of "igiene" (the Hygiene Department). The play is based on the common belief among the people of the Civita that the Italian government, (about fifty years after Sicily became part of Italy) to counter the problem of overpopulation, was creating cholera outbreaks among the population by distributing meatballs contaminated with the virus. Those who believed in this conspiracy were known as "baddisti", while those who believed that the cholera spread through a column of air that brought the virus from far away were known as "culunnisti". Don Procopio Ballaccheri, who is among the latter, tries his best and with limited success to convince the people of his neighborhood about the causes and spread of the disease. Don Procopio, like so many of Martoglio's characters, is engaged in a continuous and never-ending struggle with hunger, and lives through poorly rewarded services to the members of the community: reading and writing letters for his illiterate clients, representing them in court, teaching them how to read and write. Owing to his perennial hunger, he eats a potful of burned beans and he becomes very ill to his stomach, exhibiting the symptoms of cholera. The people of the neighborhood are convinced that he is going to die within hours. In fact, they sent the town's mortuary officer to collect his body and disinfect his house. But Don Procopio, who has begun to doubt his own "columnist" theories about the spread of the disease, eventually calls for the doctor, who is known in town as possessing the "contra," that is, the antidote to the cholera. The doctor diagnoses him with severe indigestion, gives him a little bottle of laurel extract in front of a young woman who will broadcast to everyone that Don Procopio is in possession of a bottle of the antidote, and cures him of his indigestion. When Za Mara, the richest widow in the neighborhood on whom everyone depends, fall ills with what everyone one thinks is cholera, people expect Don Procopio to save her with his antidote. At first, he refuses to be a partner with his rival to swindle the widow of a large sum of money in exchange for the antidote, openly declaring that the bottle contains only a laurel extract, readily available anywhere. His refusal to take advantage of the situation by going along with everyone's belief that he possessed the antidote is a touching testimonial to his integrity, especially in view of his desperate financial situation. When the whole neighborhood, however, rises up against him for his presumed insensitivity, he succumbs to their demands and gives in, saving the widow from her misdiagnosed indigestion and earning her gratitude and reward, as well as that of the neighbors. Don Procopio Ballaccheri is a noble figure, among so many con artists that people the Martoglio stage, who maintains his dignity even in the face of the most extreme poverty.

Another character who seems to be cut off from the same source is Mastro Delfu Trapuleri, the protagonist of the play *U riffanti*, written in 1917. Mastro Delfu is a *factotum*, a man of many faces and professions. He is the local barber, tooth puller, veterinarian, who will do anything for a buck. He is a real estate and mortgage broker, a go between, who runs an illegal lottery, in competition with the State. He is also something of an interpreter and translator of dream images into numerical values that people could then bet in the lottery. Such practices were widespread in the early part of the 20th century in Sicily. There were dictionaries that assigned such numerical values to events. For example, if you dreamed a biting dog, the corresponding number would be 55; a barking dog would be 39; a hunting dog 49 etc... Mastro Delfu has an associate who lives as a hermit with a reputation as an infallible predictor of winning numbers. In reality the woman is a wealthy moneylender who feigns poverty. She, like Don Procopio, performs little services for people who repay her with gifts. People come to her for tips on the lottery; in fact, some will do anything to extract numbers from her. At the beginning of the play a peasant couple visited her and demanded that she give them numbers to play, frightening her out of her wits. When Mastru Delfu comes to see her, she tells him what happened and he, knowing how wealthy she really is not only offers her his protection but offers to marry her, even though he is currently living with another woman, Giarsumina whose husband is serving time in jail for a murder. Giarsumina, however, refuses the financial arrangement offered by Mastro Delfu and wants revenge. She steals his lottery receipts and paper work and goes to the police. When the police Delegate interrogates him presenting his with the proof of his illegal activities, Mastru Delfu's fate seemed doomed, but his quick wit wins the day. He suggests to the Delegate that he would advance his career much better by solving the disappearance of the hermit than by putting him in jail for an insignificant numbers racket. He offers to solve the who, where and how of the disappearance. One of the receipts given to the Delegate by Giarsumina contained the numbers 50, 63, 33 69 which were played with Mastru Delfu by the peasant couple who had frightened the hermit at the beginning. The numbers had been given to the couple under duress and represented a coded message to Mastru Delfu who interpreted them as "I am being detained inside a cave with doves and they are putting sticks under my fingernails to make me talk." Armed with this information, Mastro Delfu forces a confession out of the perpetrator in front of the police Delegate who will get the credit for solving the crime. He drops the charges against Mastru Delfu. The woman is freed and Mastru Delfu marries her, vowing to give up the illegal lottery.

Martoglio made important contributions to the Sicilian theater in another way: he was responsible for discovering and promoting actors who were to become legendary not on1y in the Sicilian context but also as on the national and international stage. Giovanni Grasso, Angelo Musco, and Rosina Anselmi, to name but three of the most widely known, owe much of their fame to Martoglio. They in turn found in Martoglio's characters the vehicles to express themselves. The success of Martoglio's plays was due in part to the great acting skills of these actors. Angelo Musco's performances as Don Cola Duscio in *L'aria del continente* and as mastru Austinu Miciaciu in *San Giuvanni decullatu* certainly contributed much to making them characters whose appeal was universal.

Martoglio founded three theatrical companies in his career: the first came into being in 1903 and it was known as the Compagnia drammatica dialettale siciliana (Sicilian Dialect Drama Company). This company was active for about a year and performed not only plays by Martoglio (*Nica, I civitoti in pretura* and *Sara*), but also *Zolfara* by Giuseppe Giusti Sinopoli. In 1904, after he moved to Rome, he founded a second "Sicilian Dialect Drama Company" which included in its repertory plays such as *Malia* by Luigi Capuana and a Sicilian version of G. D'Annunzio's *Figlia di Iorio*; the third "Sicilian Dialect Drama Company" came into being in 1907 and it performed a work by Verga (Dal tuo al mio) that Martoglio translated into Sicilian; in 1910 he was responsible for an interesting theatrical initiative known as "Teatro minimo," which consisted of short one-act plays where spectators could come in continuously; and finally, in 1918 he formed the "Compagnia Drammatica del Mediterraneo" in collaboration with Luigi Pirandello and P.M. Rosso di San Secondo. After a brief and successful tournée during which the company performed, among others,

Il Ciclope, a play by Euripides translated into Sicilian by Pirandello, Martoglio was forced to disband the company because of financial difficulties.

Nino Martoglio also achieved a great deal of success as a movie director. In 1914, he became artistic director of a production company narned Morgana Films and was responsible for producing and directing three films (*Capitan Blanco, Teresa Raquin, and Sperduti nel buio*). His *Sperduti nel buio, (Lost* in *the Dark)* based on a play by Roberto Bracco, was deemed a masterpiece by those who saw it. Unfortunately no prints of this film (or of the others) have survived, but film historians regard it a forerunner of Neorealism.

If the theatre became his life after 1904, his love for poetry was the guiding light of his existence. And he loved Sicilian poetry in particular. He was the first person to organize several national conventions on dialect poetry which were attended by the best known dialect poets. Although he wrote many of his plays in Italian (most of which are no longer available), Martoglio wrote poetry only in his Sicilian language; a language he considered "ammagaturi" ("bewitching"). Many of the poems, later collected in *Centona,* first appeared in the *D'Artagnan.* In fact, as the reputation of the newspaper grew and attracted the most famous and talented dialect poets and writers of his time, such as Pascarella, Trilussa, Di Giacomo, Fucini and others, Martoglio' s reputation as a poet also crossed the straits of Messina, and grew to the point that Giosuè Carducci, the first Italian Nobel Prize winner for literature, wrote: "Nessuno ha il diritto a dirsi letterato, che non conosca il linguaggio del Meli ed in esso linguaggio i sonetti del Martoglio." (Nobody has the right consider himself a literary person if he does not know the language of Meli and in that language the sonnets of Martoglio.)

In spite of his many accomplishments, in the theatre, in poetry, as a journalist, as a theatrical producer and as a movie director, Martoglio has received scant critical attention. Even the academicians who specialize in Italian literature have not shown much critical interest in Martoglio. Very little has been written about him since his death. In the dialogue between hirnself and the personification of his book, *Centona,* which served as a preface to the work, the poet hirnself complained that his poetry had not been given any attention by the "varvasapi allittricuti" (literary big-wigs) primarily because he had not known how to promote it correctly. However, Martoglio, in defense of his poetry, claimed that while the academicians have not made a fuss about his work, the people have consistently displayed affection for it, so much so that he could say that "there isn't any town in Sicily where *Centona* has not brought people cheer." Martoglio went on to say that his poetry was a favorite of the Sicilian people wherever they may be, within Sicily, in war trenches and in foreign lands. The reason for this predilection is that *Centona,* he said, brought people the smells and sounds of Sicily, the passions that are always raging in their unhappy hearts, and the memories of their beloved and tragic land. And he concluded with aconfidence that his poetry would live on:

> as long as you leave on each street you pass
> of restless Sicily the scent and soul,
> you'll always be assured of great success.

Readers may regard this as wishful thinking, but I can testify from personal experience that it is actually true, at least in Sicily. Sicilians love Martoglio and they love his poetry. One brief story will make the point: I was browsing one day in one of the largest bookstore in Catania looking through their Sicilian language poetry section and started a conversation with the store manager. When I told him that I was working on a book about Nino Martoglio, he began to recite "Lu cummattimentu tra Orlandu e Rinardu" from memory. He went through nearly the last 8 stanzas of the poem without faltering once, showing great appreciation for Martoglio's cleverness by highlighting with shifts in tone and manner of reciting those parts he deemed most interesting. This performance, however, is not all that extraordinary. In fact, on several occasions, on learning of my interests in Sicilian literature, my interlocutors have begun reciting their favorite Sicilian poerns. The poems most commonly found in such personal repertories are by Giovanni Meli, Micio Tempio and Nino Martoglio.

The people of Catania identify with Martoglio's characters in one way or another, they recognize their own weaknesses and ignorance in them. In his poerns they hear every day voices; they see neighborhood women gossiping at their windows; they hear echoes of the street vendors' voices, mothers calling children for supper, a lover urging his beloved to come out on her balcony. Martoglio is an embodiment of Sicily and Sicilian sensibilities. Pirandello was right when he said that Martoglio was, after Giovanni Meli, the most expressive poet of Sicily. In his preface to *Centona* he said that Martoglio was for Sicily,

> "What Di Giacomo and Russo were for Naples; what Pascarella and Trilussa were for Rome; Fucini for Tuscany; Selvatico and

Barbarini for Venetia: native voices that say things about their lands as they should be said, so that they are what they are and not something else, with that flavor and color that cannot exist anywhere else, that air, that breath and that smell in which they live and breathe, and where they are enjoyed and illumined. Martoglio embodies all his Sicily, the Sicily that loves and hates, that laughs and weeps and frets, using accents and a manner that here in *Centona* are incomparably expressed."

Martoglio indeed expressed the varied aspects of Sicilian life. He sang about many things and always with freshness, ingenuity, inventiveness and truth: he sang of macho Catanese men who live in taverns where the light of the sun never shines and who speak a jargon so obscure that only God and Martoglio could fathom, of people in the tough *Civita* neighborhood where he recorded the imaginative insults of neighborhood women whose linguistic skills display the astuteness and subtlety of a master politician; he captured with uncanny subtlety the skillful verbal exchanges between two partners playing "briscula" and painted vignettes—"tranches de vie"—like the sonnet "A cira," that Pirandello rightly considered a little rnasterpiece in which one word, one gesture or one look magically discloses a world of complex motivations and emotions.

One theme that is ever present in *Centona,* is love: love as the principal reason for human life, love as the source of bitterness and pain; love that is bought, love as the source of all ecstasy, love that is full of thorns. And the "fimmina" (woman-female), which in Sicilian is not an offensive word as it is in Italian, is always on Martoglio' s mind. At times she is an angel that recalls the Angel-like women of the *Dolce Stil Nuovo;* at times she is the temptress who leads men into hell and gives them death when she tires of them; at other times, she is the lady whose eyes are sweet and traitorous at once. Often woman is seen as the eternal repose and the only goal of man. Women are the source of all the sweetness in the world. The only problem Martoglio seems to have is that he can never be sure how long a woman' s promise will last. Inevitably they abandon the poet, betray and forsake him. Martoglio seems to search for an ideal of constancy that he can never find, except in the image of the saintly mother. The image of the "donna-danno" is in fact frequently opposed to that of the mother, who alone is able to understand and comfort the poet. As a good Sicilian of the nineteenth century, Martoglio felt a special devotion to his mother, perhaps because of her many marital difficulties.

But what is it that gives Martoglio's poetry its identifying marks? Let us try a more formal analysis of two of his poems. In the dedication to the "Triple Alliance" to his brother Giulio, who ironically was to die in the war against the partners of that alliance, Nino Martoglio declared openly that he was not particularly proud of the poem. He probably would have not included it in the *Centona* if the public had not shown such affection for it. The "Triplici Allianza" seemed to Martoglio a mere "divertimento," a comic extravagance and he chides the public, calling it "a dumb beast," for not being able to distinguish it from the good poetry of *Tistimunianza*. The latter –eight sonnets that related in vivid details and in dramatic fashion the recovery of the body of a girl who jilted by her lover had committed suicide by jumping into a well—was constructed with all the technical tools that a Verist poet could muster. In terms of structure and development, tone, presence of varied stylistic devices, appropriateness of language to the situation, adherence to the rules of Veristic writing as elaborated by Capuana and Verga, whom Martoglio greatly admired, (objectivity, impersonality, scientifically correct descriptions of people and things, accurate observation of events, use of indirect discourse, use of actions to characterize and give insights into a character's psychological state of mind, logical connections between the deterministic rules of cause and effect, etc.), the eight sonnet drama was for Martoglio as a real work of art, almost a demonstration of what Verist poetry should be. fashioned with all the technical skills of a consummate artist, the latter was only a casual comical excursus of the imagination, written without paying too much attention to the rules of Verismo. The subtitle of the "Triple Alliance" "Smàfiri di mastru Cuncettu, lu tamburineri," which can be translated loosely as "Concoctions by Master Cuncettu, the Drummer," clearly denotes something less than a scientific treatise by a political scientist. But more importantly it identifies the author's position *vis á vis* the poem and master Cuncettu' s credibility. Martoglio, as the author, has intruded into the poem characterizing Cuncettu' s words as "smàfiri," that is, unbelievable imaginings of a lovable but all together risible character. While there is nothing wrong with this, it probably represented a serious breach of one of the most cherished, if flawed, rules ofVeristic art: the need for absolute impersonality. The author was not to intrude into the stories he was writing. In fact, as Verga said, the best work of art was one in which the mystery of creation remained a mystery: "the best work was the one that seemed to have written itself"

A detailed analysis of the differences between the two poems reveals that Martoglio felt that poetry had an important role in educating the public and to accomplish it had to be serious. Like the poems on the mafia, *O scuru o scuru*, which he considered totally devoid of redeeming virtues, his "Triplici Allianza" had no ambition to enlighten anyone. It was meant as *divertimento* to amuse a few friends. Nevertheless, the poem is a political satire which may have lost some of its bite because the events discussed are no longer part of current events, but which remains even today a valid indictment of the distance that exists between the origins of historical events and the people. And it is morre characteristic of Martoglio's poetry than the Deposition. In this respect, I agree with Salvatore Camilleri who claimed that Martoglio never realized that his poetic personality leaned more toward comedy and less toward drama. In the final analysis, Martoglio was at his best when he was poking fun at his compatriots and himself. His brand of humor was not unlike the humor of Giovanni Meli, which Pirandello identified as his own.

In the "Triple Alliance," when Master Cuncetto related how Umberto's warship fired a cannon against the German castle, he added that the shot was completely noiseless: "senza sgrusciu, oh! /Ca nuatri taliani, pi sapillu/ sgrusciu non sèmu facili di fàrini..." (Without noise at all...you *know!* 'cause we Italians, to tell the truth, are not easily adept at making noise!) (that is, we cannot rnake noise, even when we want to!). This type of humor is directed outwards as much as it is directed inwards. Martoglio includes himself in that statement, as an Italian. So he is not simply poling fun at Master Cuncettu who does not realize that what he is saying undermines completely the greatness of Italy that he is trying to establish. By praising the great ability of Italians to shoot cannons without making a noise he is establishing their lack of weight and power upon the world stage. Italians can't make noises even when they want to! This is satire that cuts in both directions, and it is another example of that attitude, that *ltalicum acetum* of Horatian memory which is the ltalian way of looking at the world: a way of laughing with tears in our eyes, of crying with laughter in our voices.

Nino Martoglio married Elvira Schiavazzi in 1905. They had four children: Luigi, Marco, Bruno and Maria. He met an untimely and tragic death on September 15, 1921. After visiting his son at the Vittorio Emanuele hospital which was under construction at the time Martoglio fell into the elevator shaft.

Plays

Nica (1903). A play in four acts in Sicilian, first performed at the Manzoni theater in Milan in 1903.

I civitoti in pretura (1903). A one act play in Sicilian, first performed at the Teatro Bellini in Palermo in 1903.

Sara (1904). A one act play in Sicilian (unpublished and lost), first performed at the

Arena Peloro in Messina in 1904.

Turbine (1905). This two act play in Italian was first performed at the Teatro Manzoni in Milano in 1905. It was later rewritten with the title of *Riutura.*

Il salto del lupo (1906). A three act play in Italian (unpublished and now lost) was first performed at the Teatro Margherita in Genoa in 1906. It was derived from the *Vanni Lupo* piece which Martoglio dedicated to his wife and which included in *Centona.*

*Capitan Blanco (*1906). this four act play in Italian, (unpublished and now lost), was performed at the Teatro Politeama in Livorno in 1906..

'U paliu (1906). The Sicilian version of this *Capitan Blanco*, entitled, *'U Paliu*, in four acts, was first performed in Rome at the Teatro Nazionale in 1906.

La sua famiglia (1907).

San Giuvanni Decollatu (1908). A three act play in Sicilian, first performed at the Teatro Politeama in Piacenza in 1908.

L'ultimo degli Alagona (1908). A three act play in Italian (now lost), first performed at the Teatro Filodrammatici in Milan in 1908.

Riutura (1911). A one act play in Sicilian. This is the Sicilian version of *Turbine.*

Voculanzicula (1909). A three act play in Sicilian, first perfomed at the Teatro Paganini in Genoa in 1909.

Il divo (1909). A three act play in Italian (now lost) first performed at the Teatro Argentina in Rome.

Salto di barra (1909). A one act play in Italian, unpublished and now lst was firs performed at the Teatro Nicolini in Florence.

Punto a croce e nodo piano (1912). A one act play in Italian first performed at the Teatro Quattro Fontane in Rome

Capitan Senio (1912). A two act play in Sicilian, first performed at the Teatro Malibran in Venice in 1912.

Passo Luparo (1912). A one act play in Italian never performed.

L'aria del Continente (1915). A three act play in Sicilian, first performed at the teatro filodrammatici in Milan in 1915.

'U riffanti (1916). A three act play in Sicilian first performed at the Teatro Olympia in Milan in 1916.

L'arte di *Giufà* (1916). A three act play in Sicilian, first performed at the Teatro Argentina in Rome in 1916.

Scuru (1917). A three act play in Sicilian first performed at the Teatro Olympia in Milan in 1917.

'A vilanza, (1917). A three act play also written in collaboration with Pirandello; was first performed at the Teatro Olympia in Milan 191.7

Cappiddazzu paga tuttu (1917). A three act play in Sicilian, written in collaboration with Luigi Pirandello, was first performed posthumously in 1958 at the Palazzo Corvaja in Taormina.

'U contra (1918). A three act play in sicilian, first performed at the Teatro Nazionale in Rome

Sua Eccellenza di Falcomarzano (1918). A three act play in Italian first perfformed at the Teatro Alfieri in Turin in 1918.

Taddarita (1919). A one act play, was first perfoemedd at the Treatro Argentina in Rome.

Il Marchese di *Ruvolito* (1920). A three act play in Sicilian first performed at the teatroNazionale in Rome.

"*Annata ricca. massaru cuntentu*" (1921). Originally written as a one act play in Italian, it was rewritten as a two act play in Sicilian and performed posthumously at the Teatro Angelo Musco in Catania in 1953.

Martoglio's theatrical works were published originally by Niccolò Giannotta, in Catania between 1918 and 1924. A number of editions have been published since then. Two such editions are by Il Vespro Editore, Palermo, which published 12 indvidual plays between 1978 and 1979. A more recent edition in three volumes which contains all the theatrical works and *Centona* was published by Newton in 1996. They were edited by Sarah Zappulla Muscarà with the title *Tutto il teatro e tutte le poesie siciliane.*

Poetry

O scuru o scuru, (Catania: Galatola 1896), album of sonnets on the Mafia

A tistimunianza, sonnets with illustrations by G Martoglio Catania:Giannotta, 1899.

Centona, Catania: Giannotta (1899)

Cose di Catania: la seconda Centona, ed. by Salvatore Camilleri Catania: Tringale 1985.

Criticism

AA.VV., *Nino Martoglio nel teatro nel cinema nel giornalismo,* Catania, Teatro Stabile di Catania, 1983.

AA.VV., *Martoglio. La figura e l'opera,* a cura di Giuseppe Sambataro, Roma, Edizione della Banca Popolare di Belpasso, 1984.

AA.VV., *Angelo Musco e il teatro del suo tempo,* a cura di Enzo Zappulla Catania, Maimone, 1990.

Giacomo Armò, *Martoglio,* Napoli, Chiurazzi, 1929;

Salvatore Camilleri (edited by), *Cose di Catania,* Catania, Tringale, 1983;

Salvatore Calleri (edited by), *La Divina Commedia di Don Procopio Ballaccheri,* Messina, EDAS, 1986;

Santi Correnti, *Martoglio inedito. Un ignoto canzoniere italiano della Catania "fin de siècle",* Catania, CUECM, 1993.

——. *Le opere e i giorni di Nino Martoglio,* in "Nuovi Quaderni del Meridione," Palermo, aprile-giugno 1971;

Giuseppe Gulino, *Deformazioni lessicali nelle opere* di *Martoglio,* in AA.VV., *Dialetto e Letteratura,* a cura di Giuseppe Gulino e Ermanno Scuderi, Pachino, Biblioteca Comunale "Dante Alighieri", 1989;

Francesco De Felice, *Storia del teatro siciliano,* Catania, Giannotta, 1956;

Carlo Lo Presti, *Sicilia-Teatro,* Firenze, I Centauri, 1969;

Guido Nicastro, *Teatro e società* in *Sicilia (1860-1918),*Roma, Bulzoni, 1978;

*The Poetry of Nino Martoglio, Selections from Centona,*edited and translated by Gaetano Cipolla, New York, Ottawa: Legas 1995.

Sarah Zappulla Muscarà, *Pirandello-Martoglio,* Milano, Pan, 1979 (II ed., Catania, CUECM, 1985);

——, *Contributi per una storia dei rapporti tra letteratura e cinema muto (Verga De Roberto*

Capuana Martoglio e la settima arte), in *Lette- ratura Teatro e Cinema,* Catania, Tringale, 1984;

——. *Nino Martoglio,* Caltanissetta-Roma, Sciascia, 1985;

——. "*Sperduti nel buio*" di *Martoglio: un antesignano del neorealismo,* in AA.VV., *Il neorealismo nella letteratura e nel cinema italiano,* a cura di Rosetta Brambilla, Assisi, Biblioteca Pro Civitate Christiana, 1987.

——. *Luigi Capuana, Adelaide Bernardini, Nino Martoglio* e *Angelo Musco,* in *Luig Capuana e le carte messaggiere,* Catania, CUECM, 1996, vol. Il.

Sarah Zappulla Muscarà e Enzo Zappulla, *Sicilia: Dialetto e Teatro. Materiali per una storia del teatro dialettale siciliano,* Agrigento, Edizioni del Centro Nazionale di Studi Pirandelliani, 1982 (Il ed. aggiornata, 1985);

Guido Nicastro, *Pirandello. Martoglio e il teatro siciliano,* in *Scene* di *vita e vita* di *scene* in *Sicilia,* Messina, Sicania, 1988;

Antonio Scuderi, *The Dialect Poetry of Nino Martoglio,* New York, Peter Lang, 1992;

Lia Banna Ventorino, *Il D'Artagnan* di *Nino Martoglio,* Catania, Giannotta, 1974;

Enzo Zappulla, *Nino Martoglio capocomico,* in "Otto-Novecento", Varese, VIII (1984), I (Also Catania, CUECM, 1985);

Nino Zuccarello, *Musco e Martoglio,* Catania, Camene, 1953;

Vitaliano Brancati

Vitaliano Brancati was born on July 24, 1907 in Pachino, a small town in the province of Siracusa which marks the extreme south-eastern corner of Sicily, one of the three promontories of ancient Trinacria. When Brancati was 13 years old, his family moved to Catania, a city that represents an important reference point both for his life and for his fiction. He studied at the University of Catania and received a degree after writing a thesis on Federico De Roberto in 1929. He moved to Rome and began a career as a journalist working for *Il Tevere* and then, in 1933, for the weekly Fascist literary journal *Il Quadrivio.* At the beginning of his literary career his works showed an infatuation with Fascism and Nietzchean ideals (he joined the Italian Fascist Party early), as can be seen in his first dramatic poem *Fedor*, written between the ages of 17 and 19, as well as the plays *Everest* (1928) and *Piave* (1932). He had been attracted by Fascism's promise of changing the world through action, by the "heroic" and "virile" attitudes displayed by Il Duce and embodied by Gabriele D'Annunzio. Brancati's enthusiasm started to wane and when he came to realize that the Fascist experience had been a social and moral failure he distanced himself from Fascism. Evidence of the rift between Brancati and the Fascist ideology can be deduced by the events surrounding the publication of a short novel, *Singolare avventura di viaggio*, (*Singular Journey Adventure*) written in 1933 and published in 1934 by Mondadori, while he was still an editor at *Il Quadrivio.* The book was openly condemned by Luigi Chiarini, the vice director of the journal and eventually it was pulled off the shelves of bookstores as "immoral" by the Fascist regime. Brancati resigned his position. Brancati came to be consider the years spent following the Fascist ideology as *Gli anni perduti* (*The Lost Years*), a novel written in 1936 and published in installments in *Omnibus*, a journal founded by Leo Longanesi that was shut down by the Fascist regime in 1939. The novel was eventually published in 1941. From 1933 through 1941 he taught Italian literature in several Istituti Magistrali (training schools for elementary school teachers) in Rome, Catania and Caltanissetta. In 1940 he began working on *Don Giovanni in Sicilia*, (*Don Giovanni in Sicily*) a novel published in 1941 in which Brancati introduced some of the themes he would develop in subsequent novels and which critics have regarded as the distinguishing traits of his style: namely the so called *gallismo*, a penchant for irony and satire. In 1942 he published a one-act play, *Le trombe di Eustachio* and during the rehearsals for its stage production at the theater of the university he met the actress Anna Proclemer whom he married in 1946. In 1943, his play *Don Giovanni involontario* (*Involuntary Don Giovanni*) was stopped by the Fascist censors after five performances.

In 1943, perhaps feeling that the political atmosphere had changed and that it was no longer advisable for him to remain in Rome, he returned to Sicily where he lived until 1945. In 1946 he began to collaborate with various newspapers and magazine such as *L'Europeo, Tempo Quotidiano* and *Cronache*. In 1946, he received the Vendemmia Prize for the novel *Il vecchio con gli stivali* (*The Old Man with the Boots*) which became the subject of a film in 1947 with the title of *Anni difficili* (*Difficult Years*) for which he also wrote the screenplay. He began writing for *Mondo*, founded by Mario Pannunzio. This journal, which gathered among others some of the most important names in Italian literary circle such as Corrado Alvaro, Mario Soldati, Alberto Moravia, Bonaventura Tecchi, represented an attempt to reform Italian society along the progressive and liberal lines for which the figure of the philosopher Benedetto Croce stood. Brancati who was a frequent visitor to the magazines' offices embraced the ideals of this group of intellectuals. His meeting with Croce marked an important moment in Brancati's outlook. Through an understanding of Croce's ethics he came to repudiate completely his youthful infatuation with Fascism.

In 1949 he published *Il bell'Antonio* (*Handsome Antonio*) which won the prestigious Bagutta Prize in competition with Cesare Pavese's *La bella estate (The Beautiful Summer)*. In 1952 he wrote screenplays and began working on his last novel *Paolo il caldo* (*Paolo, the Hot One*) which was published posthumously in 1955 with a preface by Alberto Moravia. In 1953 he wrote more screenplays: *L'uomo la bestia e la virtù* (*Man, Beast and Virtue*) and *Viaggio in Italia* (*Journey in Italy*). In 1954, on September 25, he died in Turin, following complications from surgery.

Vitaliano Brancati's literary figure has undoubtedly not received the critical attention that his talent and skill as a writer deserve, probably because of his initial infatuation with Fascism. Even though he came to totally repudiate his involvement as a youthful aberration, critics never fail to point out its importance in Brancati's universe, both for the early writings which were written as a conscious exaltation of the ideals that inspired Fascism, and in his more mature works that take a conscious antifascist stand. Thus politics may be identified as one of the most pervasive concerns of the Brancatian discourse. From the early plays through his collection of short stories and novels, Brancati seems to be making a political statement that is more or less transparent. The novel of the break with Fascism *Gli anni perduti* describes how in the sleepy city of Nataca (an inverted form of Catania) during the heyday of Fascism, the bored citizens are awakened by the arrival of a professor Buscaino who is full of ideas and plans for the future. He proposes to build a tall observation tower from which the view could be enjoyed and the citizens embark on the construction of it with faith and great expectation, only to find out to their chagrin, after the tower had been built, that the necessary building permits had not been obtained and so the use of the tower was forbidden. The "lost years" obviously refer to the years spent believing in the impossible political project of Fascism, a project that ultimately lacked legitimacy and proved to be an illusion. Brancati's antifascist sentiments are even more clearly stated in the short novel *Il vecchio con gli stivali*, (1944) in which the protagonist, Aldo Piscitelli, a short and insignificant little man, who wants nothing but to be able to support his family without getting involved in politics, was forced to become a Fascist to keep his job as a clerk in the town hall of a Sicilian city (Catania) and to wear the uniform (the boots in the title) of a Fascist "squadrista". Piscitelli does not have a clear understanding of why he hates fascism, but he despises it with a passion, because Mussolini took away the joy of little things like calling for an encore at the theatre or sipping a cup of coffee outdoors. He vents his anger against the regime by passing next to Fascist functionaries and calling them names, mentally. He is never able to externalize it for fear of reprisals. When Fascism was defeated, ironically he became one (indeed the only one) of the first victims of the reaction by the new political leaders who see him as an embodiment of the past regime. He is thus fired from the post he had occupied in the town hall for thirty years while his wife who had not shared his aversion to Fascism and in fact had driven him to become a member of the party, is singled out for help by the newcomers.

In a similar fashion, Brancati also disposed of his youthful infatuation with D'Annunzio and the Fascist rhetoric in the satiric tale entitled *La singolare avventura di Francesco Maria* (*Francesco Maria's Singular Adventure*) (1941) in which the myth of the one-eyed poet of the imagination is lived through by a young Sicilian provincial who discovers D'Annunzio's poetry as a way of envisioning a higher plane of existence and tries to make it a guide for life with disastrous consequences for himself and the woman he seduced: a clear parody of the Fascist fascination with the bombast and high sounding words that have no connection with real life.

While in these works the political implications are immediately evident, in other works Brancati made a political statement in an indirect way and following a tortuous path. In 1937, in a letter to his father who had advised him to steer clear of direct criticism of the Fascist regime fearing for his safety, Brancati seems to have made a choice as regards the style that he would follow in his future works. He would use a comic or ironic style. In 1938 he wrote the following sentence in the journal *Omnibus*: "At the court of Louis/ only the clown was a free man." The first important work that seems to be inspired by the newly discovered attitude was *Don Giovanni in Sicilia*, (1941). This novel presents an image of the provincial society of Catania, completely oblivious of what is happening in the world—Germany had already invaded Poland and France, Italy's entrance into the Second World War was imminent, the Fascist regime had conducted a colonial war against Ethiopia—. In their total absorption with one thing—woman—the people of Catania seem to be the opposite of what a true Fascist should be. They like to talk about women, they are more interested in imagining women, in chasing fantasies rather than meeting women of flesh and blood. These men suffer from a disease that affects Sicilian men in general that Brancati called "gallismo," defined as "a common disease of the men of the South for whom the word "honor" has its highest meaning in the sentence "to gain honor with a woman"; it consists primarily in making people believe that one is endowed with extraordinary sexual power." (*Diario romano*, p. 79 [Roman Diary]) The main character, Giovanni Percolla, a man who at 36 years of age has never known love, engages in these long and useless pursuits of the elusive "woman" who exists only in their fantasies until one day the most beautiful woman in the city, Ninetta dei Marconella, a woman from the north of Italy, looks at him. In a society where women were sheltered and protected, where contact with the opposite sex was almost nonexistent except after marriage, women were endowed by the imagination of males as mysterious and ineffable creatures who had it in their power to open the gates of paradise, Ninetta's look transforms Giovanni into a different man. He had been living the life of a lazy bachelor served by three unmarried sisters who idolize him and cater to every whim, but from the moment Ninetta singled him out, his Sicilian habits, the apartment where he had been living, the food his sisters prepared for him, even his personal hygiene habits are no longer good enough. He abandons his friends and marries Ninetta, in spite of his abhorrence of marriage. They move to Milan where his Sicilian charms make many conquests among the women. He embraces his newfound life in the North with gusto. He even manages to keep at bay his Sicilian penchant for jealousy when men fawn over his wife's charms, but as time goes by, his success with the local women, devoid of the sense of sin that always accompanied his fantasies in Sicily, becomes less fulfilling, less exciting. The pleasures that he and his friends dreamed so much about proved to be illusory. There was more pleasure in imagining them. Ironically, as a parallel, the happy and bustling, businesslike life of the north had seemed to Giovanni as the perfect antithesis to the somnolent and stagnant life he led in Catania. But when he is living in Milan he finds that his acquaintances consider life in Sicily as the better and healthier alternative. His new Milanese friends consider him an amusing relic of the Baroque age, someone who reminds them, in his use of language, of Verga's imaginative and earthy characters. In the end, having returned to Catania for a visit, Giovanni rediscovers his old habits, his old and comfortable bed, the smells and sensuality of his youth and makes peace with his Sicilianness, at least while he is in Sicily.

Il bell'Antonio, which Brancati published in installments in *Il Mondo* in 1949 is perhaps the most complex of his novels. Politics, *gallismo* and moralism that critics see as distinguishing features of Brancati's style are perfectly blended in this book, though it easily transcends these simple classifications. The novel actually, unlike *Don Giovanni in Sicilia*, which was written around the theme of *gallismo*, opens up a wider vista of Italian society under Fascism. It is no longer the sleepy provincial city of Catania that is dissected in Brancati's satire, it is the whole system of present values that comes under attack.

The theme of *gallismo* may offer a line of continuity between *Don Giovanni in Sicilia* and *Il bell'Antonio*, but the treatment of the theme is very different in the two novels. For Brancati the *gallismo* of his characters is not amusing any more. Indeed, *Il bell'Antonio* is not a humorous book.

Nor is the third novel of *gallismo* a humorous book. Brancati himself, in a note written in his *Diario romano*, that *Castorini*, (the first title of *Paolo il caldo*) turned out to be a different book from what he had originally envisaged: "I started out writing with a program of happiness, but this is turning out to be my saddest book." The third of what may be considered a trilogy, *Paolo il caldo* was published in 1955 and concluded Brancati's search for meaning through love. If in *Don Giovanni in Sicilia* the protagonist comes to feel nausea for the sexual act and in *Il Bell'Antonio* he is unable to perform it because he endowed it with too much significance, and in *Paolo il caldo*, it becomes the only way that he can feel alive, if only for a moment.

Brancati's theatrical works, while having a distinct character, run along tracks that are parallel to those of his narrative. The themes and concerns that we have identified as central to Brancati's universe are also represented in his plays with an even more direct manner than he does in the novels. Although it is clear that Brancati's reputation as an important Italian literary figure of the first half of the 20th century is primarily tied to his novels, Brancati himself did not consider his involvement with the theater as a marginal or secondary activity. Brancati's early predilection of the theater as an ideal vehicle for his art testifies to his abiding interest in it. With the exception of one or two plays, however, his theatrical works never achieved the measure of success that his novels did. Nevertheless, Vitaliano Brancati earned a prominent place among the playwrights of the post-Pirandellian era.

We will not concern ourselves with the youthful plays because Brancati himself repudiated them openly. In *Questo matrimonio si deve fare*, (*This Wedding Must Be Made*) written in 1936, that is, at about the same time as the novel *Gli anni perduti*, which as we saw marked the author's rejection of the Fascist regime, he has one of his character utter the following condemnation of his youthful mistakes:

> "I do not regret my twenty years, I despise them! [...]Fifteen years ago, a misguided young man, a silly fellow, an opportunist, a scoundrel bore my name! He threw it in the mud, he wrote it on the cover of abominable books, at the end of boring and shameful poems, of pitiful letters..."

This was the first public admission of his youthful waywardness. The play, which pits a deformed but very powerful member of the Fascist hierarchy (Paolo Pannocchietti) against a timid professor (Volfango Raimondi) as they vie for the love of Pierina who refuses both of them, clearly adopts an antifascist stance. The Fascist functionary's successful career proves to be ephemeral and ineffective in winning Pierina's love and drives him insane while the professor is overwhelmed to the point of silence by his love. Pierina is glad when the first gray hair appears signifying the end of the obligations of youth. In refusing the Fascist hymn to youth and vim, Pierina shares the conclusions reached by the character Lisa Careni in *Gli anni perduti*. Similarly, the madness that results from Pannocchietti's race for career success may be seen as a prelude to the fate that befell the protagonist of *Paolo il Caldo*. Raimondi's silence before love may be another manifestation of the impotence of Antonio Magnano in the *Bell'Antonio*.

The next play, *Le trombe di Eustachio*, (*The Eustachian Tubes*) (published in 1942) set at the time of the Italian movement toward unification of the country, may appear at first to be unrelated to Brancati's time. But the topic is a very timely one. It deals with the moral questions inherent in being an informant, and as we know the Fascist and Nazi regimes made ample use of such informants. Brancati's setting of the play in the Risorgimento is hardly a subtle attempt to avoid censorship. A boy named Gerardino discovers he has exceptional hearing and is placed in the service of State to spy on those who would pose a threat to the State, "the snakes that are hidden in the bosom of the Fatherland." Gerardino thus becomes an informant, denouncing political plots against the State and becoming immensely wealthy in the process, but he begins to question the morality of his actions asking himself at one point why there are never any monuments, or streets named after spies. Such doubts are overcome, however, but when he turns his powerful ear toward the constellation Andromeda, to try to get answers on the great questions about life after death, he hears nothing.

The play *Don Giovanni involontario* (*An Involuntary Don Giovanni*), written in 1943, is reminiscent of the novel by a similar name, *Don Giovanni in Sicilia.* It is the only play that exploits the theme of *gallismo*, present in his three major novels. Francesco Musumeci is a lazy young man not unlike Giovanni Percolla of Don Giovanni in Sicilia who has a certain reluctance to having anything to do with women in spite of the fact that he talks about them with his friend. His father who regards man's performance with women as a badge of honor encourages Francesco to assert himself in that area and after the first encounter with a woman, Francesco becomes a very successful seducer of women, albeit an involuntary one because it is the women who relentlessly pursue him. Like Giovanni Percolla whose easy conquests while living in Milan resulted in boredom, Francesco, too is bored by his many empty conquests. When Francesco finally falls in love with Claretta and he marries her, he is betrayed. At age 58, in a dream in which his past life, his futile loves, his empty relationships are put on trial, he comes to realize the sterility and emptiness of his life. The third act of the play employs some surrealistic touches, as Brancati did in the previous play, (dialogue between the Ear and Andromeda) when Francesco engages in a dialogue with the eye and mind of a lieutenant who is in love with his young wife.

In the *Don Giovanni involontario* the theme of *gallismo* is exacerbated. The boredom experienced by Francesco Musumeci is all encompassing. There is no joy in these relationships. He complains "Women! It's always the same story [...] How sad! Being bored is always a painful thing, but the tedium that a woman gives, that pungent, subtle, narrow, closed, repugnant tedium...ah, ah!"

The play *Le nozze difficili*, (*The Difficult Marriage*) written in 1943, was published posthumously by V Gazzola Stacchini in *Teatro di Vitaliano Brancati: poetica, mito e pubblico*, in 1972. The play, performed for the first time in 1977 on Italian TV, deals with the difficult relationship between men and women. Vladimiro, a timid professor, is in love with Agata but he is afraid to marry her because he imagines her sexual potentiality so great as to destroy him. In the end, after a series of turns and comedy of errors involving two other characters, Gildo and Ingeborg Vladimiro and Agata marry only to discover that she was an extremely chaste woman and he turns out to be an oversexed fiend who eventually betrays his wife with Ingeborg. Thus the play is based primarily on the apprehension and fear between the sexes.

The play *Raffaele*, written in 1946 immediately after the war has a number of situations that are similar to the story *Il Vecchio con gli stivali*. The play is set in Sicily in the period before the war and it represents an indictment of transformism and opportunism. Raffaele is an individual who is willing to bow his head to the powers that be, willing and eager to compromise moral and ethical principles for the sake of personal gain or convenience. In him Brancati represents the Italians' willingness to compromise their values to go along with the dictates of Fascism. The play castigates Italian conformism.

As the bitterness of the political struggle between the left and Christian Democratic Party increased in the immediate post war period, Brancati jumped into the fray with another play, *Una donna di casa*, (*A Housewife*) that attacked conformism, asserting that that there is nothing better in this world than "a moment of utter clarity in a mind that is honest and free." The play deals with Elvira, a housewife who has hidden her talents as a writer even from her own husband, Emanuele Rossi an actor. Indeed, not knowing that the play in which he is a star was secretly written by her, Rossi regards her disdainfully as a simple, unsophisticated woman. In the play, a politician in a high position in the Christian Democratic party comes to ask Rossi to write a patriotic propaganda play. When Emanuele learns that Elvira is the writer of the play he is performing, he asks her to write the commissioned work, but she refuses. She also refuses a similar offer from the Communists and plans to change the finale of her play by having the protagonist throw a collar and a leash to the audience as an invitation to be obedient and relinquish any semblances of individual freedom of thought.

In the highly partisan political milieu of postwar Italy, Brancati's play evoked animosities from the Left and from the Christian Democrats who would have liked him to take a stand in favor of their side. Brancati, having been burned by his experience with Fascism, opted to walk alone, rejecting all ideologies. This attitude, no doubt, was responsible for the difficulties he experienced with his next play, *La Governante*, (*The Governess*) written in 1951 for his wife, Anna Proclemer, but performed only 11 years after his death. The performance of the play was banned by the

Christian Democratic authorities who considered the topic—Lesbian love—too scandalous for Catholic Italy. Brancati himself, in a passionate defense of his play, denied that Lesbian love was the central focus of the play. He stated in unmistakable terms that "more than the love between two women, the substance of the story is calumny." Indeed, the lesbian theme is never treated in a provocative or blatant way by Brancati. The language that he uses is studied and aware of itself and made up of allusions and half measures.

The play's main character, Caterina Leher, a French Calvinist governess in the home of a well to do Sicilian family living in Rome, is a Lesbian. The patriarch of the family, Leopoldo Platania, a transplanted Sicilian who seems to believe that he has forsaken his Sicilian ways, admires Caterina for her intelligence, seriousness and for her devotion to her religion and to her work. In particular, he admires her rigid Calvinist moral code. She seems to live according to clear religious convictions, a fact that seems more impressive to Leopoldo whose Catholic religion seems more like a habit than a practicing guide to behavior. He, like most Italian men, does not feel the urgency to go to church on Sundays. Thus when Caterina accuses the family's naive Sicilian maid, Jana, of harboring vile desires toward her, Platania has no difficulty in believing her and sends the maid back to Sicily as his way of defending the integrity of his moral and religious principles. But during the trip home the maid is injured as a result of a train accident and eventually succumbs to her injuries in a hospital bed. Caterina meanwhile had hired a new maid, who is really her Lesbian lover, to replace Jana. When Leopoldo opens a door that was accidentally left unlocked, he discovers Caterina and the new maid in a compromising position. He understands now that the Sicilian maid was not guilty of the misdeed she had been accused of and realizes that her death was tragic and unjust. When he questions Caterina about her accusations against the innocent Jana, the governess replies "perché il ladro non vede che furti…" (because a thief can only see thefts…), a great line that lets the spectator surmise the inner struggle that is going on in her conscience between her moral convictions always on guard against the temptations of sin, which made her see sin—in Jana's devotion to her—where there was none. This is the beginning of a poignant confession. Burdened with the guilt of having caused the death of an innocent girl and with the guilt of her deviant behavior, magnified by her strict Calvinist ethics, Caterina commits suicide.

Since the play was banned, Brancati proceeded to publish it as an appendix to an essay entitled *Ritorno alla censura.* (*Return to Censorship*) This, as we have already seen, was not the first time he had had difficulty with censorship.

Early in his career as a playwright, Brancati had concluded that the theater had to express concrete things. This need, however, ran counter to the established order of things during the Fascist era and after its collapse. At the beginning of the first act of *Fedor*, his first youthful play, Brancati declared that he had disposed of about fifty pages of text of a scene set in a Tea House "sacrificing a great deal of the action to modern sensibilities which do not allow writers to call spade a spade". This statement uttered in 1926 was echoed by a similar complaint uttered by the writer Bonivaglia who acts as the author's spokesman in *La Governante*: "Morality? Italian morality consists entirely in the establishment of censorship. Not only do they (the Italians) not want to read or go to the theater, but they want to be certain that, in the play they do not go to see and in the books they do not read, there is no mention of the things they say and do all day long." (Act III, p. 384 Teatro, Bompiani, 1957). These remarks did not sit well in the moralistic and clerical atmosphere of the post-war period in Italy and created animosities toward Brancati. Another item that certainly did non recommend the play to his critics was the explicit association of the crucifix to the calvary of a woman who has two strikes against from their point of view: she was a lesbian and a suicide. In addition, Brancati's text appeared to undermine the time-cherished and conformist values of family and society.

La Governante is Brancati's most successful play. Unlike most of the other plays that seemed to be animated by a desire to satirize a political situation or a sexual problem, this play succeeds in representing Caterina's complex psychological situation in a believable way. The sense of play that accompanied the discussion of sex in the *Don Giovanni in Sicilia* has been replaced by the somber tones of tragedy.

As we have seen, politics and sex seem to be the central concerns around which Brancati's theater revolves. In the final analysis, the theater and the narrative are complementary aspects of the same worldview, with the theater being perhaps the more militant, the more polemical of the two.

Brancati's activities were not limited to theater and novels. Indeed, his work as a screenwriter may be considered as an outgrowth of his experiences in the theater. In this field, Brancati contributed with his talent to the success of numerous films. He wrote a screenplay for the film *Gli anni difficili*, derived from his own story "Vecchio con gli stivali" which has been credited for being a model for a series of political satire movies in Italy. Other screenplays followed: *Signori in carrozza* (1951), *Guardie e ladri* (1951) *Altri tempi* (1952), *L'arte di arrangiarsi* (1955), and *Dov'è la libertà* and *Viaggio in Italia* (1954) for Roberto Rossellini. He worked with other important directors such as Mario Monicelli, Luigi Zampa and Alessandro Blasetti. His two most famous novels *Il Bell'Antonio* (played by Marcello Mastroianni) and *Paolo il caldo* (played by Giancarlo Giannini) were made into films in 1960 and 1973 respectively.

The critical reception of the Brancatian opus has been conditioned by labels that have been applied too easily and have become, by force of repetition, characterizing elements that tend to obscure or marginalize other elements that are equally present or worthy of attention.

It is clear that having been marked once by his experience with Fascism, Brancati adopted great caution to avoid espousing any causes that were all encompassing and totalitarian. Thus, he would be the first to reject such reductive labels. He, in fact, rejected all of the "isms" that were current in his time. As Paolo Mario Sipala said in his *Vitaliano Brancati* (Le Monnier: Firenze 1978), the author was not a man who liked the cultural fads of the moment. He rejected Freud, Jung and psychoanalysis. He even poked fun at Alberto Moravia for rewriting his old themes in a new psychological vein. Sipala believes that all the antifascist, anticlerical and anticommunist attitudes in Brancati's works can be subsumed under the rubric of anti-conformism. "All his characters—in a way or another, by excess or lack—do not align themselves with common norms accepted by the society in which each of them must live." Whatever approach one may take toward Brancati's work, it is clear that after nearly fifty years of his passing it merits a fresh look.

Theatrical Works

Fedor, dramatic poem in three acts and a prologue, (written between 1924-26) Catania, Studio Editoriale Moderno. 1928. Never performed.

Everest, one-act myth, (written in 1928) Catania, Studio Editoriale Moderno. 1931. First performed at the Salone Margherita, Rome on June 5, 1930.

Piave, four-act play, published in Milano, Mondadori, 1932. First performance at the Teatro Valle in Rome in 1932.

Il viaggiatore dello sleeping N. 7 era forse Dio?, three-act play, published in "Il convegno," XIII, n. 5-6. Some unrecorded performances in 1933 and one performance in 1935 in Genoa.

L'urto, a play published in 1934, but written some years earlier. This play has never been staged.

Le trombe di Eustachio, also known as *L'orecchio di Dionisio,* play in six scenes published in 1942. First performance at the theater of the University of Rome in January 1942. It was also broadcast of the Italian radio on February 1, 1952.

Don Giovanni involontario, play in three acts and an epilogue, first performed on March 2, 1943 in Rome at the Teatro delle Arti

Raffaele, a play in three acts and a prologue, written in 1946, published in "Botteghe oscure" in 1948. First performance was on February 7, 1961 at the Teatro Verdi of Padua.

Il tenore sconfitto, a musical farce, published in A. Savinio's *Orfeo vedovo*, 1950. Never performed.

La governante, a play in three acts, written in 1951. First performance was on January 22, 1965 at the Teatro Duse in Genoa.

Una donna di casa, a play in four acts, published in *Mondo* in 1950. First performance was in Milan in 1958

Peter Ustinov, *L'amore dei quattro colonnelli* (play translated in collaboration with A. Proclemer), in "Sipario," n. 72, aprile. 1952

Teatro, Milano, Bompiani (includes the plays: *Questo matrimonio si deve fare, Le trombe di Eustachio, Don Giovanni involontario, Raffaele, Una donna di casa, La governante*). 1957.

Narrative Works And Essays

L'amico del vincitore, novel (written between 1929-30) Milano, Ceschina. 1932.

Singolare avventura di viaggio, novel (written in 1933), Milano, Mondadori. 1934.

In cerca di un sì, collection of short stories, Catania, Studio Editoriale Moderno. 1939.

Gli anni perduti, novel (written between 1934-36), Firenze, Parenti. 1941

Don Giovanni in Sicilia, novel (written in 1940), Milano, Longanesi. 1941.

Giacomo Leopardi, Società, Lingua e Letteratura d'Italia, 1816-1832, Anthology edited by V. Brancati, Milano, Bompiani. 1942.

I fascisti invecchiano, essays, Milano, Longanesi. 1943.

I piaceri -- Parole all'orecchio, essays, Milano, Bompiani. 1946.

Il bell'Antonio, novel, Milano, Bompiani. 1949.

Le due dittature -- Considerazioni sul tema diversità e universalità, Essay, Roma, Associazione Italiana per la libertà della cultura. 1952

Ritorno alla censura, essay, Bari, Laterza. 1952.

Paolo il caldo, novel, Milano, Bompiani. 1955.

Il vecchio con gli stivali e i racconti. Milano, Bompiani. 1958.

Diario romano essays written between 1947-1954, edited by S. De Feo and G.A. Cibotto, Milano, Bompiani 1961.

Il borghese e l'immensità, essays between 1930-1954, edited by S. De Feo and G.A. Cibotto, Milano, Bompiani 1973.

Lettere da un matrimonio (correspondence between Vitaliano Brancati and Anna Proclemer), Milano, Rizzoli, 1978.

Selected Bibliography

P. Pancrazi, *Brancati moralista serio,* in *Scrittori d'oggi,* Bari, Laterza, 1950.

E. Falqui, *Tra romanzi e racconti del '900,* Messina, D'Anna, 1950

L. Russo, *I narratori,* Milano, Principato, 1950.

E. Falqui, *Narratori e prosatori del '900 italiano,* Torino, Einaudi 1950.

C. Muscetta, *Brancati e la censura,* in *Letteratura militante.* Firenze, Parenti, 1953.

G. Villaroel, *Vitaliano Brancati,* in *Gente di ieri e di oggi,* Bologna, Cappelli, 1954.

A. Moravia, *Il destino di Brancati.* In "Galleria," anno V, n. 6, settembre-dicembre 1955

G. C. Ferretti, *Il teatro di Vitaliano Brancati,* in "Rinascita," anno XV, n. 2, febbraio 1958.

G. Trombatore, *Fine del gallismo,* in *Scrittori del nostro tempo,* Palermo, Manfredi, 1959.

P. Fontana, *Vitaliano Brancati,* in "Cronache sociali ," giugno- luglio 1960.

C. Salinari, "Uno scrittore antifascista, "in *La questione del realismo,* Firenze, Parenti, 1960,

G. De Robertis, *I tre libri di Brancati,* in *Altro Novecento,* Firenze, Le Monnier, 1961.

R. Dombroski, "Brancati and Fascism: a profile, " in "Italian Quarterly," n. 49, Summer 1969.

P. M. Sipala, *Per una lettura drammatica di Brancati,* in *Da Carducci a Quasimodo,* Padova, CEDAM, 1970.

V. Gazzola Stacchini, *La narrativa di Vitaliano Brancati,* F Olschki, 1970.

G. A. Peritore, "Punti di vista sulla narrativa di Brancati, " in *Belfagor*, anno XXVI, n. 3, 31 maggio 1971.

N. Borsellino, *Vitaliano Brancati,* in *Dizionario biografico italiani,* vol. XIII, 1971.

C. Licari Huffman, "Vitaliano Brancati: a reassessment," in *Forum Italicum*, VI, 1972.

E. Cecchi, *Un nipotino di Aristofane. Paolo il caldo,* in *Letteratura italiana del Novecento,* ed. by P. Citati, vol. II, Milano, Mondadori, 1972.

V. Gazzola Stacchini, *Il teatro di Vitaliano Brancati,* Lecce, Milella, 1972.

E. Lauretta, *Invito alla lettura di Brancati,* Milano, Mursia, 1972.

A. Bocelli, *La narrativa di Brancati,* in *Letteratura del Novecento,*Caltanissetta-Roma, Sciascia, 1975.

La Sala, "Rassegna di studi critici sulla narrativa di Vitaliano Brancati," in *Critica letteraria*, anno VI, fasc. I, n. 10, 1976.

La Sala, "Rassegna di studi critici sul teatro di Vitaliano Brancati," in *Critica letteraria*, anno VI, fasc. IV, n. 13, 1976.

R. Verdirame, "Posizioni critiche di Brancati giovane," in *Quaderni di filologia e letteratura siciliana*, n. 3, 1976.

L. Abrugiati, *Il primo tempo di Vitaliano Brancati,* Lanciano,Carabba, 1977.

G. Amoroso, *Brancati,* Firenze, La Nuova Italia, 1978.

P.M. Sipala, Vitaliano Brancati: *Introduzione e guida allo studio dell'opera brancatiana. Storia e antologia della critica*. Firenze, Le Monnier, 1978.

G. Santangelo, *La "siepe" Sicilia*, Palermo, S.F. Flaccovio editore, 1985.

A. Di Grado, "Per i quarant'anni del *Bell'Antonio* (1949-1989) in *Da Malebolge alla Senna: Studi letterari in onore di Giorgio Santangelo*, Palermo, Palumbo 1993.

G. Ferretti, *L'infelicità della ragione nella vita e nell'opera di Vitaliano Brancati,*

Milano 1998.

D. De Maglie, *Studio su Vitaliano Brancati*

Special issue of

"Il dramma," luglio 1971: G. C. Vigorelli, *Brancati, il fallimento laico;* P. M. Sipala, *Drammaticità e politica, Brancati;* V. Gazzola Stacchini, *Il fondo Brancati.* (Papers read at a national conference held in Siracusa-Pachino, April 1971).

And

"Le ragioni critiche": n. 1, July 1971: E. Scuderi, *Il fecondo sodalizio Brancati-Guglielmino* (unpublished correspondence) S. Zappulla Muscarà, *Brancati e il fascismo;* n. 2, Oct. Dec. 1971: S. Zappulla Muscarà, *De Roberto e Brancati;* Jan-March 1972: G. Padovani *Brancati e il comunismo* n. 4, April-June 1972: R. Verdirame, *Pirandello e Brancati;* S. Zappulla Muscarà, *Brancati e la censura;* July-Sept. 1972: G. Finocchiaro Chimirri, *Brancati "leopardista,"* n. 6, Oct-Dec. 1972: R. Verdi *Brancati lettore di Verga;* n. 19-20, Jan-June 1976 Verdirame, *Alle origini della narrativa di Brancati.*

Translating Andrea Camilleri into English

Andrea Camilleri — who seems to have replaced Gesualdo Bufalino and Vincenzo Consolo as the current writer who best expresses the island's "sicelitude"—is enjoying tremendous popularity in Italy. His books seem to be ubiquitous and he seems to have an inexhaustible supply of them stashed away in his desk drawer. So much so that I saw an article in *Arte e Folklore di Sicilia,* a quarterly pubblication of Catania, which proclaimed in capital letters "Basta, Camilleri!"which I could readily translate with "Enough already, Camilleri!" making a rhyme without attempting to do so. At any rate, everyone who dabbles in translation or has an interest in it when the subject of Camilleri comes up, inevitably ask "how in the world can you translate Camilleri?" Needless to say, I count myself among those who have asked the same question. The straight and immediate answer that comes to my mind is that you really cannot translate Camilleri, if you expect to present an English-speaking Camilleri. But I would give the same answer to the question "how can you translate Dante, or Petrarch or Calvino?" Theorists of translation can tell you in two hundred pages or more that translation is an impossible task. The reality is, however, that translation has always been part of the literary world and it has been accomplished in various degrees of fidelity since the beginning of time. As a practicing translator I am more interested in the pragmatic aspect of translation that accomplishes every day something that presumably is impossible to do. Thus, it is true, Camilleri is impossible to translate, but I venture to say that his books will in fact be translated one after the other. Already the first translation has come out. It's *The Shape of Water, La forma dell'acqua*, translated by Stephen Sartarelli and I understand that two more novels will be coming out in April. Many more of Camilleri's books have been translated into French and Spanish, although I have no data on these. I do have a copy of *La forme de l'eau*, by the French translator Serge Quadruppani and I have been comparing it to the English translation to see how the two approached the subject.

As most of you know, If you have read any of Camilleri's books, the problem of translation is complicated by the writer's intentional interspersing of his text with Sicilian words or expressions camouflaged as Italian and his frequent use of Sicilian especially in dialogues. It is clear that the conscious use of dialect, whether in an undiluted form or camouflaged, transformed or even parodic, constitutes the most obvious element of this writer's style. A translator faces three different challenges of various difficulties. The first is the fairly straight forward problem of translating Italian into English which ought not create much of a problem; the second is the frequent use of the Sicilian language—notice I said language, not dialect—in dialogues with people who for one reason or another speak in that language. This too should not represent an unsurmountable difficulty since Sicilian is a language like all the others and as such can and is normally translated to English. The easiest way of translating these dialogues is to add a qualifying sentence that says these words word were spoken in Sicilian. Another way could be to translate the dialogues into slang or colloquial speech. The third and certainly the most difficult subtext to translate in Camilleri is his unpredictable and whimsical interspersing of the narrative with Italianized Sicilian words. The use of these words, in fact, distinguishes Camilleri from other Sicilian writers such as Vitaliano Brancati, Sciascia or Bufalino, who used Sicilian occasionally but always with transparent objectives. At any rate, it is probably the most recognizable feature of his style and no doubt contributed, in some measure, to the huge success of his work.

This kind of linguistic code-switching is not discussed by academic translation theorists and practitioners. No one, at least as far as I have been able to read, has addressed the problem from a theoretical or practical point of view. Luigi Bonaffini in an article on the translation of dialect poetry confirms that the American translators he has studied completely ignore the problem and proceed as if the original texts were written by a monolingual author. But this is a serious problem, especially when you translate from Italian which is unique among the romance languages for having dialects that are not dialects but different languages that boast of a long and important literary tradition. Thus, translation theorists are not much help to us in this endeavor. In my translation of Giovanni Meli's *Don Chisciotti and Sanciu Panza* I encountered some code-switching that I tried to differentiate from the regular text by using a more archaic/poetic diction than in the normal text. The text of the *Don Chisciotti* is written in Sicilian but on two occasions the Knight of La Mancha quoted Petrarch. To encourage his squire to be more adventurous Don Chisciotti uses one of Petrarch's Italian lines: "un bel morire tutta la vita onora" which I rendered with "a worthy death brings honor to thy life", where the archaic-poetic word "thy" was meant to signal that it was a poetic quotation. But Camilleri's use of Sicilian goes beyond the occasional quotation. It constitutes an intrinsic part of his style and as such its function must be understood before any attempts can be made not to duplicate it—

because that is impossible—but to come as close to it as possible. To develop a strategy the translator must understand what Camilleri is trying to accomplish by interjecting the Italianized Sicilian into his narrative. This task is not an easy one and it certainly would require a great more study than I have been able to devote to it. Nevertheless, a few observations can help us to orient ourselves as we attempt to offer solutions to the problem at hand.

With this in mind, I picked out at random a paragraph from one of the thirty stories in *Un mese con Montalbano*, the Sicilian police inspector whom the French liken to their Inspector Maigret. The story is entitled "La Sigla". Let's read the paragraph:

> *Calorio* non si chiamava *Calorio,* ma in tutta Vigata lo conoscevanó con questo nome. Era arrivato in *paisi* non si sa da dove una ventina d' anni avanti, un *paro* di pantaloni ch' erano più *pirtusa* che stoffa, legati alla vita con una corda, giacchetta tutta pezze pezze all'arlecchino, piedi *scavusi* ma pulitissimi. *Campava dimandando la limosina,* ma con discrezione, senza dare *fastiddio,* senza *spavintare fimmine e picciliddri.* Teneva bene il vino, quando poteva *accattarsene* una bottiglia, tanto che nessuno l'aveva veduto a malappena brillo: e dire che c'erano state occasioni di feste che di vino se n'era scolato *a litri.*

The italics are mine and indicate Sicilian words and expressions that the author uses throughout the book as an intrinsic component of his style. For the moment, we will postpone any consideration of how these stylistic devices characterize the text. But, as anyone can see, their employment has a definite impact on the reader, each word or expression is charged to express significant bits of meanings, nuances and color that cannot be completely ignored by the would-be translator without flattening the text, reducing a stereophonic sound into a single speaker.

The author here is making great demands on the translator. The italicized words are in effect Sicilian words that have been modified to sound Italian by changing a vowel or two, and they can be understood because the author placed them in a context that even non-Sicilians can guess at, even though they may not know the exact meaning. Calorio is thus the shortened form of Calogero, but it is not *Caloriu,* which is the exact Sicilian name. The word *paro* is the same as *paio* in Italian, but in Sicilian it would be written as *paru.* We can guess why Camilleri chose to use "paro" instead of "paio" (it is easier for Sicilian speakers to say "paru" instead of "paio"). The etymological equivalent of *pirtusa* in Italian is "pertugi" (holes), but in Italian they would identify physical holes in structures, not holes in clothing, as the Sicilian *pirtusa* does here. "Dimandando la limosina" would be "domandando l'elemosina" in Italian, but "dumannannu a limosina" in Sicilian. The double "d" of "Senza dare fastiddio" identifies it as Sicilian. "Senza spavintare fimmine e picciliddri" in Italian would be "senza spaventare donne e bambini" and in Sicilian "senza fari scantari fimmini e picciliddri". The "ddri" ending of "picciliddri" identifies the speaker as a person from the area of Agrigento where the cacuminal sound of "ddu" as in "Turiddu" is pronounced as "Turiddru". "Accattarsene" might not be readily understood as the equivalent of "comprarsene" if the context did not come to clarify it. In Sicilian, of course, the verb "accattari" from "acheter" commonly replaces the Italian "comprare." The use of Italianized Sicilian or Sicilianized Italian as the case may be, was originally thought to be an impediment to non-Sicilians. In fact, in the first edition of *Il filo di turno,* the editor at Mondadori required Camilleri to add a glossary that would explain the Sicilian words to non-Sicilian readers. This feature has been dropped from subsequent books because it is in reality unnecessary for Italians. They can understand the text because Camilleri has become more skilled in placing them in a context that explains them better. Even if the terms are not understood exactly, Italians have a good idea of the possible meanings. At any rate, the presence of these words adds a certain strangeness to the narrative that the translator cannot ignore. The problem for non-Italians reading Camilleri in Italian is probably insurmountable because those who have learned Italian in school in a foreign country are notoriously poor at making connections between words that vary even very slightly from the dictionary meanings. Such people have difficulty equating "limosina" with "elemosina" "paro" with "paio."

Let us look at the paragraph in an attempt to discover whether the use of Sicilian adds dimensions of meaning and style that must be retained or somehow acknowledged by the translator.

The use of the form Calorio instead of Calogero has two purposes: it identifies the locus of the action and it suggests that the person has also been adopted as one of their own even though he is a foreigner. We are in Sicily and specifically in a town of which Saint Calogero is the Patron Saint. Vigàta is Camilleri's fictional town, but it could be anywhere from Sciacca to Porto Empedocle. Saint Calogero, if I am not mistaken, is in fact the patron Saint of Sciacca and a few other towns in the Agrigento province. So perhaps a note should point this out. The term "paisi" is so close to "paese" it does not need an explanation, but it begins a series of interjections in Sicilian whose presence is highly subjective and unpredictable. There are cases when the Sicilian term used does not have an Italian counterpart and Camilleri uses it because the Sicilian is far more expressive and renders better what he had in mind. But in general, there does not seem to be any logic, either linguistically determined or contextually driven for the intrusion of such terms. Their presence does not seem to emerge out of a need to make a particular statement. One could ask Camilleri why he places Sicilian words into his narrative, I am confident he has been asked although I don't know what his response may have been, but even if we knew what he said we would have to assess the effect that their presence has on the reader. I suggest that two of the reasons for the interjections are primarily to add color and to identify the narrator as a Sicilian. Ultimately it seems to me that Camilleri probably speaks like that himself, that is, from time to time, and in an unpredictable manner, he interjects Sicilian words into his speech. If that is so what purpose do the interjections have. I think that Camilleri uses this device for the purpose of making a connection with his listener, of somehow taking the reader into his confidence, by speaking a language that by its restrictive nature constitutes a "secret" jargon that both the writer and his listener understand. It is a method of drawing the readers into the web that he is spinning, an act of *captatio benevolentia.* Sicilians have been historically conditioned not to speak in their own language to strangers or anyone whom they do not know or trust. Camilleri, I think, is throwing in his Sicilian expressions as hooks to draw readers into his world. As a literary ploy this is not new. Boccaccio establishes the same kind of relationship with his readers, a kind of complicity between author and reader that excludes some of the characters themselves. As Boccaccio lets us be a knowing audience, participants in the joke, Camilleri by using his Sicilianized Italian or Italianized Sicilian is forming a bond with the reader who understands—the trick is that after a while everyone understands—and the use of a different code does not exclude anyone.

These preliminary and somewhat tentative conclusions may be sufficient to start working on a strategy for the translation of Camilleri's text. Let's try to give a straightforward rendition of the paragraph without making any attempt at signaling the shift in code in the original.

> Calorio's name was not Calorio, but in Vigata everyone knew him with that name. He had come to town, —nobody knows from where—about twenty years back, with a pair of pants more holes than fabric, tied at the waist with a rope, with a little jacket with so many patches he looked like a Harlequin, barefoot, but with very clean feet. He begged for a living, but discreetly, without bothering anyone, or scaring the women and children. He could hold his wine well, when he could afford to buy a bottle, so much so that nobody ever saw him even slightly drunk, in spite of the fact that there had been times during feast days when he had put away quite a few liters.

Few would argue that this is not a faithful rendition of the Italian text, in terms of the information conveyed. What is missing is the writer's voice, his gently mocking tone that emerges from his problematic use of the dialect. Having lost the metalinguistic component, i.e. the use of the dialect, the rendition is definitely flatter than the original. What options are open to a translator? It seems to me that if he wants to maintain a multilevel linguistic code he must couch his rendition with a least two, and possibly more, linguistic codes that would be accessible to the readers. If the audience for the novel is English, the translator could try to use standard English with American English as subtext. If he is American he might utilize expressions and idiomatic sentences that can be identified with a local dialect to render the Sicilianized Italian expressions. For example, whenever possible he might interject Brooklinese or a local jargon of some kind into the stream of standard American English. Naturally the risk is great that the translator would introduce an alien dimensions into the novel, disregarding the fact that the action takes place in Sicily and such interjections would be considered out of sync with the environment. Failing this option, it seems to me, the only option left for the translator is to develop his own multiple level language made up of sequences that he himself considers normal and interjecting from time to time expressions that deviate in a consistent way from the dominant language. The types of deviation naturally would depend on the translator's background and preparation. But the deviations would not have to coincide with Camilleri's own departures from standard Italian. An attempt to make the deviations coincide with Camilleri's would probably be counterproductive. The translator would have to listen to his own voice and from time to time revert to his own subcode in a way that would mimic Camilleri's own procedure. With this in mind let us try a different rendition of the passage we have already translated.

'The following might be an improvement:

Calorio was not his name, but in Vigata the whole town knew him as Calorio. About twenty years back, he had *turned up* in town from God knows where, with a *pair of britches* that were *draftier than a barn* on account of the many holes, tied with a rope around his waist, and with a *raggedy* jacket so patched up *he looked like a circus clown*. He walked barefoot, but his feet were *spotless*. He *scraped along* by begging but without making a nuisance of himself, *never bothering nobody*, or *scaring the womenfolk or young'uns*. He held his liquor so well, when he could *scare up* enough to buy himself a bottle, that nobody ever saw him even *slightly pickled*;tough there had been times on Feast days when he had *put away* quite a few quarts.

The italicized words were chosen to convey a subtext normally associated with a slangy, folksy, homespun, Southern vocabulary that mimics though not in an obvious way what Camilleri is doing. Questionable grammatical structures like "never bothering nobody" or the use of local jargon "womenfolk and young'uns" or colloquial terms like "scare up," "pickled," or scraped along" produce a multivoiced narrative that is akin to Camilleri's. No doubt this is only an approximation of Camilleri's style. No translator expects a perfect correspondance between his version and the original. Translation is like riding a seesaw with the translator sitting on one end and the original author on the other. The translator's goal is to keep pace with the author, but he cannot help to rise higher at times or sink lower than the author. It is impossible to synchronize his movements so that they match perfectly with the author's. The important thing is to maintain a balance that allows peaks and valleys on either side. Some time the translator will overshoot the target, sometimes he will come up short. The important thing is to remain within an acceptable range of the author's text.

The sample translation of Camilleri's text was simply meant to point the way. I think that after a while the translator would develop a sub language that would serve him well whenever his fancy called for it. But it would be almost like speaking in falsetto. The danger to overdue it, of course, would be ever present. This danger must have dawned on Camilleri himself, for as his stories develop, he seems to lighten the dosage of the code-switching to a bare minimum and often dropping it altogether. In the *Forma dell'acqua* for example, in the last few chapters, except for one or two words, Camilleri uses standard Italian, almost as if he forgot to throw in a few of his trademark words or perhaps because he wanted to develop his detective conclusions and the words would have been a distraction.

When I learned that Stephen Sartarelli had translated *La forma dell'acqua* I bought a copy to see how he had solved the problems discussed above. And I must say, he solved the problem by completely ignoring it. In all fairness to him, I think Sartarelli did a creditable job. His translation is highly readable, accurate in terms of the content of Camilleri's text. He captures Camilleri's irony fairly well and I did not find any factual misreadings of the text. Nevertheless, Sartarelli's English text is monolingual, with one exception where he translates some Sicilian dialogue with American slang or colloquialism. But the code-switching that we have talking about is completely ignored. And I must say that the French translator who addressed the problem and claimed that he would occasionally intersperse his translation with Francitan terms, that is, a kind of modern provençal, if I understand it correctly, to provide a similar code-switching as Camilleri, does not seem to do much of it, although my French is probably not good enoug to spot the code-switching. Allow me a brief comparison between the three texts:

> Pino e Saro si avviarono verso il posto di lavoro *ammuttando* ognuno il proprio carrello. Per arrivare alla *mànnara* ci voleva quasi una *mezzorata* di strada se fatta *a pedi lento* come loro stavano facendo. Il primo quarto d'ora se lo passarono *mutàngheri*, già sudati e *impiccicaticci*. Poi fu Saro a rompere il silenzio.
>
> "Questo Pecorilla è un cornuto" proclamò.
>
> "Un grandissimo cornuto" rinforzò Pino.

I have added the italics to the words that represent Camilleri's code-switching. Here is the French translation:

> Pino et Saro se dirigèrent vers leur lieu de travail en tirant chacun sa carriole. Pour arriver au Bercail, il fallait une demi-heure de route, quand on la suivait à pas lents comme eux. Le premier quart d'heure, ils le passèrent sans mot dire, dejà tout pegueux de sueur. Puis ce fut Saro qui rompit le silence.
>
> —Ce Pecorilla est un cornard, proclama-t-il.
>
> —Un cornard de premiere grandeur, rajouta Pino.

And here is Sartarelli's rendition:

> Pino and Saro headed toward their assigned work sector, each pushing his own cart. To get to the Pasture it took half an hour, if one was slow of foot as they were. The first fifteen minutes they spent without speaking, already sweaty and sticky. It was Saro who broke the silence.
>
> "That Pecorilla is a bastard," he announced.
>
> "A fucking bastard," clarified Pino.

As you can see, neither translator has acknowledged the code-switching or made an attempt to go beyond the surface meaning of the words and even at that level one could be picky and find unfelicitous renderings. Monsieur Quadruppani actually has Saro and Pino pulling a two wheeled "carriole" behind them when they are pushing it in front of them. "Carriole" is a Provençal word described as having two wheels, thus not equivalent to the one-wheel Italian "carriola" with which he probably wanted to mimick Camilleri's code-switching. In the process, however, he mistranslated the sentence. One could argue minor points in both translations, but let's take one word that both translated in a similar fashion: "mutàngheri" Surely it means more than "sans mot dire" and "without speaking". The word does not exist in Italian, but it's understood because of the context. In Sicilian it means more than "taciturn," "unspeaking," it means an unwillingness to speak, a sullenness brought about by being engrossed in one's thoughts, by mulling over things. It also means an inability to speak. *Mutàngaru* in the region of Agrigento describes also a deaf-mute who cannot speak clearly because he cannot hear. I would have said "brooding silently," or "in bleak silence" or "stubbornly silent" or something like that. The word "ammuttando" is also more than "pushing" or the French "pulling" because the Sicilian is more than "spingere". The word is strangely onomatopeic. I can't seem to pronounce it without moving my body forward, which is exactly why Camilleri chose it. He wanted to convey the considerable energy required to make the carts move forward. Simply *pushing* or *pulling* would not do.

I suppose it's fair to ask how I would translate this passage. So here is my tentative version:

> Pino and Saro started out toward their assigned work area, each leaning forward on his cart. It would take half an hour to walk to the pasture if you moved one foot after the other as slowly as they were doing. They spent the first quarter of an hour, already sweaty and sticky, stubbornly clinging to their silence. Then Saro was the first to speak.
>
> "That Pecorilla is a cuckold!" he blurted out.
>
> "A major cuckold" Pino added.

I suppose Sartarelli's use of the word "bastard" is more appropriate, but in using "cuckold" I wanted to retain a measure of the strangeness evoked by the code-switching in Camilleri's text. Americans generally do not use the word and some would have to look it up in a dictionary. Hence "cuckold" would work almost the same way for Americans as one of Camilleri's Sicilian words for Italians. In conclusion, while it is possible to achieve a similar effect in the English, it is very likely that the translator would adopt the minimax strategy, that is, he will try to obtain the maximum effect with the minimum of effort and in real life it takes too much time to imitate Camilleri's style. Hence the English translations of his work will inevitably be monovocal.

Marquis Book Printing Inc.

Québec, Canada
2007